THE CLUBS OF AUGUSTAN LONDON

BY

ROBERT J. ALLEN

JACOB TONSON

SECRETARY TO THE KIT-CAT CLUB

From a mezzotint by John Faber after the Kit-Cat portrait by Sir Godfrey Kneller

THE CLUBS OF AUGUSTAN LONDON

BY

ROBERT J. ALLEN

HAMDEN, CONNECTICUT
ARCHON BOOKS
1967

LIBRARY OF CONGRESS CATALOG CARD NUMBER: 67-11470

PRINTED IN THE UNITED STATES OF AMERICA

TO

H. H. A.

PREFACE

THE literature relating to eighteenth-century clubs has assumed, during the past hundred years, a very respectable bulk. Fascinated writers have used the old clubs as a key with which to unlock the secrets of Georgian social life. They have become interested in tracing the development of the club as an institution, and have written books dealing with the more important founders of clubs. Although most of their information came from the literary productions of eighteenth-century clubmen, their emphasis has rested largely upon the clubs themselves, not upon their literary significance.

In going over the ground again, I have avoided, where it was consistent with clearness, a mere retouching of the already vivid pictures drawn by antiquarians and social historians. I have tried simply to analyze the relations between men of letters and the club life of Swift's time, to see how far a single social phenomenon affected the literature of an age famous for its preoccupation with manners. If new light has been thrown upon the clubs themselves and the personalities of their members, so much the better.

It is a pleasure to acknowledge the many obligations which I have incurred while my study was in progress. The use of rare books in London and Oxford, made easy by the courtesy of officials of the British Museum and the Bodleian Library, became possible through the generosity of the donors of the Clark Bequest and the Charles Dexter Scholarships. To the members of the committee which directs the Harvard Studies in English, I am indebted for the appearance of the book in this series, the continued publication of which has been made possible by the use of a portion of the gift of the General Education Board to the University for the promotion of research in the humanities.

Of the illustrations, two are published with the courteous permission of Mr. Arthur M. Hind, Keeper of the Prints and Drawings in the British Museum. Another owes its appearance here to the kindness of Mrs. Flora V. Livingston, Curator of the Harry Elkins Widener Collection, who put at my disposal the wealth of material on clubs which that collection holds.

Helpful suggestions have come to me from Professor William Henry Irving, Dr. Lester Middlesworth Beattie, Mr. John d'Auby Briscoe, and many, many others. Professor Chester Noyes Greenough has contributed more than he can well realize in allowing me to reap the benefits of his advice, his genial encouragement, and his extraordinary familiarity with the literature of Augustan England. Professor Hyder Edward Rollins, by his friendly interest and his unfailing willingness to let me profit by his wide knowledge, has turned the task of seeing the book through the press into one of my most pleasant and highly valued experiences.

R. J. A.

CAMBRIDGE, MASSACHUSETTS
   October 4, 1933

CONTENTS

ILLUSTRATIONS

THE CLUBS OF
AUGUSTAN LONDON

CHAPTER I

The Rise of the Club

For, as I have before intimated, a plan of it is laid and concerted (as all other matters of importance are) in a club.

THE absorbing interest which clubs held for men of letters in the early years of the eighteenth century was thus voiced by Joseph Addison when, in the first number of *The Spectator*, he outlined his new periodical venture. During the half century in which he and Swift flourished, composition after composition came to be set in a background colored by the club life of London. A cursory glance at *The Spectator* alone reveals the preoccupation of the Town with the newly arisen societies of gentlemen; and a further study of the literature of the period shows how the club penetrated genres as varied as satire, fiction, comedy, and tracts on politics and education. Yet only a century earlier the word "club" in its collective sense was hardly known. Even the social groups for which it stands appeared in literature before 1650 with great rarity. A brief account of the extraordinary rise of the club, with emphasis upon its literary manifestations, is almost indispensable to an understanding of its hold on writers of the eighteenth century.

The word "club" is of much more recent date than the institution. According to the *New English Dictionary*, the earliest use of the word to mean "a meeting or assembly at a tavern, etc., for social intercourse," occurred in Sir William D'Avenant's "Long Vacation in London" (1648), where the town wits decide to "dissolve the club"

for the summer.[1] Ben Jonson employed the word in this
sense some years earlier. In "A Vision on the Muses of his
Friend Michael Drayton" (1627), the dramatist says that
it is not his intention to "raise a rhyming club about the
town."[2] Equally unmistakable is his usage in *The New
Inn* (acted in 1629), where Barnaby inquires of Jordan,

> How does old Staggers the smith, and Tree the saddler?
> Keep they their penny club still?[3]

The existence of another kind of society is implied in the
prologue to *A Tale of a Tub*, which was licensed in 1633.

> *No state-affairs, nor any politic club,*
> *Pretend we in our Tale, here, of a Tub.*[4]

Thus the word was used to designate a social group some
years before the middle of the seventeenth century.

From the first the noun seems to have been connected
with a verb which meant "to join forces in some common
undertaking." For example, Francis Osborne, writing not
long before his death in 1659, said of Sir Thomas Overbury:
"Ackording to the humor of his Stile, he was gracious to
men of parts as Sr Beniamin Rudiard Sir H Gu &, with
whose wite he clubed for those few things he printed."
There was also a noun meaning a contribution made by
an individual toward some joint expense. Thus James
Puckle in *The Club* (1711) wrote: "Whereat *Detractor*
being dumb-founded, threw down his Club, and left the
Room." It was, apparently, from this verb and noun and
from the practise which they indicate that the noun signi-
fying a social meeting originated. It was not until considerably later that the restricted modern meaning first
came into common use. Dr. Johnson still defined the word

---

1. *The Works of Sir W. D'Avenant* (1673), p. 289.
2. *The Works of Ben Jonson*, ed. W. Gifford and F. Cunningham (1875),
VIII, 326.
3. *Ibid.*, V, 373.   4. *Ibid.*, VI, 121.

in 1755 as "an assembly of good fellows, meeting under certain conditions," and it should be borne in mind that no stricter interpretation was generally felt until late in the eighteenth century.

The practise of clubbing is also much older than the word. Plutarch's life of Lycurgus has a lively description of Spartan dining societies of about fifteen contributing members, who added to their number by an ingenious system of secret balloting. The author of the *Sketch of the Rise and Progress of the Royal Society Club* remarks that "Justus Lipsius mentions a *bonâ fide* Roman Club, the members of which were bound by certain organized rules and regulations." [1] In a satiric poem of 1680, one of the members of a "drunken club" draws a parallel between his society and a classical one.

> The seven wise Men, of whom the *Grecians* tell us,
> Were but a Club of honest Fellows,
> They sate, and drank, and talkt, as we do now;
> until the Reckoning was come,
> Then every man threw in his Symbolum. [2]

Whether the clubmen of the eighteenth century patterned their societies after any of these is a matter of considerable doubt. There is actual evidence, however, that Cicero's account of the Roman *sodalitates* had its effect upon Henry St. John, later Viscount Bolingbroke, who founded the powerful Brothers Club. Bolingbroke reveals his familiarity with the passage in *De Senectute* in his "Letter on the Spirit of Patriotism," where, as Cooke puts it, "he fortifies his position with the authority of the elder Cato, who, in the midst of public duties, private studies, and an extreme old age, found time to frequent the sodalitates, or clubs of friends, at Rome, and to sit up all night

1. Page 6. Addison refers to this "old Roman club" and "the rules of a symposium in an ancient Greek author" in *The Spectator*, No. 9.
2. Charles Darby [?], *Bacchanalia: or a Description of a Drunken Club* (1680), p. 8.

with his neighbours in the country of the Sabines." [1] Bolingbroke, though actuated partly by political motives, was by no means insensible of the value of his club in developing friendship and harmony. Although he wrote the "Letter on the Spirit of Patriotism" some years after he assembled the Brothers, his words show a definite realization of a classical precedent.

The natural gregariousness of mankind, not the sanction of the ancients, explains the formation of the earlier English clubs. This was surely true in the case of "La Court de Bone Compaignie," whose epistle to Sir Henry Somer is to be found among the works of Hoccleve. The explanation which follows the title is worth quoting.

Ceste balade ensuyante feust, par la Court de bone conpaignie, enuoiee a lonure sire Henri Sommer, Chaunceller de leschequer, & un de la dicte Court.

The Court seems to have been a dining club of definite membership, with traditions so firmly established that they may well be called rules; for in one passage the letter reminds Sir Henry of his promise to pay his score "as dooth an othir wight," [2] indicating such clubbing as became common in the seventeenth and eighteenth centuries. The gentlemen of the Temple who made up the membership appear to have grown so extravagant in their expenditures for good cheer that they had drawn from Sir Henry a remonstrance not unlike that of Swift concerning the Brothers three centuries later. The Court suggested, in their imperturbable reply, that they were willing to reduce their outlays whenever he chose to set them an example in that direction. Meanwhile, he was to remember his promise of a dinner. The epistle ends with the exhortation:

> But keepith wel your tourn how so befalle,
> On thorsday next on which we awayte alle.

1. G. W. Cooke, *Memoirs of Lord Bolingbroke* (1835), 1, 186.
2. *Hoccleve's Works*, ed. F. J. Furnivall (E. E. T. S., 1892), 1, 65.

Similar groups of convivial gentlemen must have formed from time to time throughout the next two centuries; but for the most part their fame has died with them. Thomas Nashe has a tantalizing reference to what seems to have been a kind of club in *Have with You to Saffron Walden*, where he says of Anthony Chute:

And for his Oratorship, it was such that I haue seene him *non plus* in giuing the charge at the creating of a new Knight of *Tobacco*; . . . and, to approue his Heraldrie, scutchend out the honorable Armes of the smoakie Societie.[1]

The Ash-Wednesday suppers held at Sir Fulke Greville's house, of which Bruno gives an account in *La Cena de le Ceneri*, suggest a philosophical dining club.[2] Such companies as these, however, are so shadowy in outline that their true nature is as deceptive as that of the much-debated "Areopagus."

The next true club about which anything is known was the society extraordinary that convened at the Mermaid Tavern. Even here there has been so much romancing that it is hard to arrive at any definite facts. The imagination is kindled at the outset by the famous passage in Beaumont's epistle to Ben Jonson:

> What things we have seen
> Done at the Mermaid! heard words that have been
> So nimble, and so full of subtle flame,
> As if that every one from whence they came
> Had meant to put his whole wit in a jest
> And had resolved to live a fool the rest
> Of his dull life.

Under Beaumont's spell, actualities fade into matters of supreme indifference.

There is a more distinct picture in a letter of Thomas Coryate, of 1615, which bears the direction:

1. *The Works of Thomas Nashe*, ed. R. B. McKerrow, III (1905), 107.
2. See I. Frith, *Life of Giordano Bruno* (1887), p. 128.

To the High Seneschall of the Right Worshipfull Fraternity of Sireniacal Gentlemen, That meet the first Fridaie of euery Moneth, at the signe of the Mere-Maide in Bread-streete in London, giue these: From the Court of the Great Mogul, resident at the Towne of Asmere, in the Easterne India.[1]

The letter is devoted to an account of Coryate's travels and concludes with a request to the "Seneschall" to see that the bearer of the epistle is well used and "to exhilarate him with the purest quintessence of the *Spanish, French* and *Rhenish* Grape, which the Mermaid yeeldeth." [2] Coryate speaks of the "Seneschall" as "M. L. W.", initials which furnish a definite clue to one member of the club. When Purchas reprinted some of the traveler's letters in the 1625 edition of his *Pilgrimes,* he headed the chapter in which they appeared with a statement to the effect that they were "written to Mr. L. Whitaker." [3] Thus Whitaker must have been the seneschal.

Little enough is known about this early clubman except that he was a friend of John Donne. Reliable information about the other members of the Mermaid group is almost equally scanty. Anthony Wood's *Fasti* gives a valuable hint under the year 1616, in recording the fact that on July 9 Francis Stewart was created Master of Arts.

He was a learned gentleman, was one of sir Walt. Raleigh's club at the Meremaid tavern in Friday-street in London, and much venerated by Ben. Jonson, who dedicated to him his comedy called *The Silent Woman.*[4]

Better known references to Ben Jonson's conviviality connect him with Shakespeare. Fuller describes the wit-combats between the two poets, without mentioning the Mermaid; and John Ward speaks of the fact that "Shake-

---

1. *Coryat's Crudities* (1776), vol. III, sig. L8ᵛ.
2. *Ibid.*, vol. III, sig. M2.
3. *Purchas His Pilgrimes* (1625), I, 592.
4. *Fasti Oxonienses*, ed. P. Bliss, II (1815), 369.

speare, Drayton, and Ben Jonson, had a merie meeting, and itt seems drank too hard, for Shakespear died of a feavour there contracted." [1] If all this actually went on at the Mermaid, as Gifford and others have assumed, it would be as easy to visualize the meetings in Friday Street as those of a century later at Button's Coffee-house.

There is more certainty about the tribe of Ben who assembled years later at the Devil Tavern. Jonson's recent biographers have given a pleasant picture of the place.

Situated close to the City side of Temple Bar in the very heart of the legal and literary quarter, this hostelry, under the guidance of its notable host, Simon Wadloe ('brave duke Wadlow, king of skinkers', as he was variously called), became in the later years of James the most famous of the haunts of wit and letters. The upper chamber of this tavern, known as the 'Apollo', in which Jonson and his coterie forgathered, remained, in the eighteenth century, a speaking monument of these symposia, while to the days of Pope and Addison at least the tradition of them lingered in the neighbouring coffee-houses, spiced with a few sayings of Ben himself. [2]

Jonson is generally credited with the authorship of the set of Latin rules, called "*Leges Conviviales*," that hung in the club room to regulate the less restrained members. The first rule says definitely, "*Nemo asymbolus, nisi umbra, huc venito*," indicating that the custom of dividing the expense prevailed. Although excessive silence was frowned upon and the code insisted upon a friendly spirit, brawling was expressly forbidden. No one could be compelled to produce extempore verse, nor was anyone allowed to publish what he heard there. Other rules were concerned with the preparation of the feast, the admission of ladies, and the choice of members, so that taken together the *leges* give a fairly definite idea of how the club was conducted.

1. *Diary of the Rev. John Ward*, ed. C. Severn (1839), p. 183.
2. C. H. Herford and Percy Simpson, *Ben Jonson*, I (1925), 85.

The least familiar of the early references to the Apollo group appears in the second act of Shackerley Marmion's play, *A Fine Companion*, where Careless enters in high spirits.

Æmi[*lia*].   Whence come you, from *Apollo?*
Car[*elesse*].   From the heaven
Of my delight, where the boone *Delphicke* God,
Drinkes sacke, and keepes his *Bacchanalias*,
And has his incense, and his Altars smoaking,
And speakes in sparkeling prophesies; thence doe I come.
My braines perfum'd with the rich Indian vapour,
And heightned with conceits: from tempting beauties,
From dainty Musicke and Poeticke straines,
From bowls of *Nectar*, and Ambrosiacke dishes:
From witty Varlets, fine Companions,
And from a mighty continent of pleasure,
Sayles thy braue *Carelesse*.[1]

The convivial spirit of the Apollo Club, together with the personal magnetism of its vigorous monarch, drew the poet Herrick into its number. How well his mood at this time suited that of the society is revealed in his exuberant drinking songs. Moorman, indeed, considers it "likely enough that many of his bacchanalian and anacreontic verses, including the magnificent lines, *To Live Merrily and trust to Good Verses*, were specially indited for the ears of the chosen comrades who met in the Apollo Chamber, or at the Sun, the Dog, or the Triple Tun." [2] The famous "Ode to Ben Jonson" shows a lyric abandon and an enthusiastic gusto that were only too rare among the eighteenth-century poets of club life.

A bit of verse somewhat in Herrick's mood appeared in Alexander Brome's little book of *Songs and other Poems* in 1661. This poem, called "The Club," reappeared in the edition of 1664; and in the same volume there was also printed, for the first time, Brome's translation of the *Leges*

---

1. *A Fine Companion* (1633), sig. D3ᵛ.
2. F. W. Moorman, *Robert Herrick* (1910), p. 63.

Conviviales under the title, "Ben Jonsons sociable rules for the Apollo." This circumstance has led to the suggestion that "The Club" may have been written for the Apollo Club. The poem is a summons to carefree enjoyment. After three stanzas which bid the company incline to mirth, leaving behind them all lethargy and worry alike, the poet concludes:

> Still those *clocks*, let time attend us,
>   We'l not be to hours confin'd;
> We'l banish all that may offend us,
>   Or disturb our *mirth* design'd;
> Let the glass still run its round,
> And each *good-fellow* keep his ground,
> And if there be any *flincher* found,
>   We'l have his soul *new-coyn'd*.[1]

The verses are quite in the Apollo vein, and the inference that they were born of the tribe of Ben is tempting.

Samuel Pepys makes frequent references to his visits to the Devil Tavern, and mentions John Wadlow, son of the more illustrious Simon of Jonson's time, as vintner there, but shows no interest at all in the Jonsonian traditions connected with the place. That the traditions survived appears from Steele's allusion in *The Tatler*.

After the ceremony [a wedding], I was resolved to entertain the company with a dinner suitable to the occasion, and pitched upon the Apollo, at the Old Devil at Temple Bar, as a place sacred to mirth, tempered with discretion, where Ben Jonson and his "sons" used to make their liberal meetings . . . ; and as soon as the company were come into that ample room, Lepidus Wagstaff began to make me compliments for choosing that place, and fell into a discourse upon the subject of pleasure and entertainment, drawn from the rules of Ben's Club, which are in gold letters over the chimney.[2]

1. *Songs and other Poems* (1664), p. 98.
2. *The Tatler*, No. 79. Compare Pope's "First Epistle of the Second Book of Horace," ll. 41–42:
> "And each true Briton is to Ben so civil,
> He swears the Muses met him at the Devil."

An amusing suggestion about the origin of the Apollo's name is made in the lines from an unknown hand "On Ben Johnson's Club-Room, call'd the Apollo; at the Devil-Tavern in Fleet-street." As the "jovial bard" was sitting one day among his sons at the tavern, he called upon Phoebus to aid him in "some rare strain" which he was about to attempt. Nonplussed at the god's refusal to help him, he took a long draft of the Devil's best canary.

> Soon as this Nectar glided o'er his Tongue,
> He rous'd, and tuned his Lyre, and sweetly sung.
> Then to the Room which the rich Juice supply'd,
> Henceforth be thou *Apollo* call'd, he cry'd;
> *Apollo* let thy Name for ever be,
> That lab'ring Bards, in Time to come, may see,
> If they their Father *Ben*'s Advice will take,
> The best Inspirer is delicious Sack.[1]

That there were other societies of gentlemen who met not much later than the tribe of Ben to indulge in and discuss poetry is evident from some commendatory verses of Alexander Brome "On the Comœdies of the late facetious Poet, Mr. Richard Brome Deceased" (1659). Alexander speaks of the would-be wits who heckle novices

> With *Questions* intricate, yet catching though,
> Such as themselves can't answer, namely, who
> First made them *Wits*? How they the grace obtain'd
> Of *Poetry*? By whom they were ordain'd?
> And at what *Club*?[2]

The passage is a denunciation of the capricious, dogmatic clubmen who set up for literary authorities, and indicates that the Apollo was not without certain groups of inferior imitators.

Other bits of evidence prove that club activity was going on early in the seventeenth century and that writers took an interest in it. There is, for example, the society of

---

1. David Lewis, *Miscellaneous Poems, by Several Hands* (1726), p. 71.
2. *The Dramatic Works of Richard Brome* (1873), vol. II.

ladies presided over by Lady Haughty in *The Silent Woman*,[1] which challenges comparison with a group delineated in *The Female Tatler* a hundred years later. The "new order of drinking lately come up amongst us, call'd a drinking Schoole or Library," described in Chapter XII of Thomas Heywood's *Philocothonista* (1635), is nothing more than a drinking club which borrowed the language of the school to name its officers and customs. Heywood even gives the rules of the society and an account of its habits. Evidently before the name of club had come to be commonly applied to small, regular social gatherings, they existed and found their way into literature.

During the period of the interregnum there developed two mighty stimuli to the rise of the club. The more obvious of these forces was the establishment of a new kind of refectory known as a coffee-house. Although coffee had been used privately in England some years earlier, the first public coffee-house was opened in 1650 at Oxford, by a Jew named Jacobs. It was not until 1652 that London's first coffee-house was established. The traditional story has it that a certain Mr. Edwards acquired the coffee-drinking habit while traveling in Turkey as a merchant. Upon his return to England, he continued the practise, his coffee being prepared by a servant, Pasqua Rosee, whom he had brought home with him. Edwards's friends developed such a fondness for the beverage that they soon became a serious strain upon his hospitality. Accordingly, he devised the expedient of setting up Pasqua in the business of dispensing coffee publicly. From the first opening of the house "by Pasqua Rosee, in St. Michael's Alley, Cornhill, at the sign of his own head," the enterprise was crowned with success. Keepers of taverns and ale-houses protested vigorously at its incursions into their own traffic. But the new drink gained amazingly in popularity,

1. See also "A Speech, according to Horace," in which Jonson (*Works* [1875], VIII, 412) mentions "the Academy, where the gallants meet."

and by 1660 a number of thriving coffee-houses had sprung up, including the Rainbow, Garway's (afterwards famous as Garraway's), Miles's, and Will's.

From the beginning, the coffee-houses shared in the attraction which taverns had always held for social gatherings. Men of all stations in life assembled in them to converse with their friends and to make the acquaintance of the new, exotic liquor. The regular groups that met thus and pooled their resources toward the mutual entertainment were among the first to be called clubs. Pepys wrote, on January 17, 1660, concerning one of these societies: "So I went to the Coffee-Club, and heard very good discourse."

Although the early clubs were neither so various nor so numerous as they later became, they soon began to show the traits which were afterwards to distinguish Will's. In the pamphlet entitled *The Character of a Coffee-House* (1673), it is recorded that "the *Ingeniosi* use it for an after *Rehearsal*, where they bring *Plays* to Repetition, sift each *Scene*, examine every *uncorrected Line*, and *damn* beyond the fury of the *Rota*," [1] a picture which matches several descriptions in the later accounts of the Great Coffee-house. The same character gives an excellent idea of the heterogeneity of the company that met together.

As you have a *hodge-podge* of Drinks, such too is your Company, for each man seems a Leveller, and ranks and files himself as he lists, without regard to degrees or order; so that oft you may see a silly *Fop*, and a worshipful *Justice*, a griping *Rock*, and a grave *Citizen*, a worthy *Lawyer*, and an errant *Pickpocket*, a Reverend *Nonconformist*, and a Canting *Mountebank;* all blended together, to compose an *Oglio* of Impertinence.[2]

Surely the coffee-house was the most democratic institution of an age of unprecedented democracy; and as such it

1. Gwendolen Murphy, *A Cabinet of Characters* (1925), p. 322.
2. *Ibid.*, p. 316.

was necessarily an important factor in the rise of the club in the seventeenth century.

Another great stimulus was the trend of political events. During the ascendency of the Parliamentarians, a larger number of Londoners than ever before were actively interested in politics. Since the governing power was no longer centered in a small court circle, the English citizen was feeling his political importance, and the numerous factions needed places for forming and discussing their principles. Party leaders gravitated naturally to taverns and coffee-houses, which they found admirably suited to their ends. It was partly a genuine political need that gave an impulse to the rise of the club during the years that followed the turning of the mid-century.

One of the earliest and most active of the political groups was a club called the Rota. It seems to have taken its name from one of its leading principles: that one-third of the governing body of a commonwealth should be retired each year, in rotation, so that in three years a complete change would be effected. The prime mover of the club was James Harrington, the deviser of the scheme for a utopian commonwealth described in his book *Oceana*. The best account of the Rota (lifted in part from John Aubrey) is to be found in Anthony Wood's biographical sketch of Harrington.

And by that book [says Wood, referring to *Oceana*,] and both their smart discourses and inculcations daily in coffee-houses, they obtained many proselytes. In 1659, in the beginning of Mich. term, they had every night a meeting at the then Turk's-head in the New-palace-yard at Westm. (the next house to the stairs where people take water) called Miles's coffee-house, to which place their disciples and virtuosi would commonly then repair: and their discourses about government and of ordering of a commonwealth, were the most ingenious and smart that ever were heard, for the arguments in the parliament house were but flat to those.[1]

1. *Athenae Oxonienses*, ed. P. Bliss, III (1817), 1119.

Wood gives the names of a number of members, including Nevill, Aubrey, and "Cyriac Skinner, an ingenious young gentleman, and scholar to Jo. Milton, which Skinner sometimes held the chair." According to John Tatham, author of *The Character of the Rump* (1660), "King-killing Bradshaw" was "one of the spokes of *Harrington's Rota*, till he was turned out for cracking." [1]

By his own testimony Pepys can also be identified as a member. On January 9, 1660, he wrote in his diary: "Thence I went with Muddiman to the Coffee-House, and gave 18*d*. to be entered of the Club." [2] Wheatley's note identifying this club with the Rota is confirmed by later entries, some of which describe actual debates. The sober way in which the undaunted diarist traces the intricacies of such arguments as the following makes one smile.

So I went to the Coffee Club, and heard very good discourse; it was in answer to Mr. Harrington's answer, who said that the state of the Roman government was not a settled government, and so it was no wonder that the balance of propriety [*i.e.*, property] was in one hand, and the command in another, it being therefore always in a posture of war; but it was carried by ballot, that it was a steady government, though it is true by the voices it had been carried before that it was an unsteady government; so to-morrow it is to be proved by the opponents that the balance lay in one hand, and the government in another. [3]

Aubrey adds to the picture by describing the large oval table about which the debaters sat, "with a passage in the middle for Miles to deliver his Coffee." At this table was proposed the resolution which led Harrington to publish *The Rota: or a Model of a Free-State, Or equall Common-Wealth.* [4]

1. *The Dramatic Works of John Tatham* (Edinburgh, 1879), p. 289.
2. *The Diary of Samuel Pepys*, ed. H. B. Wheatley (1924), I, 13.
3. *Ibid.*, pp. 20–21.
4. *Brief Lives*, ed. A. Clark (Oxford, 1898), I, 289.

Before its dissolution, the Rota managed to perpetuate its memory through a tract which connects it with the name of Milton. This sixteen-page quarto pamphlet, signed with the initials of Harrington himself, bears the title, *The Censure of the Rota upon Mr Miltons Book, Entituled, The Ready and Easie way to Establish a Free Common-wealth*. The title-page carries the further explanation:

Ordered by the Rota, *that* M. Harrington *be desired to draw up a Narrative of this dayes proceeding upon* Mr. Miltons *Book, called,* The Ready and Easie way, &c. *And to cause the same to be forthwith Printed and Published, and a Copy thereof to be sent to* Mr. Milton.

Harrington begins in a pseudo-apologetic strain, stating that he writes the letter at the command of "this ingenious Convention," and that he takes "as little pleasure to repeat it as you [Milton] will do to hear it." The passage that follows gives such a lively picture of the club in action that it is worth quoting.

For whereas it is our usuall custom to dispute every thing, how plain or obscure soever, by knocking Argument against Argument, and tilting at one another with our heads (as Rams fight) untill we are out of breath, and then refer it to our wooden Oracle the *Box*; and seldom any thing, how slight soever, hath appear'd, without some Patron or other to defend it. I must confesse, I never saw Bowling-stones run so unluckily against any Boy, when his hand has been out, as the Ballots did against you, when any thing was put to the question, from the beginning of your Book to the end.[1]

Harrington proceeds to repeat a few of the scathing attacks on Milton's pamphlet, as they were made from the floor by the club members. His own speech was somewhat more restrained than the rest. The others were ridiculously abusive. One member even went so far as to say that the

---

1. *The Censure of the Rota upon Mr Miltons Book* (1660), p. 3.

Ready and Easy Way was a patchwork of falsehoods and errors, and that it was "all windy foppery from the beginning to the end." [1] This and other passages give rise to a suspicion that the *Censure* was in part a burlesque of Milton's own violent methods of pamphleteering. At least the Rota did not take him as seriously as he could perhaps have wished.

Harrington's circle proved to be the recipient as well as the author of caustic remarks. Samuel Butler, in *Hudibras*, made Sidrophel "as full of tricks, as *Rota-men* of *Politicks*." [2] Butler disliked the organization not as a club but as a political faction opposed to monarchy. His humorous little essay entitled "A Speech Made at the Rota" begins by pleading the precedent of the Roman senate for digressing into any subjects that he chooses which are of "Concernment to the Commonwealth." [3] He considers the matters of "*over-Balance and Propriety*" essentially barren; and after a few tentative thrusts at Harrington, his club, and the Commonwealth in general, he launches forth on a comical account of the name "Rump" as applied to Parliament. As the speech proceeds, Butler's criticism of the faction at Miles's Coffeehouse becomes sufficiently clear.

The Rota was famous about town for its use of the ballot to make a quick and accurate test of the opinion of the society regarding the various political questions that arose. This practise made the meetings so much more interesting than those where interminable debate was allowed that crowds flocked about Miles's to learn the opinion of the club on the problems of the day. But the popularity of the Rota was short-lived. Monck's coming into power was a serious blow to the gentlemen of Harrington's society, and they must have foreseen several weeks before the Restora-

1. *The Censure of the Rota upon Mr Miltons Book* (1660), p. 13.
2. *Hudibras*, part II, canto iii (ed. A. R. Waller [1905], p. 180).
3. *Satires and Miscellaneous Poetry and Prose*, ed. R. Lamar (1928), p. 324.

tion that their cause was doomed. A pamphlet published early in 1660 [1] urged them to accept Charles as the worthiest candidate for the leadership of England's government. When the members finally realized that a return to monarchy was about to render their deliberations superfluous, they dissolved the group. This happened, according to Wood, about February 21, 1660; and Pepys confirms the date by his entry for February 20, in which he says:

> After a small debate upon the question whether learned or unlearned subjects are the best the Club broke up very poorly, and I do not think they will meet any more.[2]

After the Restoration the rise of political clubs was rapid. So powerful did they become that in 1675 a special act was passed which closed, temporarily, all the coffee-houses of London. Roger North gives the reasons for the act in some detail, showing how malcontents used the clubs for "propagating seditious Lyes, and Misrepresentations of all the Government did." Shadwell adds his testimony in *The Virtuoso* (1676), when he makes Miranda say of the poets of the time:

> They make nonsense go down as glib without tasting, as a seditious Lie is swallowed in a City Coffee-house, or Commonwealth Clubb, without examination.[3]

Special orators were appointed to attend all political meetings and spread their factional propaganda. "And, by that Means," North asserts, "the Coffee-houses began to be direct Seminaries of Sedition, and Offices for the Dispatch of Lying, and carried on to such a Degree of Inconvenience,

---

1. *A late Letter From the Citty of Florence, VVritten By Signor Fabricio Pisani a Counsellor of the Rota, Touching these present Distempers of England* (1660). A manuscript note in the copy in the British Museum dates the publication January 4.
2. *The Diary of Samuel Pepys,* I, 59.
3. *The Complete Works of Thomas Shadwell,* ed. Montague Summers (1927), III, 154.

to the Public, as scarce any Government in the World would have endured." [1]

More objectionable to the masses than any of these "seminaries" were the clubs of papists which are known to have existed during the time when Popish-Plot hysteria was at its height. John Ward refers to such a group in his diary as early as March 8, 1674.[2] In discussing the character of Titus Oates, North speaks of a "Club in *Fuller's Rents*, where this *Smith* [an old teacher of Oates, who knew him rather too well for his safety], and one *Medburn*, . . . a Player, who was a Papist, and some other Papists used to meet." [3] In order to bring persecution upon the protestant Smith, "*Oates* did his Club the Honour to bestow an Article in his Narrative upon it, as a Papist Meeting, and named one *Smith* that frequented it, and it was made a Fault that *Smith* kept one *Medburn* Company." Many groups of Romanists must have shared the fate of this one during the bitter years that followed.

A shadowy political association known as the Club of Unanimous Voters came into existence for a short time in 1678 to thwart Charles's attempt to prorogue Parliament and save Danby. The failure of the club to gain its ends called from an unknown pen some verses entitled "Upon the Proroguing of Parliament; or, the Club of Unanimous Voters." The author gives no account of the club, but satisfies himself with protesting against the conduct of King Charles. The group was not long in reorganizing for new operations; for on May 23, 1679, according to Lemon's catalogue, a broadside appeared giving "A List of one unanimous Club of VOTERS in his Majesties Long Parliament, dissolved in 78, very fit to be thought on at the next New Choice." [4]

1. Roger North, *Examen* (1740), p. 139.
2. *Diary of the Rev. John Ward*, ed. C. Severn (1839), p. 141.
3. *Examen*, p. 238.
4. Robert Lemon, *Catalogue of a Collection of Printed Broadsides* (1866), p. 134.

It was about this time that the Whigs discovered in
the club a most useful instrument for controlling public
opinion. During the five years previous to the pope-
burning demonstrations of 1680–1682, there came into
prominence a political group known as the King's Head or
Green-Ribbon Club. Roger North gives the following explanation of the two names:

The Gentlemen of that worthy Society held their Evening
Sessions continually at the *King's Head* Tavern over-against the
Inner-Temple Gate. But, upon Occasion of the Signal of *a Green
Ribbon*, agreed to be worn in their Hats in the Days of *Street
Engagements*, like the Coats of Arms of valiant Knights of old,
whereby all the Warriors of the Society might be distinguished,
and not mistake Friends for Enemies, they were called also
The Green Ribbon Club.[1]

As president of the Whig faction, Shaftesbury was the ulti-
mate director of this militant society and the contriver of
the anti-papist demonstration.

In a letter which Charles Hatton wrote to his brother
about the middle of November, 1679, we catch a glimpse
of the activities of the King's Head group.

Monday next, being Queen Elizabeth's birthday, Sr Rob.
Peyton and ye pope are to be burnt together in effigie before
ye King's Head, nere Temple Bar, were Sr Robert's club wase
kept; but they of ye clubb have contributed 10^ll a peice for
his effigies to be burnt, wch will cost 100^ll.[2]

Such scenes, together with the violence which accompanied
them, were not long in arousing the ire of Shaftesbury's
political opponents, who rallied to an attack on the club
by way of the press. The party journalism of the time has a
number of thrusts like that of Flatman in *Heraclitus Ri-
dens*, No. 51, where a member is depicted "in such a rage,

1. *Examen*, p. 572.
2. *Correspondence of the Family of Hatton*, ed. E. M. Thompson (Camden
Society, 1878), I, 203.

as might have scar'd one that did not know the green
Ribband-men to be no Fighters."

The Green-Ribbon Club made its way into the political
verse of the period through the pen of Alexander Radcliffe. In his collection of poems called *The Ramble: an
Anti-Heroic Poem, Together with Some Terrestrial Hymns
and Carnal Ejaculations* (1682), appeared a poem entitled
"Hail to the Myrtle Shades, &c.," which ridiculed Shaftesbury's favorite, the Duke of Monmouth, under the name of
Strephon. The verses begin:

> Pitty the private Cabal,
>   Ah pitty the Green Ribbon Club;
> They've cut off poor *Strephon's* Entail,
>   And *Strephon* has met with a rub.

Radcliffe goes on to describe the vanity and arrogance of
Monmouth before his fall, and concludes:

> *Strephon* though not by his Tongue
>   Has drawn to him Parties and Factions,
> People that make the day long
>   By buzzing of private Transactions.
> *Strephon* has little to say,
>   But laughs at the Lord knows what;
> But the Club meets every day,
>   And sits with eternal Chat.[1]

The favorite weapon of the Green-Ribbon mobs was a
short but formidable club of *lignum vitæ*. Its popular
name appears in the title of Radcliffe's epigram "On the
Protestants Flail," which gives a very fair idea of the
effectiveness of the tool.

> In former days th'Invention was of Wracks,
> To dislocate mens Joynts and break their Backs:
> But this Protestant Flail of a severer sort is,
> For *Lignum vitæ* here proves *Lignum mortis*.[2]

The lines on Shaftesbury's club in the second part of
Absalom and Achitophel (1682) give a more intimate view

---

1. *The Ramble* (1682), pp. 22–24.   2. *Ibid.*, p. 51.

of the Green-Ribboners than any other. According to the
satirist, two kinds of men were in attendance at the King's
Head,

> These gloomy, thoughtful, and on mischief bent,
> While those for mere good-fellowship frequent
> Th' appointed club, can let sedition pass,
> Sense, nonsense, anything t' employ the glass;
> And who believe, in their dull honest hearts,
> The rest talk treason but to shew their parts.[1]

The passage attempts to show what a motley crew made up
Achitophel's following and to belittle his club; but the
picture has none the less an air of accuracy.

Other attacks were directed at the leaders of the Green-
Ribbon faction. One poet, writing "In Opposition to Mr.
Dryden's Essay on Satyr, 1680," admits at the outset
that the manners of the court were corrupt and then continues as follows:

> But to supplant the Government, to cry
> Allegiance down, and raze out Monarchy; . . .
> To sowce Rebellion, lay up Plots in pickle,
> And make each Tavern-bar a Conventicle;
> This would become a Muses Excellence,
> To whip the Club into Allegiance.[2]

He concludes a series of vicious thrusts at individual
Green-Ribbon men with an allusion to Monmouth.

> These are the Men who all the bustle make,
> And Empire check meerly for Empires sake.
> They lay their stamp on the revolting darling,
> And in the Club make Treason pass for Sterling.[3]

Another satirist of the time advises the court party to
adopt a policy of firm control in order to bring to time such
factionists as

1. *Absalom and Achitophel*, II, 526–531.
2. *Poems on Affairs of State*, I (1703), 262.
3. *Ibid.*, p. 265.

Chase, Lower, Negus, Tizard, all the Shrubs,
Of Kings-head, Dragon, and of *Ashley* Clubs.[1]

Prejudiced as these verse attacks are, they reveal an actual tendency on the part of the Green-Ribbon alarmists to disseminate fears which the political situation only partially justified. Roger North shows his disgust for their fanatical methods and their disregard of the truth in such passages as the following:

The Pope himself could not make Saints so readily as they Papists, . . . and a leud atheistical Fellow was as readily washed clean, and made a zealous Protestant.[2]

Whatever may have been its principles and methods, the power of the Green-Ribbon Club cannot be denied, surprising as it now seems. "But, to give a Dimission to our Treason Club," as North concludes, "I only observe that the like could scarce have subsisted in any Age but this; . . . for, until the *Rye Discovery*, their Constitution stood firm, but, immediately upon that, it fell to Pieces, like *Dagon* before the Ark, and hath not, in that Position, been heard of since." The plots of 1683 against the king's life were actually "hatched," as Trevelyan puts it, at the Green-Ribbon Club. A number of members were arrested, and the rest were glad enough to abandon the society. As late as 1685, according to Sir John Bramston,[3] one John Ayloff, who "had binn a clubber at the King's Head Taverne, a green-ribon man," was executed for complicity in one of the plots.

Evidence multiplies rapidly to prove the unceasing activity of the political clubs.[4] It must suffice here to cite the single instance of their relation to the famous Tory

1. *Poems on Affairs of State,* III (1704), 146.

2. *Examen,* p. 573.

3. *The Autobiography of Sir John Bramston,* ed. Braybrooke (Camden Society, 1845), p. 209.

4. See the account of the White-horse Club in *The Pepys Ballads,* ed. H. E. Rollins, III (1930), 68.

journalist, Sir Roger L'Estrange. On March 7, 1691, Dr. Prideaux wrote to his sister as follows:

Many persons have been taken up, as suspected, at clubbs; amongst others, Sir Roger L'Estrange, which is out on bayle.[1]

This is doubtless the same arrest as that mentioned by Viscount Sidney in his letter of March 3 to the Earl of Nottingham,[2] wherein it appears that the active old pamphleteer had recently been apprehended with damning letters in his possession. These clubs were doubtless meetings of Tory malcontents, and were as such held suspect by vigilant Whig leaders.

By this time the club had definitely begun to color contemporary literature. Sometimes it was the object of satire, as in *News from Covent-Garden: or, The Town-Gallants Vindication.* The author of this anonymous little quarto, posing as the defender of the gallant against a bitter attack in *The Character of a Town-Gallant*, showed a club of wits "assembled for the Damning of the late *Character*." His account of their meeting is in reality an ironic attack, as he makes his pamphlet a dramatization of much the same foibles that the *Character* had satirized. Mrs. Behn amused her audience at the expense of a similar society of gallants in *The Younger Brother*, which she wrote shortly before her death in 1689. In the second scene of Act I, Sir Merlin is forced to defend himself from charges of being a rake-helly scoundrel.

Sir *Merl[in]*. Lord, Aunt, I only go to the Club sometimes, to improve my self in the Art of Living, and the Accomplishments of a fine Gentleman.

Sir *Rowl[and]*. A fine Gentleman, Sot, a fine Coxcomb!
[*Beats him.*

Sir *Morg[an]*. Hold, hold, good Uncle; my Cousin has been only drawn in, a little or so, d'ye see, being Heir to a good Es-

1. *Fifth Report of the Royal Commission on Historical Manuscripts* (1876), p. 381.
2. Quoted by George Kitchen in *Sir Roger L'Estrange* (1913), p. 369.

tate; and that's what his Club wants, to pay off old Tavern Scores, and buy Utensils for Whores in Fashion.[1]

A different sort of group appears in the satiric verses attributed to Charles Darby, entitled *Bacchanalia: or a Description of a Drunken Club* (1680). As its title promises, the poem describes the rites of a club of sots in a tavern. The author's complete lack of restraint and his very indifferent handling of his modified pindaric stanzas go far to offset the vivacity of the picture. Fortunately for the literary career of the club, it was soon to fall into more able hands.

A much more sympathetic picture of a congenial society appears in a ballad called "The Good-Fellows Frollick; or, the Kent-Street Club."[2] The meeting was apparently of a casual nature, for the poem begins:

> Here is a crew of jovial Blades that lov'd the nut-brown Ale:
> They in an alehouse chanc'd to meet, and told a merry Tale.

A seaman, a weaver, a blacksmith, a nobleman, and many more are in turn presented that they may express their devotion to the "Ale that is so brown." The light-hearted spirit of the ballad is in pleasant contrast with the splenetic mood of the satire on the "Drunken Club." Samuel Butler leaves his reader somewhat in doubt as to his sympathies in his "Epigram on a Club of Sots;"[3] but the verses indicate once more the prevalence of such gatherings.

One of the most vivid scenes which Alexander Radcliffe witnessed in the course of his ramble is described in connection with a tavern which he visited.

> A Club there was in t'other Room,
> I bolted in, being known to some,
> Such men are not in Christendom
> For jesting,

1. *The Plays, Histories, and Novels of the Ingenious Mrs. Aphra Behn* (1871), IV, 356. See also p. 354.
2. *The Roxburghe Ballads*, ed. J. W. Ebsworth, VI (1889), 351–352.
3. *Satires and Miscellaneous Poetry and Prose*, p. 148.

They use a plain familiar stile,
Appearing friendly all the while,
Yet never part without a Broil
Intestin.[1]

On this particular evening the quarrel arose between a young squire and a bragging captain. Various members, of different occupations, took sides and inveighed against each other, expressing in their recriminations Radcliffe's own opinions of their various callings. When the argument finally became a general brawl, the author departed to continue his ramble, disappointed that no duel had developed.

In spite of the evidence of the increasing vogue of club life, it will be noticed that in none of the pieces written after 1660 which have thus far been mentioned has there been any indication that men of letters formed such societies. A tradition does exist which connects Cleveland and Butler with a club, founded after the Restoration, which Charles II is supposed to have visited.[2] But even such obscure societies as this were few in number, because of the supremely influential nature of the dominant literary circle. The history of the literary club of the late seventeenth century is the history of the group of wits at Will's Coffeehouse.

The story of Will's begins in the diary of Samuel Pepys. As early as 1660 there is a terse but promising entry:

So to Will's with Mr. Pinkney, who invited me to their feast at his Hall the next Monday.[3]

The passage clearly suggests some manner of group that dined regularly together. That it was not the society that later made Will's famous becomes clear, however, in a passage written down February 3, 1664:

1. *The Ramble,* p. 91.
2. John Aubrey, *Brief Lives,* 1, 175. See also *The Poems of John Cleveland,* ed. J. M. Berdan (New York, 1903), pp. 47–48.
3. *The Diary of Samuel Pepys,* 1, 16–17.

In Covent Garden to-night, going to fetch home my wife, I stopped at the great Coffee-house there, *where I never was before*; where Dryden the poet (I knew at Cambridge), and all the wits of the town, and Harris the player, and Mr. Hoole of our College. And had I had time then, or could at other times, it will be good coming thither, for there, I perceive, is very witty and pleasant discourse. But I could not tarry, and as it was late, they were all ready to go away.[1]

Although Pepys's half-dozen scattered references to the Covent-Garden Will's show that he was only an occasional visitor, his tribute is notable because of its early appearance.

"It was Dryden," Pope later remarked, "who made Will's Coffee-house the great resort for the wits of his time." [2] Here, before the composition of *Annus Mirabilis*, and as early as the production of *The Wild Gallant*, Dryden began to gather about him the ever shifting coterie which distinguished the place for some forty years. The early pictures of him and his following are largely satiric. In 1673 Richard Leigh wrote a pamphlet, published at Oxford, entitled *The Censure of the Rota. On Mr Driden's Conquest of Granada*. Leigh shows a debate between "the *Athenian Vertuosi* in the *Coffe-Academy* instituted by *Apollo* for the advancement of *Gazett Philosophy Mercury's, Diurnalls*, &c." [3] Although Leigh's wits ridicule many of the actual weaknesses of the play, especially the improbability of the action and the extravagance of the style, they do not hesitate to strike below the belt. The tone of their criticism is best illustrated in the speech which describes Dryden's typical hero.

It is but framing the character of a Huff of the Town, one that from breaking Glass-windows, and combating the watch, starts

1. *The Diary of Samuel Pepys*, IV, 30–31. The italics are mine.
2. Joseph Spence, *Anecdotes, Observations, and Characters*, ed. S. W. Singer (1858), p. 199.
3. *The Censure of the Rota. On Mr Driden's Conquest of Granada* (Oxford, 1673), p. 1.

up an *Heroe*: him you must make very saucy to his superiours, to shew he is of the same stamp with *Achilles* and *Rinaldo*; then tame the savage with the charming sight of the *Kings Daughter* (or wife) whom this *St George* is to deliver from the *Dragon*, or greater dangers: to heighten his character the more, bring in a sheepish King with a Guard of poultrons to be kick't by him, as often as he thinks fit his Miss. should be a witnesse of his Gallantry.[1]

Although both the title and the method are patterned after Harrington's tract against Milton, the Rota itself could have had nothing to do with this attack on Dryden. One of the wits is supposed to be a "grave Gentleman *that us'd to sup in Apollo and could tell many Storys of Ben. Jonson,*" which heightens the effect of spuriousness produced by the whole tone of the piece. It seems likely that Leigh was burlesquing the critical discussions at Will's and turning a purely fictitious group against the rising monarch.

The satire on Dryden was carried further in *The Friendly Vindication of Mr. Dryden from the Censure of the Rota, by His Cabal of Wits* (1673). This pamphlet purports to be a reply to "the Academick Rota of Oxford." The reader is presented with a meeting of Dryden's cabal of wits, presumably held at Will's, at which the admiring members begin a discussion of the late attack on their hero. In the course of their ironic speeches, Dryden and his circle are held up once more to ridicule, and the vindication proves to be simply another attack.[2] A true friend eventually entered the controversy[3] and set about methodically to refute the *Friendly Vindication*; but the damage was done. When Shadwell turned on Dryden with *The Medal of John Bays* nine years later, there was ample precedent for his

1. *Ibid.*, p. 18.
2. There is an interesting implication (p. 9) that collaboration went on between Dryden and his cabal.
3. With *Mr. Dryden Vindicated, in a Reply to the Friendly Vindication of Mr. Dryden: With Reflections On the Rota* (1673).

scurrilous picture of the great poet and his followers. And a poem entitled "A Days Ramble in Covent-Garden" contains the lines:

> To *Wills* I went, where Beau and VVit
> In mutual Contemplation sit;
> But which were VVits, and which were Beaus,
> The Devil sure's in him who Knows.[1]

Many of the more amiable descriptions of Will's have already become common tradition.[2] Ned Ward lays a scene in *The London Spy* at the Great Coffee-house. Dr. Johnson gleaned some interesting details from two of his contemporaries who had known Dryden, one of whom related "that at the house which he frequented, called Will's Coffee-house, the appeal upon any literary dispute was made to him, and the other . . . that his armed chair, which in the winter had a settled and prescriptive place by the fire, was in the summer placed in the balcony; and that he called the two places his winter and his summer seat." [3] The witty manner in which Dryden exercised his dictatorship appears in a manuscript note pasted in a British Museum copy of the third volume of Theophilus Cibber's *Lives of the Poets*. According to this note, the wits agreed one evening to write extempore verses, of which Dryden was to be the judge. The Earl of Dorset nonchalantly tossed off the following lines:

> I promise to pay to John Dryden, Esq; or order, on demand, the sum of five hundred pounds.
>
> Dorset.

In awarding the bays to the earl, Dryden is supposed to have remarked, "I must confess that I am equally charmed with the style and the subject. . . . This kind of writing

---

1. John Dennis, *Poems in Burlesque* (1692), p. 12.
2. See John Timbs, *Clubs and Club Life in London* (1872), pp. 315–322.
3. Samuel Johnson, *Lives of the English Poets*, ed. G. Birkbeck Hill (Oxford, 1905), I, 408–409.

exceeds any other whether ancient or modern. It is not the essence but the quintessence of language."

During the last decade of Dryden's life, three separate clubs arose at Will's. John Dennis wrote to Cheek from the country in 1693, saying that a friend of theirs "has a hundred times, since he came to this Place, regretted the Rabble, nay he has regretted the *Grave Club*; nay, has wish'd himself even in the *Witty Club*, which he believes is by this time erected." [1] A letter from Moyle to Congreve, two years later, says:

I believe not a Man of the Grave Club durst assist at this ridiculous Scene, for fear of laughing outright. . . . Would to God I could laugh with you, for one hour or two, at all the ridiculous things that have happen'd at *Will*'s Coffee-house since I left it, 'tis the merriest place in the World. [2]

In the same year, Congreve had written to Moyle:

All here wish for you, from the President of the Grave Club, to the most puny Member of the Rabble.

Beyond what the names tell, it is difficult to ascertain anything about these three clubs except that they were fairly distinct. Malone's supposition that the Grave Club was made up of politicians is placed under suspicion by a letter from Congreve to Moyle in which he urges his friend "not to come up again like a Politician," because in so doing he would "add a new Monster to the Coffee-house, that was never seen there before." [3] As Malone points out, the dominating position of the Witty Club is reflected in the practise of referring to Will's as the Wits' Coffee-house. [4]

Stories of Julian, the inebriate lampoon-monger, and of Will Urwin, the proprietor, are almost as common as those

1. *The Select Works of Mr. John Dennis* (1718), II, 537.
2. *Ibid.*, p. 534.
3. *Ibid.*, p. 536.
4. *The Critical and Miscellaneous Prose Works of John Dryden*, ed. Edmond Malone (1800), I, i, 490.

of Dryden. Because it is less well known than the rest, one copy of verses deserves partial quotation. The lines were addressed "To Will's Coffee House" in 1691.

> *Tell* me sage *Will* thou that the town around
> For wit & Tea & Coffee art renown'd
> Tell me, for as the common rumour goes
> Thy house is cramm'd eternaly with beaus,
> How shall I that strange Animal define
> What are his marks, his Virtues, or his sign?
> So may'st thou still keep in the wits' good graces
> And never loose a farthing more at races.[1]

In the eight remaining lines Will replies with a none too flattering character of a beau, in whom he finds the chief faults of some of his leading customers, including the inevitable Thomas D'Urfey. Will's death in 1695 produced much sadness and elegy among the wits his patrons. It was not, however, until after the death of Dryden that the place became perceptibly changed. In the opening number of *The Tatler*, Steele wrote from Will's:

This place is very much altered since Mr. Dryden frequented it; where you used to see songs, epigrams, and satires in the hands of every man you met, you now have only a pack of cards; and instead of cavils about the turn of the expression, the elegance of the style, and the like, the learned now dispute only about the truth of the game.

Its traditions had survived, however, to such an extent that Steele chose it as the place whence the poetical part of his paper emanated; and even later references show that it was not soon forgotten as the seat of poetry and wit. More than any other society that existed before 1700, the gathering of wits at Will's was responsible for the nature and literary importance of the clubs of the early eighteenth century.

1. MS. Harl. 7317, p. 247.

CHAPTER II

The Club and the Town

THE SOCIAL IMPORTANCE OF THE CLUB

TO SHOW the relation between the clubs of London and the life and writings of its inhabitants is not an easy matter. Even to estimate the importance of the societies of gentlemen is difficult enough. It is possible to know much about the Kit-Cats and Addison's society at Button's Coffee-house. There is plenty of evidence that literally hundreds of minor societies existed, the nature of which can only be surmised. Few periods in English social history are better documented than this one. Its fashionable obsession with manners has become proverbial. Yet many clubs inevitably faded from the scene, as the century wore on, without leaving the slightest trace of their existence, except for the incalculable part they played in regulating the thoughts and actions of their unsung members. The only way to present this sort of influence would be to set down at large all the wealth of allusion to club life which does occur and allow the reader to draw his own conclusions. To do so is, of course, out of the question.

In spite of the imponderable element, the character of the general influence is clear enough. During the reign of Queen Anne, or somewhat earlier, the club began to usurp the place of the tavern and the drawing-room in the routine of London life. It became the place to which the gentleman or the citizen retired after dinner to converse with his peers over a bottle of wine or a tankard of ale, to

be joined at supper, perhaps, by more companions just
returned from the theatre. The comedy of manners, the
comedy of Westminster Hall, the execution of a highwayman, the stabbing of a minister, the latest skirmish on the
Danube or on the queen's back stairs, the soundness of a
horse or of an investment, — these were the subjects of
conversation.

Not only were events discussed, but principles were
evolved and business transacted. One club united in defense of a translation of Homer; another in defense of the
Hanoverian succession; a third in defense of freethinking;
a fourth in defense of the ancients against the moderns.
Since every man tended, in associating himself with a club,
to seek his own kind, the societies of gentlemen took on a
factional character, whether their interests were literary,
political, economic, or philosophical. If this factionalism
did not always lead to dispassionate thought, the concerted
opinion and action which resulted produced important
consequences. Witness the outcry of a dissenter in a poem
entitled "The Address, 1704":

> Ye Men of Might, and muckle Power,
>   Our Representing K[nave]s;
> Who High-Church Zealots to restore,
> And Toleration Acts devour,
>   Would make us all your Slaves. . . .
>
> You meet in Clubs, and strong Cabals,
>   To controvert Elections:
> But Party Interest there prevails,
> Merit and Sense of Honour fails,
>   And meets with no Protection.[1]

One of the greatest uniting influences of the time was
politics. Often there were other ties in political gatherings,
— friendship, social equality, community of affection for
the bottle. But party sympathy generally proved a
stronger link than any of these. The different political

1. *Poems on Affairs of State*, IV (1707), 68–69.

clubs of the period, and particularly those of Anne's reign, were frequented by men of all ranks and professions, each group having a character and purpose of its own. Praise and censure were showered upon the clubmen by pamphleteers. They themselves talked over the progress of their rivals at their meetings. The Town kept an eye of concern on their proceedings, and from the pulpit came torrents of admonition and exhortation.

THE KIT-CATS AND THE TOASTERS

The greatest political society of the day was the Kit-Cat Club. The name of this august assembly has been of enough curiosity to call forth a number of explanations. That most frequently quoted is in the famous "Epigram on the Toasts of the Kit-Cat Club, Anno 1716," generally attributed to Dr. John Arbuthnot.

> Whence deathless *Kit-Cat* took its Name,
>   Few Criticks can unriddle;
> Some say from *Pastry Cook* it came,
>   And some from *Cat* and *Fiddle*.
>
> From no trim Beau's its Name it boasts,
>   Grey Statesman, or green Wits;
> But from this Pell-mell-Pack of Toasts,
>   Of old *Cats* and young *Kits*.[1]

This ingenious theory, well as it agrees with the club's practise of toasting the reigning beauties of the day, was obviously not advanced with the expectation of belief. The "Cat-and-Fiddle" explanation, though widely accepted, is almost equally incredible. It became traditional through Ned Ward's account of the Kit-Cat Club, which has done much to obscure the facts concerning both the origin and the nature of the society. Ward maintains that a pastry-cook named Christopher kept a shop at the sign of the

---

1. Motte's *Miscellanies in Prose and Verse*, III (1732), 67–68.

Cat-and-Fiddle, where the club was accustomed in its early days to forgather. The name, according to Ward, resulted from the combination of Kit, the inevitable shortening of Christopher, and the first word of the pie-man's sign.

Much more likely than either of these explanations is the suggestion that the proprietor of the shop was one Christopher Cat,[1] from whose name the club directly derived its own. This theory harmonizes with the common practise of referring to the shopkeeper by the name of Kit-Cat, as William King does in the lines,

> His glory far, like SIR-LOIN's KNIGHTHOOD, flies;
> Immortal made, as KIT-CAT by his Pies.[2]

A portrait of honest Kit done by Sir Godfrey Kneller was extant as late as 1867.[3] In the light of the contemporary occurrences of the contracted form of his name, it seems clear that the noble Kit-Cats called themselves after the well-known publican.[4]

The origin of the club itself has been debated even more extensively than its name. Malone looked somewhat doubtfully for the predecessor of the group in a society of gentlemen who achieved some fame before 1700 as the Knights of the Toast. Although no date can be definitely assigned to the foundation of the order, Malone was able to cite abundant evidence of its existence.

In one of Settle's pieces, purchased some time ago, Mr. Bindley found a loose sheet containing a manuscript poem written

1. Thomas Hearne asserts (*Remarks and Collections*, I [1885], 116–117) that the club was named for Christopher Catling, "wth whose Puddings & Conversation the first Founders of the Society were extremely well pleas'd." The entry is for December 6, 1705.

2. *The Original Works of William King* (1776), III, 83. Compare Addison's usage in *The Spectator*, No. 9, Blackmore's in *The Kit-Cats*, and Pope's in his account of the club to Spence.

3. *Notes and Queries*, 5th Series, III (1875), 259–260.

4. A skeptical devotee of *Notes and Queries* (5th Series, III, 117) explained the name as the product of a natural human fondness for reduplication.

by him, addressed "to the most renowned the President, [probably either Lord Dorset or Mr. Montague,] and the rest of the Knights of the most noble Order of the TOAST;" in which the poet endeavours to propitiate the person to whom the verses served as a begging Petition, by asserting the dignity and antiquity of this illustrious Society. They appear to have been written in 1699.

> "Why should the noble Windsor garters boast
> "Their fame, above the Knighthood of the Toast?
> "Is't on their first original they build?
> "Their high-priz'd knighthood these to you must yield.
> "A lady dropp'd a garter at a ball;
> "A toy for their foundation; — was that all?
> "Suppose the nymph that lost it was divine;
> "The garter's but a relique from the shrine:
> "The Toast includes the deity; — not one star,
> "But the whole constellation of the Fair." [1]

Other poetical accounts of the order are more accessible. Shadwell seems to have been referring to the members when he wrote in *The Scowrers* (1691):

> You're all meer Sops in Wine, your Brains are Bogs;
> A Toast is equal to a common Drunkard. [2]

Among the *Poems on Affairs of State* is a "Letter from J. P. to Colonel H. occasion'd by the Colonel's two late Letters," which proves even more illuminating than Settle's verses. Henry Heveningham, the aspirer to wit referred to as "Colonel H.", had apparently written a verse epistle on the Knights that J. P. did not consider worthy of them, for he begins:

> O *Harry*, canst thou find no Subject fit,
> But thy best Friend, to exercise thy Wit;
> No Order but the Toast to ridicule?
> Why with things sacred dost thou play the Fool? . . .

---

1. *The Critical and Miscellaneous Prose Works of John Dryden*, ed. Edmond Malone (1800), I, ii, 115 n.

2. *The Complete Works of Thomas Shadwell*, ed. Montague Summers (1927), V, 139.

Is this thy Gratitude for all the Wine
The Knights bestow'd, who never tasted thine?
And dost thou thus our Mysteries disclose,
And in rude Rhime our President expose? [1]

Clearly the Knights took themselves very seriously. If the objectionable poem of Heveningham had survived, it would doubtless throw much light upon the intimate affairs of the order.

Malone also calls attention to a reference in one of Dryden's letters (of February, 1700) to a "Ballad of the Pews," whose author was "sayd to be Mr. Manwareing, or my Lord Peterborough." [2] This poem is probably identical with "A New Ballad, Call'd, The Brawny Bishop's Complaint," a lampoon on Bishop Burnet, which represents him as petitioning the queen to prevent his services from being spoiled by the inattention of the ladies during the sermon. The ballad begins:

When B[urne]t perceiv'd the beautiful Dames,
Who flock'd to the Chappel of hilly St. *James*,
On their Lovers the kindest Looks did bestow,
And smil'd not on him while he bellow'd below,
     To the Princess he went
     With pious intent,
This dangerous Ill in the Church to Prevent:
O Madam! quoth he, our Religion is lost,
If the Ladies thus ogle the Knights of the Toast.

Only the old ladies heed him, the bishop complains.

The rest with their Tattle my Harmony spoil;
And *Bur[ling]ton*, *An[gle]sey*, *K[in]gston* and *B[oy]le*
     Their Minds entertain
     With thoughts so profane,
'Tis a Mercy to find that at Church they contain;
Ev'n *Hen[ning]ham*'s Shapes their weak Fancies intice,
And rather than me they will ogle the *Vice*.[3]

1. *Poems on Affairs of State*, II (1703), 255.
2. Dryden, *Prose Works*, I, ii, 109.
3. *Poems on Affairs of State*, III (1704), 372–373.

Malone would identify Burlington, Anglesey, Kingston, and Boyle with certain of the offending ladies, who were reigning toasts of the day.[1] The syntax of the passage is ambiguous, however, and the names allow interpretation as referring to four famous noblemen of the time, a reading which is more significant, especially when considered in connection with the passage about "Henningham's shapes" which follows.

Some vague relationship seems to exist between the Knights of the Toast and the Kit-Cat Club; for Burlington, Kingston, and Boyle were all members of the latter society, and here is indication of their connection with the former. If Arthur Maynwaring, another Kit-Cat, wrote the poem, — and he is one of the two possible authors suggested by Dryden, — there is another connection between the order and the club. A much more impressive bit of evidence appears in a letter from Addison to Abraham Stanyan (February, 1700), in which the poet writes:

I thank you for the news and poetry you were pleased to send me, though I must confess I did not like either of them. The votes had too much fire in them and the verses none at all: however I hope the first will prove as harmless to the ministers of state as the others are to the knights of the toast.[2]

This reference can hardly be to anything but the poem by Heveningham to which J. P. versified his objections. The passage implies that the two correspondents had an interest in the order which may have meant membership. Since Addison and Stanyan were both members of the Kit-Cat Club, here is still another connection between the two societies.

The best description of the Knights' proceedings is given by Addison in *The Tatler*, No. 24, where he traces the custom of toasting back to a ludicrous incident of the reign of Charles II.

1. Dryden, *Prose Works*, I, ii, 116.
2. *The Works of Joseph Addison* (1856), v, 329.

Though this institution had so trivial a beginning, it is now elevated into a formal order; and that happy virgin who is received and drank to at their meetings, has no more to do in this life, but to judge and accept of the first good offer.[1] The manner of her inauguration is much like that of the choice of a Doge in Venice: it is performed by balloting; and when she is so chosen, she reigns indisputably for that ensuing year; but must be elected anew to prolong her empire a moment beyond it. When she is regularly chosen, her name is written with a diamond on a drinking-glass.

The expression, "a formal order," refers directly to the Order of the Toast, the fame of which had evidently survived till 1709. Although the Kit-Cats also inscribed verses to their toasts on their wine-glasses,[2] it is not necessary to assume that the two clubs were identical, obviously related though they were.

A bit of gossip written by Prior to Stanyan on the nineteenth of January, 1700, settles the question.

To-morrow night Batterton acts Falstaff, and to encourage that poor house the Kit Katters have taken one side-box, and the Knights of the Toast have taken the other.[3]

The two societies were distinct enough, then, that they could occupy the opposite sides of a theatre. Originally they were probably very different. Oldmixon says that the Kit-Cat Club "grew up from a private Meeting of Mr. *Somers*, afterwards Lord *Chancellor*, and another Lawyer,

1. The distinction conferred in electing a toast appears in the mock treaty which was drawn up between Swift and Mrs. Long in 1709. It is reprinted with Lord Wharton's toast to Mrs. Long in *The Prose Works of Jonathan Swift*, ed. Temple Scott (1897–1908), XI, 383–386.

2. Some of the verses which accompanied the ladies' names have been preserved in Tonson's *Miscellany Poems*, V (1716), 60–70. The fifty-four poems are grouped under the caption, "Verses Written for the Toasting-Glasses of the Kit-kat Club, in the Year 1703." Although many are anonymous, a number are signed with such names as Addison, Congreve, Garth, Maynwaring, Lord Carbery, Lord Halifax, and Lord Wharton. Two similar toasts by Lord Lansdowne are printed in John Nichols's *A Select Collection of Poems*, V (1782), 276.

3. *Calendar of the Manuscripts of the Marquis of Bath*, III (1908), 394.

now in a very high Station in the Law, and Mr. *Tonson, sen.* the Booksellor, who before the *Revolution*, met frequently in an Evening at a Tavern, near *Temple-Bar*, to unbend themselves after Business, and have a little free and chearful Conversation in those dangerous Times."[1] The Whig historian speaks of the famous mutton pies, and then continues:

Other Gentlemen of the same good *English* Principles, joyning themselves afterwards to this original Society, it became the most Noble One, and the most Pleasant, that perhaps ever was in the World.

By "good *English* Principles" Oldmixon meant, of course, good Whig principles; for the club was unified, in its later days, by party loyalty. The group which gathered about Somers and Tonson was composed at first, in all likelihood, of rising young wits. As the last decade of the century wore on, the more brilliant of the Knights of the Toast deserted their order for the new club, bringing with them the custom of toasting. If Lady Mary Wortley Montagu was presented at the Kit-Cat Club when she was only eight years old, as Lady Louisa Stuart relates,[2] the evolution was complete by 1697. Prior's reference, however, is the first one known that uses the famous name.

How the sagacious publisher, Jacob Tonson, maintained his position in this distinguished group is a matter of some curiosity. Clearly he was the social inferior of most of the Kit-Cats, a fact of which he was constantly reminded by his enemies. Rowe, among others, jibed at his presumption, in "The Reconcilement between Jacob Tonson and Mr. Congreve" (1714). The poem, in the form of a dialogue between Tonson and Congreve, is imitated from the ninth ode of the third book of Horace. Congreve says:

1. John Oldmixon, *The History of England*, III (1735), 479.
2. *The Letters and Works of Lady Mary Wortley Montagu*, ed. Moy Thomas (1893), I, 52–53; and D. Crane Taylor, *William Congreve* (Oxford, 1931), p. 197.

While in your early Days of Reputation,
You for blue Garters had not such a Passion;
While yet you did not use (as now your Trade is)
To drink with noble Lords, and toast their Ladies;
Thou, *JACOB TONSON*, wer't to my conceiving,
The chearfullest, best, honest, Fellow living.[1]

In spite of such taunts, Tonson continued to occupy a
leading rôle in Kit-Cat affairs as long as the society lasted.
In 1703, upon his acquisition of Barn Elms, the headquarters of the club were moved there, though meetings continued to be held at times, for the sake of convenience, in
London taverns. It was at Barn Elms that Tonson arranged the special club-room, in which the famous portraits by Sir Godfrey Kneller, himself one of the club, long
hung. Sir John Vanbrugh, one of Tonson's most intimate
friends among the clubmen, testifies again and again to
the bookseller's importance in the affairs of the society.
When Jacob was away in Amsterdam in 1703 and wrote
back that he missed the congenial gatherings, the dramatist replied:

In short, the Kit-Cat wants you, much more than you ever
can do them. Those who remain in towne, are in great desire
of waiting on you at Barne-Elmes; not that they have finished
their pictures neither; tho' to excuse them (as well as myself),
Sir Godfrey has been most in fault. The fool has got a country
house near Hampton Court, and is so busy about fitting it up
(to receive nobody), that there is no getting him to work.[2]

The forty-eight members whose memory Kneller perpetuated in his portraits [3] were the most distinguished

1. *The Miscellaneous Works of Nicholas Rowe* (1733), I, 11.
2. *The Complete Works of Sir John Vanbrugh*, ed. B. Dobrée and G. Webb
(1928), IV, 7. See also the next page, where Vanbrugh says, "The Kit Catt too,
will never meet without you, so you see here's a generall Stagnation for want
of you."
3. For a list of the portraits, see James Caulfield, *Memoirs of the Celebrated
Persons Composing the Kit-Cat Club* (1821). In 1735 John Faber published *The
Kit-Cat Club Done from the Original Paintings of Sir Godfrey Kneller*, a handsome book of engravings dedicated to the Duke of Somerset.

Whigs of the time. Along with the names of Sunderland, Marlborough, Godolphin, and Walpole, appear those of Addison, Steele, Congreve, Vanbrugh, Walsh, and Garth, so that the literary world was not ill represented. Prior was at one time a member; but when he lost his "good English principles" in 1707 and became a Tory, his membership terminated abruptly. His portrait is not to be found among those of the Kit-Cat collection. Macky informs us that "this *Club* can have but *Thirty-Nine* Members." [1] When one considers that the club existed for some twenty years, the nine odd portraits tell their own story. Certain turbulent spirits appear to have been admitted, with due qualms, because of their influence. In this connection, Pope remarked to Spence that "the day Lord Mohun and the Earl of Berkley were entered of it, Jacob said he saw they were just going to be ruined." [2] The numerous anecdotes of the members give colorful pictures of the Kit-Cats in session. [3]

The society had not lived long when it began to draw the fire of satirists. Among the first verse attacks was a passage devoted to Tonson in *Faction Display'd*, an anonymously printed satire on the Whigs which came in 1704 from the hand of William Shippen. The poem pictures a heterogeneous gathering of Whig leaders, and identifies the club with the party in the lines:

> Beaus, Biters, Pathicks, B——rs and Cits,
> Tosters, Kit-Kats, Divines, Buffoons and Wits
> Compos'd the Medly Crew. [4]

Among the caricatures of the various leaders who address the assembly is one of Tonson, under the name of Bibliopolo, three lines of which, according to Malone, are stolen

---

1. *A Journey Through England* (1714), p. 188.
2. Joseph Spence, *Anecdotes, Observations, and Characters*, ed. S. W. Singer (1858), p. 256.
3. See John Timbs, *Clubs and Club Life in London* (1872), pp. 49–53.
4. *Faction Display'd* (1704), p. 14.

from Dryden.[1] The opening lines of Tonson's speech intimate, in spite of their ircny, the strategic nature of the
bookseller's position in the spreading of Whig propaganda.
Bibliopolo is then made to continue bombastically:

> 'I am the Founder of your lov'd *Kit-Kat*,
> 'A Club that gave Direction to the State.
> ''Twas there we first instructed all our Youth,
> 'To talk Prophane and Laugh at Sacred Truth.
> 'We taught them how to Tost, and Rhime, and Bite,
> 'To Sleep away the Day, and drink away the Night.'[2]

An undated broadside advertisement attacking Tonson
seems to refer to this passage from Shippen's satire. It
purports to be a statement by Tonson on his expulsion
from the club in January, 1704, "for his ill-timed freedom
with some of the Principal Members, at the Reading of a
Late Satyr upon his Parts and Person." Tonson earnestly
denies that he was beaten on this occasion and insists that
he "did of his own free Motion valiantly withdraw himself
from the said Society, in scorn of being their Jest any
longer." The fact that Jacob's name was subscribed to the
advertisement need be taken no more seriously than the
announcement of the speedy publication of a poem called
"Jacob's Revenge. Being a Comical Account of the
Grounds and Reasons of the Bookseller's quitting the
K—t-C—t Club." Tonson's connection with the Kit-Cats
does not elsewhere appear to have been broken, and the
whole advertisement was only a piece of amusing irony.

Political animosity was behind another aspersion on the
club in 1705. In a pamphlet entitled *The Tackers Vindicated; or, an Answer to the Whigs New Black List*, a Tory
journalist had at his opponents with a *tu quoque*. If the
Tories desired to blacklist the enemies of church and
queen, says the author, "the KIT-KAT CLUB in the *Pall-*

1. Dryden, *Prose Works*, I, i, 525.
2. *Faction Display'd* (1704), p. 15.

Mall, might also Furnish them with sufficient Heads for such an Undertaking; they being given to understand that they are fall'n off the Design of their first Institution; and from turning *Criticks* upon Wit, are fall'n into *Criticisms* upon *Policy*, I might say AGENTS in it." Before its enemies had done with the Kit-Cat Club, they were to build up for that noted body a reputation for inebriety, blasphemy, and political intrigue, which it only partially deserved.

The passages just adverted to were merely the opening guns. In 1708 a much more elaborate attack came from the tireless hand of Sir Richard Blackmore. His motives are obscure. Perhaps it is enough to recall that as a non-member he may well have been envious of the distinction which had fallen to most of the Kit-Cats, and that he had previously suffered from the pens of Garth and Steele.[1] When the mock-heroic entitled *The Kit-Cats* appeared in a collected edition (1718) of Blackmore's shorter pieces, it was accompanied by a statement that although it was "writ some Years ago . . . and not design'd for the Press," it was now being published because "the Author, having unwarily let a Copy of it go out of his Hands, which he has not been able to recover" had "Reason to believe it will otherwise come Abroad by Means of the Copy beforemention'd." Since Curll had already published the poem separately in a thin folio ten years before, Blackmore's statement is of no great consequence.

The Kit-Cats throws much light on the later misconceptions about the club's origin. The poem begins with a florid invocation of "great Bocai,"[2] who according to Blackmore was the leader of the society, having founded it in the reign of King William. It is here that Tonson first appears in the rôle of guardian angel to neglected young poets.

1. Samuel Garth, *The Dispensary*, IV, 172, and Steele's contribution to the *Commendatory Verses on the Author of the Two Arthurs*.
2. Obviously an inversion of "Jacob."

He still caress'd the unregarded Tribe,
And did to all their various Tasks prescribe;
From whence to Both great Acquisitions came,
To him the Profit, and to them the Fame.[1]

The satirist mentions the weekly meetings of the club at
the Fountain Tavern in the Strand, where Jacob feasted his
hungry protégés.

Hence did the Assembly's Title first arise,
And *Kit-Cat* Wits sprung first from *Kit-Cat*'s Pies.

As Blackmore describes the quality of their literary efforts,
his praise is ironically fulsome. Their fame, he says, spread
rapidly.

Their brighter Beams eclips'd the fading Toast,
That long before unrivall'd rul'd the Roast.
Now Crowds to Founder *Bocai* did resort,
And for his Favour humbly made their Court.
The little Wits attended at his Gate,
And Men of Title did his Levee wait;
For he, as Soveraign by Prerogative,
Old Members did exclude, and new receive.
He judg'd who most were for the Order fit,
And Chapters held to make new Knights of Wit.

The remainder of the poem deals with an effort to break
up the club with internal strife, made by the votaries of the
God of Dullness. In his temple in Ireland, the god holds
a meeting to discuss the plot. The delegation from England includes Dr. Knightly Chetwood, Henry Dodwell,
Martin Lister, Sir Hans Sloane, Tom Brown, and other
writers and virtuosos whom for various reasons Blackmore
wished to abuse. As the satire concludes, the God of Dullness is assuring the convention that they may return to
their homes confident of the destruction of the Kit-Cats
and the downfall of Tonson.

1. Richard Blackmore, *A Collection of Poems on Various Subjects* (1718),
pp. 105-106.

This mediocre mock-heroic does not enhance its author's reputation. It has a certain importance, however, because of its relation to the more widely read account of the club by Edward Ward, who followed Sir Richard in describing the origin of the Kit-Cat group. Ward devotes a comparatively long section of his *Satyrical Reflections on Clubs* (1710) to ridiculing the Kit-Cats. Like Blackmore he explains the club's inception as a business enterprise of Tonson's, adding graphic details as to the nature of the meetings, including the elusive Cat-and-Fiddle where Christopher was supposed to have had his pastry shop. Although the young wits whom Tonson collected were a set of mercenary scandal-mongers, according to Ward, "every Week, the Listening Town was Charm'd with some wonderful Off-spring of their Teeming-Noddles: And the Fame of *Kit-Cat* began to extend it self to the utmost Limits of our learned Metropolis." [1] Ward also agrees with Blackmore that the fame of the poetical club drew the nobility to its meetings and insists upon the priority of the writer-members. Giving free rein to his imagination, Ned even mentions the poetical works for which the club should receive credit, citing particularly "that most accurate Banter upon the *Hind* and *Panther*, call'd the City-Mouse and the Country-Mouse." The implication that Prior received much less credit than he deserved for his share in the piece appears in four epigrams, bad enough to have been of Ward's own composition, the last of which concludes:

> But mastiff Poets oft are doom'd to Starve,
> Whilst Lap-dog Wits are hug'd, who less deserve. [2]

Ward ends his account with some irreverent verses describing a Kit-Cat feast.

There is no reason for taking Ned's *Satyrical Reflections* as an authority on the Kit-Cats. His Tory sympathies

1. *Satyrical Reflections on Clubs* (1710), p. 363.
2. *Ibid.*, p. 367.

alone would be enough to cast suspicion on his veracity. This particular essay is full of envious sarcasm and reveals on every hand its author's resentment at the distinction achieved by the poetical members. John Macky's less prejudiced account, written about 1713, says nothing of the club's having arisen from the rapacity of Tonson and asserts that "the late Great Earl of *Dorset*, was One of the first Founders." [1] William King's editor confirms this fact and adds that "a ludicrous account of it is also in Ned Ward's 'History of Clubs,' which represents Mr. Tonson as the first institutor." [2]

Much more serious in its tone, though not so influential, was the attack of Mary Astell in the dedication to her essay entitled *Bart'lemy Fair: or, an Enquiry after Wit*, which appeared in 1709. The bitterly ironic address "To the most Illustrious Society of the Kit-Cats" extends over fourteen astonishing pages. The author's insinuations ascribe to the club every sort of vice, from oppression of the weak to treason and blasphemy. The members are accused of extravagance, loose living, and even cowardice in not going to the wars, their conduct in these matters being contrasted with that of Prince Eugene.

According to Miss Florence Smith,[3] the thirty-second number of *The Tatler*, in which Mary Astell's educational theories are roughly handled, is a reply to this attack on the Kit-Cat Club. This number is generally supposed to be largely the work of Swift, who was not a member of the club. In 1709, when the paper was written, however, Swift was not yet so militantly attached to the Tory cause as to shatter his Whig friendships. It is thus possible that he wrote the essay partly in defense of Addison, Steele, and other of his Kit-Cat friends, and partly because he was

1. *A Journey Through England* (1714), p. 188.
2. *The Original Works of William King* (1776), III, 307.
3. *Mary Astell* (New York, 1916), p. 25.

genuinely amused at the educational methods suggested by the lady whom he was lampooning.

Mary Astell was not alone in objecting to the godlessness of the Kit-Cats. Some hint of their reputed attitude toward religion has already appeared in the passage quoted from *Faction Display'd*. Swift delicately implies their tendencies to atheism in the introduction to his essay on *Mr. C[olli]ns's Discourse of Free-Thinking*, when he says:

> I could see no reason why these great discoveries should be hid from our youth of quality, who frequent White's and Tom's; why they should not be adapted to the capacities of the Kit-Cat and Hanover Clubs, who might then be able to read lectures on them to their several toasts.[1]

Charges of this sort upon the whole club were doubtless based upon the known indifference of many individual members to matters of religion and upon the open atheism of such men as Dr. Garth. Although the accusations were in a sense founded upon fact, there is no evidence that the club fostered freethinking or was in any way responsible for the somewhat elastic philosophy of certain of the members.

During the administration of the queen's Tory ministry (1710–1714), the Kit-Cats were looked upon as the leaders of the opposition, and as such were showered with abuse. The sixth number of the Tory *Examiner* protested angrily against the prestige of the great Whig gathering.

> The *Collective* Body of the Whigs have already engross'd our Riches; and their *Representative* the Kit-cat, have pretended to make a Monopoly of our Sense. Thus it happens that Mr. P[rio]r, by being expell'd the Club, ceases to be a *Poet*; and Sir Harry F——e becomes one, by being admitted into it. 'Tis here that Wit and Beauty are decided by a plurality of Voices: The *Child*'s Judgment shall make H[arle]y pass for a Fool; and

1. *The Prose Works of Jonathan Swift*, ed. Temple Scott (1897–1908), III, 170.

Jacob's Indulgence shall preserve Lady *H[arcour]t* from the
Tallow-Candle.

Somewhat similar is the lively abuse of John Lacy in the
second canto of his satire on Steele,[1] where he gives a description of "Fame's Burlesquing Court" too quotable to
omit.

> *Baker*'s large Picture the first Entrance grac'd,
> Then *Bocai*'s *Kit-Cats* were in Order plac'd;
> *G[ar]ters*, *W[hi]te St[a]ves*, and *Bays*, amuse the Eye,
> And deck Sedition's Motley Gallery.
> This Gen'ral, whom Paneg'ricks make a God,
> And holds a Staff, should smart beneath a Rod;
> Pert *Dulness* here acquires unjust Renown,
> And *G[art]h*'s a *Wit*, for Verses not his own.

Lacy writes as if he were walking among the pictures, and
scanning contemptuously the faces, of the poets, ministers,
and Knights of the Garter. Indeed, he must have seen the
portraits, for Kneller painted Marlborough with the staff in
his hand, just as he appears in Lacy's stinging allusion.
A note at the end of the canto identifies Bocai with Tonson
and adds airily that the publisher "has a Collection of the
Images of the *Kitcats*, each of whom is within a few Degrees of being as Illustrious as their *Chairman*."

Some of the political attacks were much more pointed.
John Oldmixon records the fact that "*Abel Roper* was
order'd to insert in his Paper, of *November* 22, [1711,] a
Paragraph reflecting on the KIT-CAT CLUB."[2] According
to Abel Boyer's equally Whiggish account of the affair,[3]
there was some justification for Roper's attack in *The Post-
Boy*. Effigies of the pope, the devil, and the Pretender were
found on November 16 in an empty house, where they had
been placed preparatory to being burnt in the celebration

---

1. *The Steeleids, or, the Tryal of Wit* (1714), pp. 22–30, 40 n.
2. *The History of England*, III (1735), 478.
3. Abel Boyer, *The History of the Reign of Queen Anne, Digested into Annals*,
x (1712), 279.

of Queen Elizabeth's coronation on the seventeenth. Anti-Jacobite feeling was running high, and this year there was to be a great demonstration against the Pretender. Boyer denies indignantly that the club raised a mob on this occasion to do violence to the persons and property of the queen's subjects. Neither did the Kit-Cats spread the report that the queen was on her death-bed. All they did was to pay for having the effigies made! Boyer concludes his account of the episode by freely expressing his opinion of "the infamous Authors of a *News-Paper*, mainly calculated for the Service of the *Jacobite Party*, [who] had the Impudence to slander the most Noble and most Ingenious *Whig* Society in *England*."

The club was clearly implicated, and Roper made the most of the situation. In *The Post-Boy* of November 29 he continued his attack. He even gave the following directions for solving the mystery of the initials G. G. G. S. S. S. W. H. M., by which he had referred to a junto of Kit-Cats:

> This is to inform the Publick, that, without giving themselves any farther Trouble, they may apply to *Jacob Door-holder* to the Club, who can shew the effegies of that ignoble Society, or to the *Dispensatory* [Garth], who, *I profess*, can satisfy them of every Particular . . . , and shew the Originals, which ought rather to be burnt with the Pope, Devil, and Pretender, than disturb the quiet of Her Majesty's *Good*, *Faithful*, and *Loyal Subjects*.[1]

Roper recommended that the Kit-Cats read *The Conduct of the Allies*, where they "will find innumerable Truths which only will make them equally angry with my Paper of the 22nd instant."

The most deft of the attacks upon the club was that of Swift entitled *A Letter of Thanks from my Lord W[harto]n to the Lord B^p of S. Asaph, In the Name of the Kit-Cat-Club*, printed in 1712. With remarkable economy, Swift

1. *Tory Annals Faithfully Extracted* (1712), p. 80.

killed three birds with one stone: Lord Wharton, in whose
character he wrote; the club, whom he pretended to represent; and Bishop Fleetwood, whom he was actually addressing. Swift's thrusts at the Kit-Cats were directed
chiefly at their religion and politics. Their religious laxity
is ingeniously exposed through some damning admissions
of Lord Wharton. In the realm of politics Swift ridiculed
their opposition to the peace. The club, says Lord Wharton, will favor peace "when the Dutch could get nothing
by the war, nor we Whigs lose anything by a peace; or to
speak in plain terms, (for every one knows I am a free
speaker as well as a freethinker) when we had exhausted
all the nation's treasure, . . . and so far enriched ourselves,
and beggared our fellow-subjects, as to bring them under a
necessity of submitting to what conditions we should think
fit to impose."[1] Thus a club was made to bear the brunt of
the attack of the opposing party. As will appear later, the
Tory clubs shared this fate with the Kit-Cats; but the
Tory groups were the more fortunate, in that they found
no opponent with the annihilating faculty for irony which
Swift possessed.

A curious bit of satiric verse has escaped the notice of the
club's numerous historians. In 1718 Edmund Curll printed
a collection of letters and poems, obtained by those de-
vious methods that he best knew, which documents, as he
announced on the title-page, were "now first published
from their respective originals, found in the cabinet of the
celebrated toast Mrs. Anne Long, since her decease." The
thin little volume contains among other things an exceed-
ingly scurrilous poem entitled "An Essay to Restore the
Kit-Cat-Members to their lost Abilities." The clubmen
are represented as

> Your Men of wondrous Might, who boast,
> How many Bumpers they can toast,[2]

1. Swift, *Prose Works*, v, 266–267.
2. *Letters, Poems, and Tales: Amorous, Satyrical, and Gallant* (1718), p. 85.

and are ridiculed for drinking themselves nightly into a stupor. The rancorous author treats Garth and Steele with particular severity. The toasting scenes could not possibly have been as debauched as the verses imply. They merely furnished one more excuse for an unscrupulous attack which probably issued from personal or political animosity.

The later history of the club is difficult to trace. Pope told Spence that it broke up soon after 1709.[1] A letter from Steele to Philips in 1712, however, gives evidence of a meeting, and Aitken draws a pleasant picture of the summer gatherings during that year at the Upper Flask in Hampstead.[2] Austin Dobson quotes part of a letter from Steele to Welsted, written in 1716, in which the essayist admits having just written "three Couplets for the Toasts ... to be printed under their names for the Kitt Catt Club."[3] An explanation made by Sir Richard to Lady Steele enables us to prove its survival for at least one year more. On March 30, 1717, he wrote:

> The omission of last post was occasioned by my attendance on the Duke of Newcastle, who was in the chair at the Kit-Cat.[4]

By 1725 the club was a thing of the past. In that year Vanbrugh wrote to Tonson of a journey which he and his wife had made with Lord Carlisle and his daughters, during which they talked of their "former Kit-Cat days." Sir John tells of "eating a Chearfull Cold Loaf at a very humble Alehouse, I think the best meal I ever eat, except the first Supper in the Kitchen at Barns." Later in the same year he wrote, concerning the Duke of Newcastle:

> He will chearfully accept of the Clubs Invitation, to dine with them one day, or one hundred, if so God pleases. I'm sorry

1. Spence, *Anecdotes*, p. 257.
2. *The Life of Richard Steele* (1889), I, 344.
3. *Richard Steele* (1886), p. 53.
4. H. R. Montgomery, *Memoirs of the Life and Writings of Sir Richard Steele* (Edinburgh, 1865), II, 113.

a meeting cou'd not be on the day and at the Place you mention; both I am sure, would be highly agreeable to the Members of it. But they will not so soon be within Call: when they are, we'll try to find some other day of Happy Remembrance.[1]

It is pathetically plain that the surviving members were assembling to indulge in reminiscences rather than to re-enact the brilliant scenes of twenty years before. The Duke of Somerset lived to see Faber's fine book of engravings, made after the Kit-Cat portraits, dedicated to him in 1735, and, like Walpole, lived on into the 'forties. But the merry society of Whig wits and statesmen was no longer the talk of the Town as it had been when it toasted the beauties of Queen Anne's reign, staunchly supported the Hanoverian succession, and patronized young writers. That its fame was not at once forgotten appears from Fielding's allusion in *Tom Jones* [2] and the tribute of the son of a distinguished member, who pronounced the Kit-Cats "in reality the patriots that saved Britain." [3]

TWO MINOR TOASTING SOCIETIES

The success of the Kit-Cats led to the formation of at least two similar Whig toasting clubs which sought to gain prestige by emulating the more distinguished society. About 1712, according to Oldmixon, there was founded a society known as the Hanover Club, "that met once a Week at *Charing-Cross*, and took the Name from that Illustrious Family, for whose Service they assembled." [4] The list of members given by the Whig historian includes Pulteney, Lord Lumley, Steele, and Addison, all of whom were Kit-Cat men. The society "was very instrumental in keeping up the *Whig* Spirit in *London* and *Westminster*, and

---

1. *The Complete Works of Sir John Vanbrugh*, IV, 170.
2. Book IV, chapter ii.
3. Horace Walpole, *Anecdotes of Painting in England* (1849), II, 591.
4. *The History of England*, III (1735), 509.

consequently throughout the whole Kingdom." Macky's account also connects the new Whig club with the Kit-Cats.

> The *Hannover-Club*, also composed of Noblemen of the first Quality, and Officers of the Army, . . . have their Meeting as the former [*i.e.*, the Kit-Cat Club]; they are, as all the other innumerable Clubs, kept within this Great City, prescribed by Rules; and have their *President, Secretary, &c.*[1]

The secretary was the gaily caparisoned Ambrose Philips.

The Hanover Club followed the practise, by now well established, of toasting the leading Whig beauties. In 1713, pursuing his duties as secretary, Philips published a broadside on which were printed the names of thirty-one "Toasts Elected by the Hanover-Club" for that year. The list was headed by the Duchess of Cambridge, and included Lady Mary Wortley Montagu, the Duchess of Bolton, the Countess of Sunderland, Mrs. Steele, Mrs. Dunch, and other famous ladies, some of whose names had already appeared on the wine-glasses of the Kit-Cats. At the bottom of the sheet were printed the following verses, probably by Philips:

> The reigning *Fair* on polish'd Crystal shine,
> Enrich our Glasses, and improve our Wine.
> The favorite Names We to our Lips apply,
> Indulge our Thoughts, and drink with Extasie.

> While These, the chosen Beauties of our Isle,
> Propitious on the Cause of Freedom smile,
> The vain *Pretender*'s Hopes we may dispise,
> And trust *Britannia*'s Safety to their Eyes.

Contemporary allusions to the Hanover Club are few and inconspicuous,[2] and accounts of its activities are not to be found. It is not even possible to tell when the society

---

1. *A Journey Through England* (1714), p. 188.
2. *E.g., The Lay Monk*, No. 6. In exonerating his club from charges of papistry, Sir Arthur Wimbleton explains "that Mr. Freeman, one of our Number, was a Member of the *Hanover*-Club."

ceased to exist. Dr. Arbuthnot mentions it in a letter to Swift dated August 6, 1715, and there is no reason to believe that it survived much longer. The definite political end for which it had been established had been achieved.

One other Whiggish toasting club has recorded its existence by means of an unpretentious literary monument. In 1734 there appeared a little collection of verses entitled *The Toasts of the Patriots Club at London*.[1] As the poems were printed in London, the last two words of the title are a sufficient indication of the club's insignificance; no one would have thought of speaking of "the Kit-Cat Club at London." The toasts are inscribed, oddly enough, "To the Reverend the Clergy in and about the City of London," with the design of securing political aid from the pulpit. Just what sort of faction made up the Patriots' Club is not difficult to determine. The ladies eulogized were the wives of famous Whigs. At least five of the poems contain reflections upon Walpole. Obviously the Patriots were recruited from the Whig opposition. The political note is sounded much more often in these verses than in the more gallant tributes of the Kit-Cats. Indeed, these later toasts seem less likely to have emanated from witty sessions of the club than from the pen of a single roused patriot, who took upon himself the rôle of spokesman.

Bourgeois Clubmen: Calves-Head and Mug-House

Not all the clubs of Whigs were as aristocratic as the toasting societies. From time to time the London populace formed political clubs which were as widely discussed as the more influential organizations. No club connected with

1. These same toasts were printed in folio as *The Toasts of the Rump-Steak Club* (1734). This book contains three additional toasts, but has no dedicatory epistle. Both names seem to have been applied to the same club. This "Rump-Steak Club" is not to be confused with the Beefsteak Clubs.

the Whig party caused more speculation and comment than the strange society that flourished about London for nearly half a century under the name of the Calves-Head Club. The contemporary stories of its exploits, duly toned down with certain necessary reservations, furnish the following details. Among the adherents of the Commonwealth party, there developed not long after the Restoration a group of irreconcilables who assembled to register their disapproval of the new régime. Actuated by their hatred of royalty and their bitterness over the downfall of the Commonwealth, these fanatics instituted at their secret sessions various treasonable rites by which they celebrated the downfall of Charles I. The day set aside for England to repent of the crime of the decollation, January 30, was for them a season of rejoicing. On this occasion they met at various taverns about London, drank to the Good Old Cause, sang blasphemous songs about the beheaded monarch, and indulged in certain symbolical rites in which the head of a calf played a conspicuous part.

Just what may be believed in the contemporary descriptions of these meetings is hard to decide. A secret organization of this nature, which furnishes no respectable account of itself even by way of defense, inevitably gives rise to conjectures. How the awful doings of the society captured the imagination of the London populace appears in a curious broadside of 1704, which purports to give "A most Strange, but True Account Of a Very Large Sea-Monster, That was found last Saturday in a Common-Shore in New Fleet Street in Spittle-Fields." To prove the ominous nature of this strange phenomenon, the author catalogues a whole list of similar portents, the following among others:

And so when *Oliver Cromwel's* Usurpation was at end, the Members of the *Calves-head-Club* Confederate the Devil fetcht him away in a terrible Whirlwind.[1]

1. *The Bagford Ballads*, ed. J. W. Ebsworth (1878), 1, 60.

Since the literature on the Calves-Head Club consists largely of satiric attacks and attempts to exonerate the dissenters from implications of membership, our evidence about the nature of the society must be surveyed with some caution. Indeed, a few have gone so far as to consider the group entirely mythical; but as Wilson suggests in his life of Defoe, its existence is "rendered probable by the frequent notice of it by the writers of the times." [1]

The most certain evidence was given by Samuel Wesley in the course of his controversy with Samuel Palmer over the dissenting academies. Wesley's *A Letter . . . Concerning the Education of the Dissenters in their Private Academies*, printed without his consent in 1703, drew a reply from Palmer entitled *A Defence of the Dissenters Education*. In 1704, Wesley defended his original letter in a pamphlet signed with his own name. In explaining how he came to write the letter in the first place, Wesley told that he was at supper one evening with a party of dissenters (1693), when they

fell a railing at *Monarchy*, and blaspheming the memory of King *Charles* the Martyr, discoursing of their *Calves-head Club*, and producing or repeating some *Verses* on that Subject. I remember one of the Company told us of a Design they had at their next *Calves-Head Feast*, to have a *Cold Pye* serv'd on the Table, with either a *Live-Cat* or *Hare*, I've forgot whether, enclos'd: and they had contriv'd to put one of their Company who lov'd *Monarchy*, and knew nothing of the matter, to cut it up; whereupon, and on the leaping out of the *Cat* or *Hare*, they were all to set up a *Shout*, and cry, *Haloo! Old Puss!* To the Honour of the *Good Old Cause*, and to shew their affection to a Commonwealth.

Wesley added in a marginal note that since writing this passage he had seen some Calves-Head songs in print. In one song, dated 1694, he found the verses,

1. Walter Wilson, *Memoirs of the Life and Times of Daniel De Foe* (1830), ii, 108.

Then to Puss, Boys, to Puss, Boys,
Let's drink it off thus, Boys,

"on which, if I mistake not," he adds, "this story will be a good comment."[1] The verses quoted by Wesley are to be found in *The Secret History of the Calves-Head Club* (1703) on page fifteen. It is inconceivable that a man of Wesley's integrity would have stooped to invent the story only to make a point. He was no cheap satirist nor Grub-Street sensation-monger. In the light of his statement, one must be over-fastidious to doubt the existence of the club.

The first document to be considered in connection with the Calves-Head Club, both because of the details it gives and because of its astonishing popularity during the reign of Queen Anne, is attributed to Edward Ward. It appeared first in 1703 as a quarto pamphlet of twenty-two pages, bearing the title, *The Secret History of the Calves-Head Clubb, or, The Republican Unmasqu'd: Wherein is fully shewn the Religion of the Calves-Head Heroes, in their Anniversary Thanksgiving Songs on the Thirtieth of January, by them called Anthems.* The preface states that the "anthems" were published because they were being privately circulated among the proselytes of the members, and "some honest Men have thought there could be no more Effectual Remedy for the Mischief it might do, or a surer Way to stop the Career, than a Publication." As to the history of the verses, Ward says:

These Lines (for such Ribbaldry and Trash deserve not the Name of Poems) were compos'd and set to Musick for the Use of the CALVES-HEAD CLUBB, which was erected by an Impudent Sett of People, who have their Feast of Calves Heads in several Parts of the Town, on the *30*th of *January*, in Derision of the day, and Defiance of Monarchy; at divers of which Meetings, the following Compositions were sung, and in Affront to the Church call'd *Anthems*. These which are here Publish'd, are

---

1. *A Defence of a Letter* (1704), pp. 4–5.

said to have been Written by Mr. *Benj. Bridgewater*,[1] and that he was largely rewarded by the Members of the Club for his Pains.

Ward concludes his preface by expressing the hope that the publication may prove a check to the evil practises of the club.

The "secret history," which serves as an introduction to the anthems, begins with an encomium of Charles I and a protest against these insults to his memory. Ward gives as one source of his information "a certain active Whigg, who in all other Respects, was a Man of probity enough." It was this same Whig who confided to the author that the society had been instituted by "*Milton*, and some other Creatures of the Commonwealth" during the Interregnum.[2] After the Restoration, the club had met with great caution for some years. "But now, says he, (and this was the Second Year of King *William*'s Reign) they meet almost in a Publick Manner, and apprehend nothing." Another gentleman, who was supposed to have actually attended the meetings, told Ward that they met at twenty fixed places, and that they consisted of Independents and Anabaptists. Ned proceeds to describe their rites, and concludes the history with an appeal for the suppression of the group in the interests of humanity, religion, and lawfulness. The anthems, five in number, occupy the remainder of the pamphlet. Ward's critical opinion of them, as quoted above, is not inaccurate. Some are scurrilous, some are blasphemous, and all are incredibly bad.

That the anthems were actually written to be sung and are not spurious poems manufactured for the purposes of Ward's book is everywhere evident. The versification of the following stanza will bear witness.

1. The *Term Catalogue* takes this name to be a pseudonym for John Dunton.
2. *The Secret History of the Calves-Head Club* (1703), p. 9. Milton's connection with the club is, of course, incredible.

Then Boys let's drink a Bumper, since their Actions
(made us great,
Let us lay our Trophies at their Feet:
The Cause gave Courage to the Soldiers, taught them
(how their Foes to beat,
That alone cou'd free a Captiv'd State.[1]

Only one of the songs appeared elsewhere than in Ward's collection.[2] A careful study of the two versions shows variants that could not well have resulted from editing, and leads to the conclusion that the songs were learned by ear and written down for publication by two different persons.

The *Secret History* was from the first an enormous success. By September 18, 1705, it had reached its fifth edition, which, as the title-page promised, contained large additions. This edition begins with a vigorous personal attack upon John Tutchin, "Observator, and *Censor Morum* general: Supervisor of the Admiralty, Victualling-Office, Playhouse, *Bartholomew*-Fair, Bear-garden, Defender of Parliaments and Protestant *March* Beer, &c." The thickness of the volume was five times multiplied by its reduction in size to an octavo and the insertion of new material. The principal additions are "The Character of a Calves-Head Clubbman," presumably by Ward; five new songs; "A Vindication of the Royal Martyr King Charles I," here ascribed to Samuel Butler; and a character of a Presbyterian, in verse, assigned to Sir John Denham. The last two pieces have no connection with the club except that they are directed against the enemies of the church and throne, the Calves-Head men among others. At this point in the history of the little book it becomes evident that Ward's purpose was a general attack on his political enemies and not simply an effort to suppress a degraded society of fanatics.

1. *Ibid.*, p. 15.
2. *I.e.*, "A Psalm sung the 30th of January, 1696. At the C - - - - s-H - - d Club," printed in *Poems on Affairs of State*, II (1703), 406.

Further editions, successively augmented, continued to pour from the presses of London and Dublin. Even John Morphew published one. The success of the remarkable book, which began its career in 1703 with twenty-two pages and in 1714 entered what was really its eleventh edition with more than two hundred pages, is difficult to explain on its literary merits. The verses which originally formed its nucleus are entirely negligible as poetry. The prose sections consist of separate tracts, many from the pen of Ward, which are unified only by their bearing on some phase of the club's program and are of little credit to the age of refined prose in which they appeared. The success of Ward's undertaking must be attributed primarily to its journalistic nature. Although the editions did not come out regularly at the rate of one a year, each thirtieth of January revived sufficient interest in the club to make the book sell. The reason for this interest was the treasonable nature of the scandalous rites in which the members indulged. Aside from the fascination of the grotesque scenes which the book conjured up, there was much patriotic feeling in the matter, particularly among the Tories. Both of these caprices of his public Ward humored by giving vent through sensational journalism to his outraged feeling of loyalty to the throne. As a result the Calves-Head Club was probably more talked of about the streets of London, mean as it was, than any other club of its day.

Its invasions of contemporary writing, exclusive of Ward's *Secret History*, were by no means inconsiderable. What seems at first sight to be the earliest piece connected with the custom of eating calves' heads on the thirtieth of January was published as the work of Samuel Butler in the *Posthumous Works* (1715), under the title, "The Morning's Salutation: or, a Friendly Conference Between a Puritan Preacher and a Family of his Flock, upon the 30th of

January." [1] This short satiric poem, arranged in dramatic form with the husband, the wife, and the preacher as speakers, reveals the pleasure with which the preacher drinks wine and eats of the calf's head on this day. The implications of the author are obvious; and if the piece could be regarded as authentic, it would move the literary appearance of the club back some twenty years. But since it is omitted from the *Genuine Remains* and is almost certainly spurious, it may have been written only a short time before its publication.

The only important attack upon the club before Ward's occurs in Tom Brown's *Letters from the Dead to the Living*, in which there is an exchange of letters between Ludlow, the regicide, and the Calves-Head Club. A passage from Ludlow's epistle from the infernal regions will suffice to show the harshness of Brown's assault.

Lucifer and all his Kingdom of *Hob-gobblins*, drink a Health to your Society every Thirtieth of *January*, in burnt Brandy, and are well assur'd the Interest of these infernal Territories can never sink, as long as there is a *Calves-Head-Club* upon Earth, to glory in the Remembrance of the worst of Villianies. [2]

The letter contains other hints at the high esteem in which the club was held there below and at the applause which the damned accorded to the yearly celebrations. The reply from the Calves-Head Club praises Ludlow for his bloody deed and applauds all regicides. Brown anticipates Ward in casting suspicion upon John Tutchin, for the club informs Ludlow:

The Author of the Dialogue between *Vassal* and *Freeman*, is our Secretary; you guess'd his Name very right in your Letter, and a notable Fellow he is either in Verse or Prose, for the

1. Also printed as a broadside (Dublin, 1721) under the title: "Dialogue between a Dissenting Minister and the Calves-Head-Club, on the 30th of January, being the Martyrdom of King Charles."
2. *The Works of Mr. Thomas Brown* (1720), II, 258.

Justification of our Principles; . . . had he liv'd in the happy Days when you erected a *High Court of Justice*, he would have been the fittest Man in the Universe for two Posts under you; *First*, To have been *Attorney-General*, and then *Executioner*.[1]

Though Tutchin cannot with absolute certainty be exonerated from these charges, it is quite possible that both Brown and Ward were merely using a newly discovered weapon to wound a political opponent.

The Calves-Head Club was not long in becoming a regular satiric bludgeon with which the Tories belabored the Whigs in all sorts of party writing. William Shippen used it in 1704 by describing Bishop Burnet as

> A *Scotch*, Seditious, Unbelieving Priest,
> The Brawny Chaplain of the *Calves-Head-Feast*.[2]

Tom Brown derided the company in a coffee-house as being "of as much Diversity, and as many Humours, as the Calves-Head-Club." [3] Arbuthnot picked up the weapon in *The History of John Bull*. In describing the habits of Timothy Trim, who is subsequently identified with Jack, the Calvinist, the satirist wrote:

> The witnesses further made oath, that the said Timothy . . . refused to dine upon salt-fish, only to have an opportunity to eat a calf's head (his favorite dish) in private.[4]

Swift went as far as any in connecting the club with the Whigs for offensive purposes. In *The Examiner*, No. 40, he inserted a passing accusation; but he went much farther in

1. *The Works of Mr. Thomas Brown* (1720), II, 262. It is curious to note that Ward casts a similar reflection upon Brown in his reference to the letter in the *Secret History* (1705), where he writes in the preface to "A Vindication of the Royal Martyr" (sig. L3): "The Author of *Ludlow's* Letter may be reckon'd amongst the first of these, one that always set up for a Patron of Faction, and a Promoter of the *Good Old Cause*."

2. *Faction Display'd* (1704), p. 4.

3. In "A Walk round London and Westminster" (*The Works of Mr. Thomas Brown* [1720], III, 304).

4. G. A. Aitken, *The Life and Works of John Arbuthnot* (Oxford, 1892), p. 260.

"Toland's Invitation to Dismal," [1] which purports to be an invitation to a meeting of the Calves-Head men from John Toland, the deist and Whig pamphleteer, to the Earl of Nottingham, who had just bolted the Tory party. A lively picture of the feast is drawn in the following lines:

> Toland to you this invitation sends,
> To eat the calf's head with your trusty friends. . . .
> To-morrow we our mystic feast prepare,
> Where thou, our latest proselyte shalt share:
> When we, by proper signs and symbols, tell,
> How by brave hands the royal traitor fell;
> The meat shall represent the tyrant's head,
> The wine, his blood our predecessors shed;
> Whilst an alluding hymn some artist sings,
> We toast, Confusion to the race of kings!
> At monarchy we nobly show our spight,
> And talk, what fools call treason, all the night. [2]

Swift goes on to enumerate the company at the banquet, naming more than a dozen Whig leaders as certain to be present. The effectiveness of the device is obvious. The idea of associating prominent Whig statesmen like Godolphin and Halifax with the rabble that frequented the Calves-Head Club was in itself sufficiently irritating to Swift's political enemies. To offer the hospitality of the club to a man of Nottingham's moral severity was nothing short of monstrous.

One Tory account of the society is so moderate in comparison with the rest that it must in all justice be described. It was printed in 1712 with the title:

The K[en]tish Spy: or, a Memorial of the C[al]ves H[ea]d Club: Particularly Of Three Members of the said Society that Absented themselves from the Parish Church of W[e]st[en]ham in *Kent*, the 30th day of *January* last. With What pass'd most remarkable between them at their Cabal. *Turn'd into* Hudi-

---

1. The story of the composition of this poem appears below, pp. 251–252.
2. *The Poems of Jonathan Swift*, ed. W. E. Browning (1910), II, 156.

brastick *Verse*. Inscrib'd to the *K[e]ntish* Petitioner. *By* T. W. *an Enemy to Faction*.

The moderation of the author agrees with the character of Thomas Wood (a nephew of the antiquarian), who may well have been responsible for the little tract.[1]

The first section narrates easily and rapidly the manner in which the author came to write the poem. He had happened to be riding towards London from Tunbridge Wells on the previous thirtieth of January and had been alarmed at the activity of the Calves-Head groups in the churches of the Kentish towns. When he came to a Tory community, he ventured to stop and rest, since only three Calves-Head men seemed to be celebrating there. From information gleaned from the loyal townspeople, he formed the picture of the activities of these three which went into his hudibrastic poem. The verses which follow this lengthy introduction reveal the author's sympathy with monarchy and the Tories from the time of Charles I down to that of Oxford's ministry. He shows no great alarm over the meetings, but considers it a matter for national shame that a whole countryside should be diverted from decent church services to attend such demonstrations as he had just witnessed in Kent. He adopts the wise plan of ridiculing the three who serve as his example, rather than pouring contumely upon them. The poem concludes with a round Tory prayer for peace and the safety of the queen. The calm method of dealing with these violent Whig factionists is a welcome relief from the exaggerated censoriousness of the other reproofs.

The extravagances of the Calves-Head Club were fathered not only upon the Whig party, but also upon the

1. Two of Wood's early works, mentioned by his biographer in the *D.N.B.*, show an interest in dissent. The attitude of *The Kentish Spy* agrees with that of a letter from Wood to Parker, printed by John Nichols in *Illustrations of Literary History*, iv (1822), 117. The assignment is tentative, however, and relatively unimportant.

dissenters. As early as 1705, Charles Leslie had roughly suggested that these sects "put down their *Calves-Head Clubs*, in which they *Feast* every 30*th* of *January*." [1] Although for the most part the Whigs ignored the charges of complicity in the club's affairs, the dissenters were inclined to take them seriously. In *The Rights of Protestant Dissenters* (1705), dedicated to the queen, Viscount Barrington earnestly condemned the "Scandalous and Opprobrious Feasting and Jesting" of the clubbers, "which the Dissenters know nothing more of than their Accusers." Nevertheless the charge continued to be hurled in the faces of the dissenters. On the day following the unholy festivities of 1714, Samuel Wright, an able young dissenting minister, preached a sermon on *The mischievous Consequences of publick Strife and Envy*, in which he indignantly denied any sympathy with the treasonable proceedings. Thomas Bradbury, in *The Lawfulness of Resisting Tyrants* (1713),[2] put the blame on "those High-flying Preachers that give the Irritation." A passage directed at the efforts of the dissenters to get control of the national religion, in *The Entertainer* for December 17, 1717, shows that the fear of the club still persisted in the minds of the high-churchmen; for the author asks, "Are the Members of the *Calves-Head-Club* one whit more moderate than their *Fore-Fathers*?" A reference to "the annual keeping of a *Calves-Head-Club*" in a later number points to the fact that the meetings were still thought to be going on.[3]

How strong a hold the club had on the popular imagination is revealed by the sensation caused by a supposed meeting at the Golden Eagle in Suffolk Street in 1735. L'Abbé le Blanc wrote the current version of the incident to one of his countrymen as follows:

1. *The New Association* (1705), part i, p. 13. Compare Leslie's *A Case of Present Concern* (1703), in which there is a similar outburst.
2. Sig. A4ᵛ.
3. *The Entertainer*, Nos. 7, 13.

Il y a quelques années que des jeunes Gens de Condition choisirent, pour se livrer à cette sorte de Débauche, le 30. Janvier, jour auquel l'Eglise d'Angleterre impose un jeûne général en expiation du Meurtre du Roi Charles I. qu'elle honore comme un Martyr. Si-tôt qu'ils furent chauds de vin, ils se mirent à chanter. Le Peuple scandalizé, s'arrêta devant le Cabaret, & leur cria des injures. Un de ces jeunes étourdis mit la tête à la fenêtre; & but à la mémoire de l'Armée qui détrona ce Roi, & des Séditieux qui lui firent perdre la tête sur un Echaffaut. Les Pierres à l'instant volérent de toutes parts; les vitres de la Maison furent brisées; la Populace furieuse y vouloit mettre le feu. Ces jeunes insensés eurent bien de la peine à se sauver eux-mêmes.[1]

Henry Boyle adds to the picture a display of calves' heads to the crowd, and the timely arrival of the guards to save the feasters from the violence of the mob.[2]

The incident was not slow to find its way into print. *The Weekly Oracle* of February 1 told of the extravagances of these "young gentlemen of distinction . . . calling themselves the Calf's Head Club."[3] Epigrams on the club appeared in *The Grub-street Journal* (Nos. 267, 270, and 271), one of which describes picturesquely the dismay of the merrymakers when the mob made its assault on the house. A contributor to *Notes and Queries* tells of three prints in his possession which portray the scene of the brawl, one of them supposed to have been taken from a drawing by Hogarth.[4] There was also a broadside headed "Leucifer's Grand Emessarys found out, or the Calves Head Club Discover'd," which narrates the occurrence in sensational detail, not forgetting the calf's head, the fire, nor the treasonous healths.

The whole affair, however, seems to have sprung from a

---

1. *Lettres de Monsieur l'Abbé le Blanc* (Amsterdam, 1751), II, 114–115.
2. Henry Boyle, *The Chronology of the Eighteenth and Nineteenth Centuries* (1826), p. 75.
3. Reprinted in *Notes and Queries*, 1st Series, VIII (1853), 315.
4. *Ibid.*, XI (1855), 405.

THE CALVES-HEAD CLUB

The true Effigies of the Members of
The Calve's Head Club, Held on yᵉ 30ᵗʰ of January 1734. at
yᵉ Golden Eagle in Suffolk street in yᵉ County
of MIDDLESEX.
From a satiric engraving in the Collection of Prints and
Drawings in the British Museum

misunderstanding. The gentlemen at the Golden Eagle were supping more boisterously than usual, it is true, but were supremely unconscious that it was the day of Charles's martyrdom. Some citizens misinterpreted their noise and healths, and tried to enter the tavern by force. Realizing that their position was as serious as if they were guilty, the gentlemen resisted the fast-gathering mob. After two hours they were rescued and escorted thence by the guards.[1] Thus the meeting cannot be looked upon as a survival of Calves-Head activities. It is merely a startling bit of evidence that the fame of the society was still remarkably persistent.

This sporadic outburst constitutes the final chapter in the journalistic history of the Calves-Head Club. Politically the members were outcasts. In the eyes of the Tories they were a dangerous gang of king-killers, whose anti-monarchical intriguing might conceivably prove an actual menace to church and crown. To the Whigs they seemed immoderate fanatics, who by their heedless enormities brought the whole party into disrepute. Their name has been preserved chiefly because to connect one's enemy with the club was a convenient way to vilify him, a method to which even Swift stooped with gleeful abandon. Yet in the first two decades of the century public interest in the surreptitious meetings waxed from year to year, while Ned Ward beamed amiably and prepared larger and better editions of the *Secret History*.

The most violently Whiggish of the bourgeois clubs is said to have originated with no other end in view than inno-

---

1. Joseph Spence (*Anecdotes*, pp. 304–305) received two letters early in February, 1735, which relate the whole incident from the point of view of the gentlemen involved. The version of Lord Middlesex, who was actually present, ends thus: "This is the whole story from which so many Calves heads, Bloody napkins, and Lord knows what has been made, it has been the talk of the Town and the Country, and Small beer and Bread and Cheese to my friends the Garretters in Grub street for these few days past."

cent diversion. This was the assembly at the Mug-House, which was already flourishing in 1714 when John Macky published his description of the clubs of the time.

The most diverting, or amusing of all, is the *Mug-House-Club* in *Long-Acre*, where every *Wednesday* and *Saturday*, a mixture of Gentlemen, Lawyers and Tradesmen, meet in a Great Room, and are seldom under a Hundred.

They have a grave Old Gentleman in his own Gray Hairs, now within a few Months of Ninety Years Old, who is their *President*; and sits in an arm'd Chair some Steps higher than the Rest of the Company, to keep the whole Room in Order.[1]

This great company amused itself with singing to the accompaniment of a harp and with drinking ale, for which every man had his separate and particular mug. "The Room is always so diverted with Songs," says Macky, "and drinking from one Table to another to one another's Healths, that there is no Room for *Politicks*, or any Thing that can sow'r Conversation."

If this pleasant picture is accurate, the Mug-House Club was on the verge of a sudden change of purpose. During the ensuing years it was to play a prominent part in the affairs of the Whig party. The city mob, who did not readily forget Queen Anne and the days of the Sacheverell demonstrations, remained Tory at heart, and greeted George I without any great warmth. The fires kindled by Swift and others during Oxford's ministry blazed merrily on, to the embarrassment of the new régime. When party strife became hot in 1716 and 1717 over the repeal of the Triennial Act, it was clear that the Tory element in the London mob had to be dealt with. An important share in keeping the mob at bay fell to the Mug-House Club.

By 1716 the political character of the club was so well established that a number of subsidiary Mug-House Clubs had sprung up in various parts of London and the sub-

1. *A Journey Through England* (1714), p. 189.

urbs,[1] where staunch Whigs met to toast the memory of King William, the Duke of Marlborough, and the Hanoverians. A contemporary collection of ballads contains "The Prologue spoke by Mr. Smyth, at the opening of his Mug-House in St. John's Lane," in which the proprietor assures his guests of good ale and sound political principles. In soliciting patronage, he remarks:

> In short, our only Trust's in *Whiggish Friends*,
> Let's have their Favour, and we gain our Ends.[2]

A curious little pamphlet[3] attributed to John Dunton gives an excellent picture of Smith's Mug-House, with an account of the company and characters of mine host and hostess. It even prints a Mug-House song. The club made short shrift of any enemies who wandered in by mistake. *The Weekly Packet* for January 5, 1717, reported that "Mr. Humphreys, lately committed to Newgate for cursing King George at the Mug-house in Salisbury-Court, has petition'd the Secretary of State to be admitted to Bail, but we hear the same was deferred."[4] It was not long before these festivities became intolerable to the Tory mobs which gathered outside in the streets.

> The Day before Parson *Paul* was hang'd they fell upon the *Mug-house* in *Southwark-Park*, crying out, *High-Church and Ormond, down with the Mug-house*; but the Society sallying out upon them, after the Windows of the House had been all

1. John Oldmixon (*The History of England*, III [1735], 621) enumerates six, besides the original Mug-House. They were the Roebuck in Cheapside; Smith's at St. John's, Clerkenwell; Read's in Salisbury Court, Fleet Street; another in Tower Street; a fifth in Tavistock Street, Covent Garden; and a sixth in Southwark Park.

2. *Pills to Purge State-Melancholy* (1718), part ii, p. 59. See also pages 43–44.

3. *Royal Gratitude. . . . To which is added, The High-Church Gudgeons. . . . Also, A Trip to the Loyal Mug-House at Night, to Drink a Health to King George and the Royal Family* (1716).

4. Two weeks later Humphreys was sentenced to a fine of twenty marks and six months' imprisonment. See *The Weekly Packet*, January 19, 1717.

broken, the Rascals ran away from Drubing, leaving several of their Clubs and Sticks behind them.[1]

It was such brawls as this that led in 1715 to the passage of the Riot Act; and it was not long afterwards that the inevitable party pamphlets began to appear.

Enough contemporary comment has survived to give a very fair notion of the excitement which the clubs occasioned. The pamphlet which aroused the most controversy was a Tory attack by Sir Humphrey Mackworth, which appeared in 1717 under the title, *Down with the Mug: or, Reasons for Suppressing the Mug-Houses; Humbly offer'd to the Consideration of the Parliament of Great-Britain*. In spite of Sir Humphrey's Tory prejudices, most of his arguments sound reasonable enough. The Mug-Houses used such violent measures that they antagonized the mob and roused factional disputes, thereby disturbing the peace. The meetings fostered idleness and debauchery. The riots which they precipitated often ended in bloodshed. The clubs were set up by a notorious dissenter and so, according to Mackworth, must have had designs upon the established church. On the whole, Sir Humphrey makes a fairly strong case for suppressing these militant Whig organizations. He attacks *The Flying Post* for defending the clubs, and records with marked approval the sermons preached against such societies, including the one by the Reverend Luke Milbourne, who made the inevitable comparison between the Mug-House and Calves-Head Clubs. In conclusion, Mackworth says that he is reprinting one of their songs "as a Specimen of their insipid Wit, the rather, because 'twas compos'd . . . by an Eminent Presbyterian Teacher, and a noted *Dealer in many Words*." Assuring King George of his loyalty, he retires in favor of the Mug-House poet, "T. B." The "Mug-House Song" is not of a quality to inspire one to rescue its author from oblivion.

1. John Oldmixon, *The History of England*, III (1735), 621.

It satirizes the Jacobite tendencies of the Tories, makes personal attacks on Oxford and the rest, and dwells with particular complacence on the flight of Bolingbroke and Ormonde. Although the poem is not short, it was probably meant, as its title indicates, to be sung. Otherwise its six-line stanza would be an anomalous satiric medium.

This attack on the Mug-Houses did not go long unanswered. In the same year (1717) there appeared a six-penny pamphlet entitled *The Mug Vindicated.... Being an Answer to the popular Objections of the Faction against them, contain'd in Sir H. M's Malicious and Scurrilous Libel.* The preface by "S. W." (probably Samuel Wright) gives an interesting and dispassionate history of the club at the Mug-House in Long Acre. The reply to Mackworth's "reasons" is more violent and abusive. Another answer to *Down with the Mug,* which appeared in *A Collection of the Occasional Papers for the Year 1717,* attempts to shift all the blame to the Tory mob. *The Entertainer,* begun when the controversy was at its height, took up the cudgels on the Tory side. Number 5 indignantly accused the Mug-House men of pretending to defend the throne "with Blasphemous Rants, and Lewd Lampoons, upon the best of her Sex, and the most pious of Princesses that ever adorned a Sceptre;" and on January 22, 1718, the whole paper was given over to exposing their seditious principles.

So the pamphlet war raged. Meanwhile, the scenes of violence which were enacted about the taverns where the Mug-House men assembled lent credence to all manner of extravagant reports, and eventually, in 1722, led to a discontinuance of the gatherings by an act of Parliament.

SWIFT'S TORY CLUBS

The Tories were not, on the whole, as active clubmen as the Whigs. If one considers the history and make-up of the Tory party, this fact is not difficult to understand. Since

they first received their name, the Tories had stood for the
old order of things — in the mode of government, in the
succession, in the national religion. Their traditions were
anti-democratic. They took no pains to propitiate the in-
creasingly important upper middle class of London, the
class which was rapidly becoming banker to the nation.
The political and social aloofness of the Tories explains in
part the fact that they were less clubbable than the Whigs.
Another explanation is more definite. The bulwarks of the
Tory party were the country squires and the clergymen of
the Church of England. Neither of these classes was essentially urban in its way of life, and indeed most of the members of both were absent from London during a large part
of the year. Naturally, then, the Tory clubs were less
prominent than the Whig.

Of the three most important Tory societies, we know two
only from within and one only from without. The October
Club resembled the Calves-Head Club in that no one approved of it except the members, who kept a discreet
silence in spite of the attacks of pamphleteers. The Saturday Club and the Brothers were hardly known to the
Town at all. Information concerning them comes chiefly
from the confidential writings of their members. None of
the three acquired so much fame as the Kit-Cat; none
called forth so much journalism as the Calves-Head.

The story of the Saturday Club and of the Brothers can
be told only from the point of view of Swift. The manner
in which the Irish vicar became connected with the Tory
party does not require discussion. It is enough to recall
that when he returned to London in 1710 on his old mis-
sion in behalf of the church in Ireland, he soon found himself hand in glove with Robert Harley and his ministry.
Swift not only became an enthusiastic member of both of
the clubs of the ministry; he was the only considerable
recorder of their doings. Since he was unusually discrim-
inating in the choice of company, it seems strange to find

him a complacent participator in the meetings of these groups of politicians. The casual talk of the coffee-house bored him. He delighted in the Saturday Club and the Brothers because they were small and exclusive, and because he had a personal liking for most of the members. Furthermore, he was working among potentates over crucial affairs of state, engaging in activities which gave him an exhilarating sense of power.

By Swift's own account the Saturday Club was formed in 1710.

> It was Mr. Harley's custom every Saturday, that four or five of his most intimate friends, among those he had taken in, upon the great change made at court, should dine at his house; and after about two months acquaintance, I had the honour always to be one of the number.[1]

At the outset only Harcourt, Rivers, St. John, Swift, and Harley were present at these meetings, where "after dinner, they used to discourse and settle matters of great importance." These matters were the policies of the government of which Harley was the head. No club, not even the Kit-Cat, was more closely connected with affairs of state.

Swift's presence was highly desirable. As the trusted literary henchman of the ministry he needed to know all the intricacies of state problems in order to carry on his pamphlet warfare to the greatest advantage. So fully did Swift justify the confidence placed in him that he was received on the most intimate footing. It is interesting, as one reads the *Journal to Stella*, to watch his assurance grow until his letters achieve a tone of positive arrogance. His exact status at the club is a trifle uncertain. Sometimes he leaves no question about his standing as a member, but in a letter to Archbishop King he describes the club as made up of the other four and adds, "and sometimes they used to let

1. *Prose Works*, v, 384.

me be of the company." [1] Probably Swift's presence was expected, although the ministers were in the habit of giving him a special invitation each week. On May 12, 1711, he wrote to Stella:

> I dined with Mr Harley and the old club. . . . They rallied me last week, and said I must have Mr St John's leave, so I writ to him yesterday, that, foreseeing I should never dine again with Sir Simon Harcourt, knight, and Robert Harley, Esq., I was resolved to do it to-day. [2]

Regardless of such technicalities, Swift evidently looked upon himself as a member and was held in high esteem by his lofty confreres.

The club had not been meeting long when its progress was halted abruptly (March 8, 1711) by Guiscard's attempt upon Harley's life. A month later Swift wrote to Stella:

> I went in the evening to see Mr Harley; and, upon my word, I was in perfect joy. Mr Secretary was just going out of the door; but I made him come back, and there was the old Saturday club, Lord-Keeper, Lord Rivers, Mr Secretary, Mr Harley, and I; the first time since his stabbing. [3]

During the summer when the court had departed to Windsor, the ministers met only at irregular intervals. The *Journal to Stella* records only one Saturday Club dinner between May and December, 1711. By the latter month the queen had returned to town, and her ministry, aided by the creation of the new peers, had weathered the severest storm of its career. During the season that followed, Swift's interest in the club dwindled, and he often deliberately absented himself from the meetings. They had sadly degenerated, in his opinion, because of the admission of new members, a procedure against which his exclusive

1. *The Correspondence of Jonathan Swift*, ed. F. E. Ball (1910–1914), i, 256.
2. *Prose Works*, ii, 175.
3. *Ibid.*, pp. 170–171.

nature rebelled. On January 9, 1713, he wrote to Stella, lamenting former glories:

I was of the original club, when only poor Lord Rivers, Lord-Keeper, and Lord Bolingbroke came; but now Ormond, Anglesey, Lord-Steward, Dartmouth, and other rabble intrude, and I scold at it; but now they pretend as good a title as I; and, indeed, many Saturdays I am not there. The company being too many, I don't love it.[1]

Although he continued to dine reluctantly with the "Saturday company," as he came scornfully to call it, he seems to have gone, toward the end, rather out of policy than for his own enjoyment.

Just what happened at these Saturday dinners will probably never be known. Swift was discreet on the subject even to Stella. Supposedly the members reviewed the political gains and losses of the week and mapped out a course of action for the days which lay before them. No one can say how many of the schemes of Harley and St. John were first discussed in Harley's dining-room. But during their ascendency the Saturday Club must have seen the formulation of their most important policies.

The ministry soon saw that making decisions was not enough. Provisions had to be made for securing sufficient unity among the party leaders outside the inner circle to put their plans into execution. The Tories had to contend at this time not only with the imperfectly subdued Whigs but also with the Jacobites and the high-flying members of the October Club, who were causing dangerous rifts in the party. To prevent such defections Henry St. John conceived the idea of gathering the party leaders in a club. He related his plans to Lord Orrery as follows:

We shall begin to meet in a small number, and that will be composed of some who have wit and learning to recommend

1. *Ibid.*, p. 413.

them; of others who, from their own situations, or from their relations, have power and influence, and of others who, from accidental reasons, may properly be taken in. The first regulation proposed, and that which must be inviolably kept, is decency. None of the extravagance of the kit-cat, none of the drunkenness of the beef-stake is to be endured. The improvement of friendship, and the encouragement of letters, are to be the two great ends of our society. A number of valuable people will be kept in the same mind, and others will be made converts to their opinions.[1]

There are many striking similarities between this club of St. John's and the Kit-Cat Club. Both were unified by being composed of men of a single political party. Both admitted members for their prestige, either social or literary. Both extended patronage to writers. This resemblance and the reference to the Kit-Cats in the letter just quoted lead inevitably to the conclusion that the Tory secretary had the older group in mind when his plans were forming; and although his society never achieved the renown of the Kit-Cat Club, its history might have been more distinguished had its career not been so abruptly terminated by the fall of the Tory party.

During the time in which St. John was putting his project into execution, Swift was at Wycombe spending a fortnight with Lord Shelburne, entirely unaware of his approaching connection with the club. On the day following his return to town (June 21, 1711), he found himself dining with the new society at Sir William Wyndham's, in the capacity of its secretary.

There were ten of us at dinner. It seems in my absence they had erected a club, and made me one; and we made some laws to-day, which I am to digest, and add to, against next meeting. Our meetings are to be every Thursday: we are yet but twelve:

1. *Letters and Correspondence of Visc. Bolingbroke*, ed. G. Parke (1798), I, 246–247.

Lord-Keeper and Lord-Treasurer were proposed; but I was against them, and so was Mr Secretary, though their sons are of it, and so they are excluded; but we design to admit the Duke of Shrewsbury. The end of our club is to advance conversation and friendship, and to reward deserving persons with our interest and recommendation. We take in none but men of wit or men of interest; and if we go on as we begin, no other club in this town will be worth talking of.[1]

The friendship between the members became so intimate that they habitually spoke of each other as "brothers" and of the club as the "Brothers Club." Thus Swift wrote to Stella, "I walked before dinner in the Mall a good while with Lord Arran and Lord Dupplin, two of my brothers"; and when he visited Lord Masham's son, who was ill, he spoke of the child as his nephew. This custom gained such a hold on the society that it persisted long after the meetings had ceased.

The position of Robert Harley, now Earl of Oxford, was a curious one. His exclusion from membership at the request of his friends, Swift and St. John, may have been due to the fact that his presence at the meetings would have caused an undesirable restraint. Again, the two may have known that he wished to remain away out of policy or that he was too much occupied to give up every Thursday evening. Certainly he showed no animosity over his exclusion. He playfully rallied Swift in company, two weeks after he was denied membership, over this discrimination against him. Swift later recorded with some glee that

1. Swift, *Prose Works*, II, 194. The twenty-two members who finally made up the club were Sir William Wyndham, "young Harley" (son of the lord treasurer), "young Harcourt" (son of the lord keeper), Sir Robert Raymond, the Duke of Shrewsbury, George Granville, Samuel Masham, Lord Dupplin, the Earl of Jersey, Henry St. John, Lord Orrery, Colonel Disney, Colonel John Hill, Lord Bathurst, the Duke of Ormonde, Robert Benson, the Duke of Beaufort, the Earl of Arran, Dr. Freind, Dr. Arbuthnot, Matthew Prior, and Swift. Thomas Harley, cousin of the Earl of Oxford, who was a member for a time, was "turned out . . . for gross neglect and non-attendance" in January, 1712.

when the society dined with young Harcourt, the lord keeper had to "sneak off and dine with Lord-Treasurer" to avoid being in the way. Throughout the club's life, however, Oxford was kept informed of its activities,[1] and was looked upon as its leading patron, a rôle which he did not fill entirely to Swift's satisfaction.

St. John had chosen the worst possible time of the year for founding his club, and its meetings during the summer of 1711 were casual and irregular. Oxford further prevented the dinners in the autumn by fixing upon Thursday for a series of dinners of his own. It was not until late November that the Brothers began to assemble regularly. The practise of dining in the homes of the members had by this time proved so unsatisfactory that a permanent meeting-place was taken in the Thatched-House Tavern, conveniently situated near St. James's. The responsibility for providing the feast was passed from one member to another in a manner described by Swift in the *Journal*.

This was our Society day; Lord Dupplin was president: we choose every week; the last president treats and chooses his successor. I believe our dinner cost fifteen pounds beside wine.[2]

To Swift, who was living on the modest income of a country parson, the sum seemed exorbitant, but he took his turn with the rest, grumbling to Stella at the expense.

The later history of the club shows that it gained some distinction and that membership in it was deemed no small

1. Prior's invitation to Lord Oxford to be present at a meeting of the Brothers in his quarters is preserved (*Poems on Several Occasions* [1718], pp. 286–287) in his verses entitled "An Extempore Invitation to the Earl of Oxford, Lord High Treasurer. 1712," which begins:
> "Our Weekly Friends To-morrow meet
> At Matthew's Palace, in *Duke-street*;
> To try for once, if They can Dine
> On Bacon-Ham, and Mutton-chine."

2. *Prose Works*, II, 311.

honor. Yet the report of its activities was not spread abroad, though Swift mentions no pledges to secrecy. There is one reference to the society in a threepenny pamphlet, published in 1713, entitled *Two Letters Concerning the Author of the Examiner*. The author sets about defending Steele and his works, pretending ironically to exonerate the ministry from all connection with the Tory periodical. "Is it probable," he queries rhetorically, "that any of the present Ministry, who are remarkable for their Encouragement of Learning and Ingenuity, and who have erected a *Society* for the Promotion even of Men of *obscure Merit*, should be pleased with the *Examiner*'s Railing at Mr. *Steele* . . . ?"[1] Direct allusions of this nature are rare.

The decay of the Brothers as an organization is difficult to trace. Swift departed for Ireland before they ceased to meet, and so the record of their doings stopped while the club was still in existence. It is evident from the *Journal* that before his departure Swift had lost much of his interest in the society. The reasons are not far to seek. In the first place, the members had become too extravagant to suit his thrifty nature. After each had taken his turn as president, they reverted to the practise of clubbing, but the evil still persisted.[2] Then, too, the delinquencies of the lord treasurer as a patron seem to have discouraged Swift. The club had accomplished something in the way of encouraging writers, as a later chapter will show, but the results did not reach the dean's expectations. A third cause of his discontent, as in the case of the Saturday Club, was the increased size of the gatherings. It was for this reason that he sent his excuses on society day, two months before he set off for Ireland. "Duke of Ormond chid me," he wrote to Stella, "for not being at the Society to-day, and said sixteen were there. I said I never knew sixteen people

1. Pages 17–18.
2. See Swift, *Prose Works*, II, 357.

good company in my life; no, fais, nor eight either." [1] The
last meeting which he records (April 9, 1713) he failed to
attend because Parliament was likely to sit longer than he
cared to fast.

In a letter to Swift from Paris, written at just this time,
Prior expressed a hope that after the peace was settled the
society would flourish and that he himself would "have
nothing to do but to partake of that universal protection,
which it will receive." [2] Prior's hope was not realized.
With the fall of the Tories which accompanied the death
of Queen Anne, the club lost both its prestige and its purpose; and by 1717 the poet-diplomat was able to write only
the melancholy news:

Our brotherhood is extremely dispersed; but so as that we
have been three or four times able to get as many of the Society
together, and drink to our absent friends.[3]

Such was bound to be the fate of a group held together
primarily by its devotion, however loyal, to an unstable
party.

The October Club

The Tory society which occasioned the most journalistic
writing during the early years of the eighteenth century
was the October Club. Coming into prominence in 1710,
this militant assembly became so dangerous an enemy to
Oxford's ministry that it drew the fire of his two most re-
doubtable apologists, Defoe and Swift. It caused a breach
in the party unity which was closed, with great difficulty,
only through the acumen of the Tory leaders; and its name
passed into contemporary literature as a byword for ramp-
ant factionalism. A detached study of the group is ren-

---

1. *Prose Works*, II, 434. Note the contrast of his attitude of a year earlier
(p. 363), when he wrote: "I met Lord-Treasurer to-day, at Lady Masham's.
He would fain have carried me home to dinner, but I begged his pardon. What!
upon a Society day! No, no."
2. Swift, *Correspondence*, II, 18.   3. *Ibid.*, p. 398.

dered difficult by the character of the available sources of information concerning it. The contemporary accounts are so violently partizan that they must be carefully interpreted with an eye to the political leanings of their authors.

Those who wrote seriously on the origin of the society agree on the conditions which brought it forth. Since the rise of the opposing parties there had been a general understanding that when a new party came into power its supporters at once fell heir to the vacant positions of their routed adversaries. When Harley's ministry took over the administration of the state, certain Whigs were not replaced. The conservative Tory leader tried moderate methods and attempted to bring about the change with as little disturbance as possible. His motives, as was often the case, were not clear. In *An Enquiry into the Behaviour of the Queen's Last Ministry*, Swift maintained that the policy arose from the queen's moderation, not Harley's. His account of the situation to Stella, however, came nearer the truth. In the *Journal* (October 6, 1710) he admitted having heard a report that "Mr Harley himself would not let the Tories be too numerous, for fear they should be insolent, and kick against him; and for that reason they have kept several Whigs in employments, who expected to be turned out every day."[1]

The danger of this ingenious scheme for keeping the reins in his own hands soon became evident. Oldmixon's account of what happened comes close to the truth. A number of loyal gentlemen had entered Parliament on the crest of the wave of high-church enthusiasm which had been aroused by the trial of Dr. Sacheverell.

And getting into the House by the Influence of the Doctor and the new Ministers, [these] were at first ready to vote according to the Treasurer's Conscience, if that Term is pardonable,

1. *Prose Works*, II, 22–23.

rather than their own; but falling short of their Expectations from him, they began to be restless, and enquire into the Reason of things, which was not the Business he had cut out for them.[1]

It was this group of Tory malcontents who in 1710 began to hold indignation meetings at the Bell Tavern in King Street, Westminster, under the name of the October Club. Despite Defoe's humorous contention to the contrary, the name seems to have been derived from the inordinate fondness of the members for October ale. The club numbered about one hundred fifty, "most of them young gentlemen of estates that has never been in Parliament before, and are not very close, but declare to every body what they designe, to have every Whig turn'd out, and not to suffer that the new Ministry shou'd shake hands as they see they do with old."[2] Oldmixon lists twenty-one members of Parliament as being the leading spirits of the club, among them John Aislabie, William Bromley, Sir Thomas Hanmer, Sir John Packington, William Shippen, and Sir William Wyndham.

The brief modern accounts of the October Club treat it as an unprecedented organization that sprang up over night early in the Harleian régime. Such, however, does not appear to have been its origin. Although it may be going too far to accept Defoe's statement that the club was a survival of the Jacobite societies which had been formed at the time of the Revolution, the October group undoubtedly grew out of Tory clubs which were already in existence. In describing the activities of William Bromley, later an October man, in pushing the bill against protestant dissenters, Oldmixon writes:

There were several Debates in the *Tory* Clubs, whether it should be brought in or no. Those Clubs consisted chiefly of

1. John Oldmixon, *The History of England*, III (1735), 482.
2. *The Wentworth Papers*, ed. J. J. Cartwright (1883), p. 180.

Country Gentlemen, better known afterwards by the Appellations of *October* Men, and *Fox-hunters*.

A little farther on Oldmixon speaks of "a long Consultation in their Chief Club, that of the *Vine* Tavern in *Long-Acre*." [1] This club at the Vine was in many respects a close parallel to the later and more famous October group. Walsh sought to imply that it had tendencies toward rabid Jacobitism, for he wrote in a poem called "The Golden Age Restored":

> The faithful clubs assemble at the vine,
> And French intrigues are broach'd o'er English wine,
> Freely the S[ena]te the designs proclaims,
> Affronting W[illia]m, and applauding J[am]es.[2]

Similar insinuations are made by Charles Davenant in his pamphlet entitled, *Tom Double Return'd out of the Country: or, the True Picture of a Modern Whig*.[3] In addition, Davenant makes clear the Tory aversion to continuing the war, particularly in the passage where Tom Double tells Whiglove that "every Night at the *Vine*-Tavern, the whole Club of 'em drank Confusion to the Emperor, Prince *Eugene* of *Savoy*, and the *German* forces in *Italy*." [4] The charges of Jacobitism need not be taken literally when they come from the pens of such partizan writers as these two. Defoe's *Review* of October 7, 1707, refers to the "Vine-Club" as simply a Tory organization, implying that it was a source of some annoyance. Thus the October Club was merely a fusion of a number of high-flying societies, which united naturally enough in 1710 for the purpose of securing vigorous action against the retained Whig leaders. That these minor societies kept, in some measure, their

1. *The History of England*, III (1735), 344.
2. *The Works of the Most Celebrated Minor Poets* (1749), II, 129.
3. Another reference to the Vine Tavern as a seat of the Tory opposition occurs in *The Tackers Vindicated* (1705), pp. 3-4.
4. *Tom Double Return'd out of the Country* (1702), p. 65.

separate identity, even after their union, is indicated in John Macky's brief account of the October Club, which may well be quoted entire.

That of the *OCTOBER* hath made a great Noise all over *Europe*; and we have seen in *Holland* Books printed for and against this *Society*. In the City of *London*, almost every Parish hath its separate Club, where the Citizens, after the Fatigue of the Day is over in their Shops, and on the *Exchange*, unbend their Thoughts before they go to Bed.[1]

By February, 1711, they were fairly established and already doing mischief. On the eighteenth of that month, Swift wrote to Stella:

We are plagued here with an October Club; that is, a set of above a hundred Parliamentmen of the country, who drink October beer at home, and meet every evening at a tavern near the Parliament, to consult affairs, and drive things on to extremes against the Whigs, to call the old ministry to account, and get off five or six heads. The ministry seem not to regard them, yet one of them in confidence told me, that there must be something thought on to settle things better.[2]

With the October Club railing at the ministry "as much as the Whigs do, but from topics directly contrary," Harley's followers were in dire straits, and Swift's letters at this time are full of references to the activities of the October men.[3] On one occasion he barely escaped being drawn into a club dinner. On April 13, 1711, the dean happened to be dining with Charles Ford at the same tavern where one of their meetings was in progress. When Swift sent in for his friend, Sir George Beaumont, "out comes Mr Finch, Lord Guernsey's son, to let me know, that my Lord Compton, the steward of this feast, desired, in the name of the club, that I would do them the honour to dine with them. I

1. *A Journey Through England* (1714), p. 189.
2. *Prose Works*, II, 123.
3. *Correspondence*, I, 236, 244, 249, 253-254.

sent my excuses," Swift concludes his account to Stella, "adorned with about thirty compliments, and got off as fast as I could. . . . The club is about a hundred and fifty, and near eighty of them were then going to dinner at two long tables in a great ground room." [1]

The steps taken by the ministry to combat this dreaded faction were of three sorts. The first step was to reconcile the less violent members by acceding to their request to remove the surviving Whigs from office. Swift explained the process to Lord Peterborough in his letter of May 4, 1711.

We believe Mr. Harley will soon be Treasurer, and be of the House of Peers; and then we imagine the Court will begin to deal out employments, for which every October member is a candidate.

It is worthy of note that Bromley, Hanmer, Mostyn, and other members of the club were given positions of some importance about this time, and the action in their behalf may well have been intended as a sop to the October faction. The program was carried on at such a rate that by December the gossip was abroad that "there shou'd not be a Whig in place by Lady-day." [2] Swift saw, however, that it was impossible to close the party breach by this means; for he realized that there were not enough positions to go round. "Consequently," he discerned, "nine in ten must be disappointed; the effect of which we may find in the next session." [3]

A less obvious step was the deftly managed campaign to destroy the club by splitting it with internal strife. How this move was attempted comes to light in an amusingly graphic letter from Peter Wentworth to his brother, the third Earl of Strafford.

1. *Prose Works*, II, 156–157.
2. *The Wentworth Papers*, p. 226.
3. *Correspondence*, I, 253–254.

I was told by two or three of this club last Sunday, that they begin to send the old Fellows among them, but damn they won't be bite so, and that neither their weadles nor threats shall bring them under government, what has once been carried by the majority of their club they will stand to to a man in the house.[1]

Wentworth's friends must have been of the more radical and more suspicious members, for according to Swift the plan met with some success.

The ministers gave every where out, that the October Club were their friends, and acted by their directions: to confirm which, Mr. Secretary St. John, and Mr. Benson, afterwards chancellor of the exchequer, publicly dined with them at one of their meetings. Thus were eluded all the consequences of that assembly; though a remnant of them, who conceived themselves betrayed by the rest, did afterwards meet under the denomination of the March Club, but without any effect.[2]

This March Club, according to Tom Burnet,[3] split off with about eighty members early in 1712, and the Whigs were delighted at the further dismembering of their opponents. One of Wentworth's letters asserts that St. John's election to the presidency of the October Club was an important factor in the withdrawal of the March Club.[4] Thus the second method of disposing of the October difficulty was much more effective than the first.

A third instrument in the club's downfall was the press. In 1711 Harley had at his disposal the services of two of the best controversial writers of the day, Daniel Defoe and Jonathan Swift, and it is not surprising to find them both coming forward with pamphlets designed to heal the party wound. In addition to their two productions, there are

1. *The Wentworth Papers*, p. 180.
2. *Prose Works*, v, 386.
3. *The Letters of Thomas Burnet to George Duckett*, ed. D. Nichol Smith (Oxford, 1914), p. 6.
4. *The Wentworth Papers*, pp. 283–284.

enough others devoted to the club to leave it fairly well represented in the topical writing of the day.

The most amusing of these works is the satiric piece written by Defoe. The first part was published April 21, 1711, as *The Secret History of the October Club: From its Original to this Time*, and was signed "By a Member." This curious little book of eighty-six pages is an admixture of pseudo-history, humorous prose fiction, and expository journalism. The first thirty pages trace the leading political factions from their beginning to the author's time, in order to show how the October Club was simply the outgrowth of the old Jacobite faction of the time of William and Mary. After following the history of the Tories to the point where the ministry changed in 1710, without "the Plunder, the Blood, the Persecution, the Impeaching" which the more violent ones demanded, Defoe turns abruptly to the story of how Picolomin and Edgar founded the October Club.

Pico, "a Northern Hero of *Gothic* Original," perceiving that politics were going ill for such high-fliers as himself, fell to musing upon his misfortunes until he managed to work himself into a rage. As he was walking distractedly about one day, he met, "not far from a place call'd HELL, an Old Friend of his of *Saxon* Race, Cousin *German*, about a thousand times remov'd from King *Edgar*, and still bearing his Coat of Arms." When their wrath finally permitted them to speak, they fell to cursing incoherently.

And unable to speak out, they part. Will you meet us says *Edgar?* Where says *Pico?* At the *Bell* says *Edgar?* How strong are you says *Pico?* Twenty, and Increasing says *Edgar.* Have you any Members yet says *Pico? Pox! Devil!* says *Edgar, and shakes his head*; we shall — what's the word says *Pico?* OCTOBER says *Edgar*, and so they part.

SEE HOW GREAT A MATTER A LITTLE FIRE KINDLETH.[1]

---

1. *The Secret History of the October Club* (1711), p. 33.

After some ironic remarks on the humble origin and ulti-
mate harmlessness of the club, Defoe concludes the first
part of his essay.

Part II continues the history of this violent group of malcontents under Pico and Edgar, and describes the use of the
word "October" as a token of membership, presented at
the bar of the tavern. Defoe asserts that the October men
first met in groups at various houses, but eventually came
together under the new watchword. His account of how
the ministry dealt with the club and eventually brought
many of the members into an unnatural alliance with the
court party follows in its general outline the facts set down
by more disinterested writers. A considerable section of
Part II is entirely independent of the club and is merely a
defense of Harley's policies. Toward the end Defoe gives
another explanation of "October," which he pretends to
quote from "Sir *Robert Dandylyon*'s Choice Manual, Entitled, *Loyal Table Talk*, where we have an Account of a
Conference between two Country Gentlemen upon these
State matters." [1] It appears that these two gentlemen
used the word as a password for their high-flying club because Sir Thomas had once used it in a fox-hunting club,
and was too dull to think of a new countersign.

In Part III the progress and resolutions of this second
group are described, in order to show what violent measures they favored against the Whigs. Defoe even inserts a
daring implication that they had a hand in the Guiscard
affair,[2] so great was their hatred for Harley. He returns, at
length, as he does near the end of each part, to the name of
the club and explains the manner in which the password
developed into a designation for the society. One of the
drawers was the first to blunder on to the combination
"October Club." His mistake was repeated by a stupid
footman of one of the members in the hearing of three

1. *The Secret History of the October Club*, p. 59.
2. *Ibid.*, p. 75.

others, who were just going in to a meeting. When these three arrived, a debate was in progress over "some Honourable Designation to bestow on themselves to Eternize the memory of their Assembly." One of the newcomers told the story of the stupid footman and suggested the name "October Club," which was forthwith adopted. The few remaining pages of the pamphlet are of an expository nature, being devoted to an account of the club's violent program and a defense of the queen's ministry.

The *Secret History* was obviously written, not as a serious account of the club's origin, but as an attack upon an opposed political faction. The statements of fact are hence suspect. Defoe endeavors to leave the impression that very few members of Parliament belonged to the club,[1] which is, of course, utterly false. His insinuation that the October men were connected with Guiscard's stabbing of Harley is not now credited, and the suspicions of violent Jacobitism which he casts upon them are only partially justified. As a piece of deft pamphleteering, however, the piece is admirable. Although the constant shifting of style and point of view mars the unity of the tract, it produces a variety that the reader of an eighty-page political pamphlet cannot but find pleasing. The amusing narrative bits are inserted with the same adroit art which characterizes the swift changes from pure exposition to irony and sarcasm. In each of his several manners, Defoe is deft and spirited, and his pen seems to have left untouched hardly a vulnerable spot in the program of these enemies of the ministry.

A similar tone of ridicule pervades the second attack which Defoe made upon the October Club. Somewhat later in 1711, he published a pamphlet entitled *Eleven Opinions about Mr. Harley*, the fifth of the promised [2] eleven being "the October-Club's opinion." Here he follows the same

---

1. See pages 37, 42, 79, for example.
2. Defoe gives only eight.

plan of refusing to recognize the power of the faction, and contents himself with highly participial jeering at their impotent rage. A single choice passage will illustrate his method.

> The *October-Club* are a Faction of the hot exasperated Part of the People, called *Tories*, composed of Swearing, Oath-taking, abjuring *Jacobites*, self-contradicting, Moon-blind, *High-Flyers*; Men that walk in their Sleep, dream waking, see with their Eyes shut, and are blind with their Eyes open; that were *Fools enough* to think they were coming into Play, *wise enough* to know they *are not*, and *Mad-men enough* to think *now* that they can help it.[1]

When he has poured forth sufficient contumely upon the heads of the members, he turns to a justification of Harley. The seven pages which make up this "opinion" do not attempt to give "a Character of the Clubb," that being the province of the "author of the *Secret History*, who, I am told, is bringing out a Second Part, more comical than the first." All that Harley's apologist was here undertaking was to belittle the attacks upon his patron and to show that the minister's stand on party matters was not discreditable.

Swift's method of dealing with the factionists was much more serious. *The Examiner*, No. 29, shows that he realized the danger of Harley's middle course, and his genuine interest in the club's position comes to light in the *Journal to Stella*, where he wrote on April 22, 1711:

> I was an hour with him [St. John] this morning deep in politics, where I told him the objections of the October Club, and he answered all except one, — That no inquiries are made into past mismanagement.[2]

It is possible that in this very interview he was collecting ammunition to be used against the enemy in *Some Advice*

1. *Eleven Opinions about Mr. Harley* (1711), pp. 55–56.
2. *Prose Works*, II, 162.

Humbly Offer'd to the Members of the October Club in a Letter from a Person of Honour, which was published the following January. At any rate his pamphlet is a straightforward appeal to the intelligence and party loyalty of the disaffected group, rather than an effort to make it seem ridiculous. Swift insists that if Harley's motives were known his vindication would be complete; that the Tories were, after all, in a much stronger position than they had dared to hope for a few months earlier; and that the Whigs' dread of Harley's power was sufficient testimony to that minister's skillful management. The conclusion pictures the calamity which might easily result from the extravagances of the rebellious spirits of the club. The whole tone of the pamphlet, indeed, is one of frank remonstrance, magnanimous and not unfriendly.

Swift's *Advice to the October Club* did not meet with a particularly warm reception. On January 28, 1712, he wrote to Stella:

The little two-penny Letter of Advice to the October Club does not sell; I know not the reason; for it is finely written, I assure you; and, like a true author, I grow fond of it, because it does not sell: you know that it is usual to writers to condemn the judgment of the world: if I had hinted it to be mine, every body would have bought it, but it is a great secret.[1]

The anonymity of the pamphlet was fairly complete; for Oldmixon refers to it as "said to be the Work of Lord Keeper *Harcourt*." [2] Although Swift was shortly to report to Stella that the "Letter" was gaining in popularity, it is doubtful that it influenced the group to whom it was directed as much as it served to turn public opinion against them. Its appeal was not of the sort which would move any but the least fanatical of the October men.

Not all the attacks on the club came from the pens of

1. *Ibid.*, p. 327.
2. *The History of England*, III (1735), 482.

Tories. Since it was, after all, a faction of the Tory party, there opened to Whig writers an excellent opportunity for attacking their opponents by attributing to the whole party the violent notions of its secessionists. Perhaps the most vigorous of these attacks was that of the unidentified Whig who wrote *A Collection of Hymns and Poems, for the Use of the October Club. By Dr. S—l, Dr. A—y, Dr. S—e, Dr. M—ss, and little T—p of Oxford, Ch[aplai]ns to the said Club.*[1] The church background suggested by the word "Hymns," though not sustained throughout all the poems, extends to the fiercely sarcastic dedication to the "right worshipful members of the October Club" by their worships' "Poor Beadsmen." The author designs these hymns to be used in the services of the club held at every festival in the year. The dedication concludes:

It's possible some wanton People may turn so grave a Composure into Ridicule, as they have done by several Immortal Pieces that have come from our Hands. . . . But we being by Principle Passive, except we are angred, pass by the injudicious Censures of those Airy Souls, who are more Transported with a Jigg, than the solemn Numbers of Ch[ur]ch Musick; and directly Appeal to your Worship's, who are the most excellent Judges of Proper Time, the Divine Harmony of Four Bottles of Claret, a Man at the B[e]ll, and of all the Graces (without shaking) of old Oct[o]ber in the Country.

The nine satiric poems which follow are written upon a variety of subjects and in a variety of meters. The first, called "The O[cto]br Feast," composed in pentameter couplets in a mock-heroic vein, contains an interesting reference to the password of the club.

1. The names to be supplied are as follows: Sacheverell; Atterbury; George Stanhope, D.D., Dean of Canterbury and chaplain to Queen Anne; Robert Moss, D.D., chaplain in ordinary to William III, Anne, and George I; and Joseph Trapp, poet and controversialist, who was Professor of Poetry at Oxford (1708–1718) and is mentioned in Swift's *Journal* as chaplain to Lord Bolingbroke.

Gay was the Treat and spacious was the Board,
The Hour was Two, *October* was the Word;
The Doughty Knights in Buskins led the Van,
The Squires in Socks Devoutly clos'd the Train.[1]

The poet inserts a mock grace, delivered by a caricature of Dr. Sacheverell, and gives a graphic account of the feast, which ended only when

The Drunken Squires were carry'd off the Stage,
And Couchant C——ch was cramm'd into the Cage.[2]

The second poem, which parodies the story of the Levite and the Samaritan, is directed against the resentful attitude of the October men toward the Whigs. The Tory churchmen, the author implies, held the theory

That 'twas a Damning Sin to give Relief
To Beggars of a different Belief.[3]

The remaining poems are equally pointed. One attacks high-church intolerance, another the corruptions of Harley's ministry, a third the Tory program for peace. By vilifying the club and subtly identifying it with the party, the satirist makes his verse a trenchant weapon in spite of his poetic limitations.

A Whig *Letter to a Member of the October-Club: Shewing That to yield Spain to the Duke of Anjou by a Peace, wou'd be the Ruin of Great Britain* follows similar tactics, though in a different manner. The letter begins, without any preliminary remarks on the club, by enumerating the dangers of such a peace as the title suggests, emphasizing the profit that would accrue to the French king from this new source of troops and revenue. The author stresses particularly the economic upheaval that would accompany the resulting jeopardy to England's American trade. Curiously enough, he connects *The Examiner* with the October Club

---

1. *A Collection of Hymns and Poems, for the Use of the October Club* (1711), p. 1.
2. *Ibid.*, p. 4.   3. *Ibid.*, p. 6.

rather than with the ministry. His delight is manifest as he points out that the policies of the nation had not altered materially since the change of 1710; but he is anxious for the October Club to leave the ministry in peace and resents mightily "the *Examiner*, and such other Writers."

As for these Men, I consider them as so many second-hand Hirelings to carry on the interest of *France*.[1]

Whether this is a wilful misrepresentation of the facts or a genuine misapprehension is not perfectly clear. What is everywhere patent is that another Whig pamphleteer had conceived the possibilities of directing his attack upon the Tories through their vulnerable offshoot, the October Club.

Although the literary productions which deal with the group in anything like a sympathetic manner are insignificant enough, one or two are worth mentioning. In 1711 there appeared anonymously, without even the imprint of a publisher, a group of poems entitled *Æsop at the Bell-Tavern in Westminster, or, a Present from the October-Club, In a few Select Fables from Sir Roger L'Estrange*. The preface, written ostensibly by the publisher, gives a peculiar explanation of how he came by the work.

To account with the Reader for the Title of this little Pamphlet, tho' I am altogether in the Dark, as to the Author of it, He is to be told that the following Papers were taken up by a Gentleman, in the Great Room at the *Bell-Tavern* in *Westminster*, where the Celebrated Club, of worthy *Patriots*, that goes by the Name of OCTOBER, was daily held, during the last Session of Parliament, and may justly be suppos'd to be drop'd there by One of that Honourable Society. The Method they are written in will convince the Intelligent, that a Person of Understanding, as well as Education, is the Composer of them.

1. *A Letter to a Member of the October Club* (1711), p. 47. Equally bitter accusations are implied in the ironical praise of *The Character and Declaration of the October Club*, another anonymous pamphlet of 1711.

If the matter of the fables were satire on the Club and this preface ironic, the natural conclusion would be that the remarks just quoted were pure subterfuge in the interest of anonymity. When one considers, however, the point of view of the fables themselves, the statement in the preface seems plausible enough, except for the casual way in which the publisher obtained the manuscript. Certainly it contained no satire on the October Club.

In the introductory fable of the coat, the author issues a caution against reading too much into his lines. This attempt to fortify his somewhat hazardous position leads him to conclude with the following quatrain:

> I made the Coat, 'tis very true,
> All Fools to ridicule,
> But if 'tis own'd by one of you,
> 'Tis He that *makes the Fool.*

The fables attack both the Whigs and the ministry. The former are dealt with on such matters as their commonwealth tendencies, their journalistic defenders, the prolongation of the war, occasional conformity, Godolphin's resignation, and the rapacity of Marlborough. Indeed, the preponderance of the author's spleen is vented upon the Whigs and their policies. But he identifies himself with the disaffected element in Fable X, on "The General Peace," in which he uses a variation of the cock and fox story to show his disgust at the ministry's failure to terminate the war. The fourteenth fable, on "The Naturalizing Act," shows the author's opposition to the Hanoverian succession. Most representative of all is Fable XII, called "The late Ministry's Pocket-Looking-Glass," which reveals the old rebellious spirit of the loyal country gentleman who sees himself ruled by men whom he considers his inferiors. The "moral" begins:

> So *'twas when* Rebels *had pull'd down*
> *The* Mitre, Scepter, *and the* Crown,
> *By Way of* Moderation:

> *Thieves of Commissioners of Safety,*
> *Of all Things, Ye were worth, bereft Ye;*
> *And most demurely talk'd of* Sequestration.[1]

The author's point of view throughout is such that this satiric Æsop must be taken as having emanated, directly or indirectly, from the October Club itself.

Following hard upon the calumny which the satirists poured upon the group, came some laudatory verses which found their way into D'Urfey's *Pills to Purge Melancholy*. These "Lyrical Verses: Set to a pleasant Aire, made for the Entertainment, and most humbly Dedicated to the Honourable and Worthy Members of the October Club" were written, judging from internal evidence, between the peace of Utrecht (April 12, 1713) and the death of Queen Anne (August 1, 1714). The first two stanzas give the testimony of Jove and Apollo to the truth of the refrain:

> Of all Clubs here below,
> The *October* deserves most praise.[2]

In conclusion the poet pledges the loyalty of the club to the Hanoverian succession, wishing, at the same time, "long happy days" to the queen. The hint of the social nature of the October gatherings which appears in the song is the more welcome because this feature was so generally neglected by the satirists who immortalized the club.

Although the power of the faction was broken by the withdrawal of the March Club in 1712, it was not at once forgotten. When the Triennial Act was brought up for reconsideration in 1716, a party writer came forward with *An Humble Petition from the October-Club to a certain eminent M - - - r of the H. of C - - - s.* As a living organization, however, its day had passed, and it is now remembered only because it drew the attention of the two great pamphleteers of the period, Defoe and Swift.

1. *Æsop at the Bell-Tavern* (1711), p. 27.
2. *Pills to Purge Melancholy*, II (1719), 258.

It should not be thought that the history of London's political clubs ends before 1720 with the Tory October Club or with the Whig Mug-Houses. The partizan society had become so generally accepted as a valuable political instrument that it was a veritable institution. In 1738 *The Gentlemen's Magazine* reprinted from *Old Common Sense* (No. 61) a "Project for curing Corruption and Venality," in which is proposed a system of political clubs throughout the kingdom, each distinct from the rest but allied to a central organization. The author of the scheme even offers a set of articles for the establishment of the societies, showing that he, at least, took the project seriously. The coffee-houses of the 'sixties were the meeting-places of party groups as truly as they had been half a century earlier; and Wildman's and Almack's [1] harbored Whigs and Tories respectively, somewhat as the Bell and Button's had in the reign of Queen Anne. But the appearance of these clubs in contemporary letters had become rare. The period when most of the distinguished men of letters devoted a large part of their energy and literary effort to supporting a party had gone for ever; and the political club became less and less preoccupying to writers during that evolution of the literary profession which ultimately released them from taking part in politics.

PHANTOM SOCIETIES

Important as were the various Whig and Tory societies in the background of early eighteenth-century literature, they made up only a small fraction of the total number that existed in this club-forming age. The non-political clubs, indeed, present so much diversity that they almost defy classification. A glance at Ned Ward's satirical *His-*

1. See Charles Churchill's poem, "The Candidate," lines 237–238 (*Poetical Works* [1892], II, 205):
> " Each dish at Wildman's of sedition smacks;
> Blasphemy may be gospel at Almack's."

tory of Clubs or an excursion through the pages of *The Spectator* is sufficient to establish their variety. The loose application of the word "club" is, of course, partly responsible. The Christ Church wits who assisted Charles Boyle in writing *Dr. Bentley's Dissertations . . . Examin'd* in the Phalaris controversy, for example, are referred to by Budgell as the "Club of Wits at *Christ-Church*;" [1] and Lady Mary Wortley Montagu mentions them as "Atterbury and his club," [2] though there is no reason to suspect the group of any organization. The literature of the period abounds in such vague references to clubs as that of Breval in his lines to Addison.

> For *Thee* at Home the zealous Songsters pore,
> Shun Clubs of *Port*; and turn their *Classicks* o'er.[3]

Similarly informal was the little group of Swift's friends in Dublin who frequently assembled about the card table; yet Swift refers to it more than once as a club.[4] Thus the term was extremely broad in its application, and it is necessary to consider the similar latitude in our modern use of the word in order not to reject as unworthy of the name a number of the associations so described.

Many of the non-political clubs instituted during the lifetime of Swift and the years immediately following must be passed over in silence because they do not figure prominently in contemporary letters. To this group belong the various societies for the reformation of manners, which sprang up at the turn of the century, and the Society for Promoting Primitive Christianity, in which William Whiston was prominent. It was during these years that the interest in antiquarian studies brought about the re-

1. *Memoirs of the Life and Character of the Late Earl of Orrery* (1732), p. 194.
2. *The Letters and Works of Lady Mary Wortley Montagu*, ed. Moy Thomas (1893), II, 255.
3. *An Epistle to the Right Honourable Joseph Addison* (1717), p. 3.
4. *Correspondence*, I, 121; II, 67; III, 191.

vival of the Society of Antiquaries, founded in the six-
teenth century, and the establishment of other groups in
the Peterborough Society, the Society at Spaulding, and
Lord Sandwich's Egyptian Club. Closely allied were the
clubs of Royal Society men, who held meetings from the
time of Pepys [1] to the time of John Byrom,[2] and then,
about 1743, became definitely established as the Royal
Society Club. There were also professional groups, such
as the Rose Club, composed of lawyers, to which Mrs.
Pilkington refers.[3] The Artists' Club, which met at the
Bull's Head in Clare Market, claimed William Hogarth as
a member, and the famous Dilettanti Society, formed in
1734, eventually included such men as Charles Fox, Colman, Garrick, and Sir Joshua Reynolds. Although little
was written about these clubs in their own day, taken together they show in a striking manner the hold which the
new social phenomenon was gaining upon eighteenth-
century society.

The clubs which played the greatest part in London life
were not these specialized societies which were erected for
a definite purpose. It was the informal groups, assembled
with the primary end of good fellowship and conversation,
that really colored Augustan literature. The more famous
clubs, such as White's and the beefsteak clubs, have left a
distinct impression on the writings of the time; but the less
definite allusions to club life in the end establish its importance. *A Choice Collection of New Songs and Ballads*
(1699) bears on the verso of the title-page the following
inscription:

To the Steward in Being, And the rest of the Worthy Society Meeting on Wednesdays, at the St. *Alban's* Tavern in

1. *The Diary of Samuel Pepys*, ed. H. B. Wheatley (1924), IV, 331; V, 292.
2. *The Private Journal and Literary Remains of John Byrom*, ed. R. Parkin-
son (Manchester, 1854), vol. I, part i, pp. 50, 51, 54, etc.
3. *Memoirs of Mrs Letitia Pilkington*, ed. Iris Barry (1928), p. 145. A poem
on an Archers' Club is included in *Poems on Several Occasions* (1723), p. 113.

St. *Alban*'s-*street*; This first Collection of New Songs, made to
several Pleasant Tunes, is Dedicated by,
Gentlemen,
Your most Oblig'd and Humble Servant,
T. D'urfey.

Here is a club sufficiently interested in poetry to be considered a possible source of patronage. The regularity of
its meetings implies some sort of organization, and the
place where it met is definitely stated. Yet we know precisely nothing of its activities and its membership.

Similar will-o'-the-wisps appear on every hand. An unknown satirist drew a hauntingly vivid picture of a nameless club in some verses "On the Author of a Dialogue
concerning Women, pretended to be writ in Defence of
the Sex."

> Near Covent-Garden theatre, where you know
> Poets their sense, players their shapes do shew,
> There is a club of critics of the pit,
> Who do themselves admire for men of wit;
> And lo! an arbitrary power assume
> On plays and ladies both to pass their doom;
> Censure all things and persons, priest and prince,
> And judge them by the standard of their sense:
> But scan these sparks, or by their words and mien,
> You'll find them fop without, and fool within.
> One of these brats dress'd up in shape of satire,
> Comes forth to be the ladies vindicator:
> And since for chivalry he claims no warrant,
> Instead of knight sets up for poet-errant.[1]

This attack on William Walsh came in response to that
poet's ironic *Dialogue Concerning Women, Being a Defence
of the Sex: Written to Eugenia.* The references to the club's
judgments on "plays and ladies" suggest the Kit-Cats, of
whom Walsh was one. The situation of this club of critics,
however, and the absence of any indication that they were

1. *A Supplement to the Works of the Most Celebrated Minor Poets* (1750),
p. 108.

men of rank are against any such identification; and it must reluctantly be put down among the many societies which defy all attempts to trace their history.

Evidence of an equally shadowy group of wits appears in the letters of Thomas Burnet. On March 15, 1712, Burnet wrote to his friend George Duckett:

I have worn off all the Spleen the Club had at me and am become once more a very acceptable member. Nay, having lost you the Supporter of my mirth and gaiety, I begin to be *humdrum* enough even for them. . . . I write with great ease and with no constraint, because this will be brought you by so safe a hand as is that of Jack Bromfield, a True Mitre Man.[1]

Some months later Burnet concluded a letter to Duckett by giving him the services of "Denny and Jack Bond, George Trenchard and all our Club."[2] In the absence of external evidence we can deduce a society, probably called the Humdrum Club, composed of Burnet, Duckett, and a number of their friends, which met at the Mitre Tavern. In *The Spectator*, No. 9, Addison mentions "the Humdrum Club, of which I was formerly an unworthy member," where some "very honest gentlemen, of peaceable dispositions . . . used to sit together, smoke their pipes, and say nothing till midnight." The two accounts fit together very well until one remembers that Tom Burnet was at this time making a considerable reputation as an undisciplined young rake, which mars the tempting conclusion that his club was the placid society of which Mr. Spectator was a member.

Edward Young gave Spence a suggestive account of a noble society "held at the King's Head in Pall Mall, that arrogantly called itself 'The World.' Lord Stanhope, then (now Lord Chesterfield) Lord Herbert, &c. &c. were members." Dr. Young tells how he was asked to write some verses upon a wine-glass, according to the custom of

1. *Letters*, p. 2.   2. *Ibid.*, p. 18.

the club. Having no diamond of his own, Young provided himself with Lord Stanhope's and wrote the couplet:

> Accept a miracle, instead of wit;
> See two dull lines, with Stanhope's pencil writ.[1]

Early in 1715 a large club of Welshmen came together as the Society of Ancient Britons, for the purpose, apparently, of securing court favor for Wales. Noting that by a lucky coincidence their princess's birthday and St. David's day fell together on March 1, the shrewd founders met on this day and resolved to make it the annual festival of their society. A small group of stewards was chosen to hold monthly meetings in the interests of Wales, and such was their activity that the prince himself was persuaded to become president of the society. In 1717 Sir Thomas Jones, as secretary and treasurer, published in a letter to his countrymen a history of *The Rise and Progress of the Most Honourable and Loyal Society of Antient Britons*. The little book gives a complete account of the club's celebrations on the two anniversaries which had occurred since its foundation. It also contains a song written and "performed" by Thomas D'Urfey, and "An Ode for Two Voices, for the Birth-Day of Her Royal Highness the Princess of Wales" by John Hughes. There is also a curious "Poem on St. David's Day," dedicated to the society by a schoolboy, who was sent in return a vote of thanks. Sir Thomas Jones's book can in no sense be called a contribution to literature, but it forms an interesting bit of evidence as to the great variety of purposes for which clubs were organized during these years.

Many of the clubs to which writers of the time refer are altogether nameless. Such is the financially embarrassed society that on June 5, 1712, inserted in *The Daily Courant* the following advertisement:

1. Spence, *Anecdotes*, p. 288.

THE BOXKEEPER TO THE CLUB AT THE TWO BLUE Posts in Shoemaker-Row near Aldgate, (finding that several of the Contributors to the said Club do make delay in paying of their weekly Contributions,) doth hereby give Notice to all such Contributors, That if they do not bring in their weekly Contributions as formerly, as also all their Arrears, on or before Saturday next, shall be quite excluded the Benefit of the said Club.

Such, too, is the projecting club mentioned in *The Quack Vintners: or, a Satyr against Bad Wine* (1712).[1] Almost equally obscure is the group suggested in the "Song for the nonsensical Club, sung annually on the 24th of June," which appeared in *The Gentleman's Magazine*.[2] Two stanzas of the song run as follows:

> Should nonsense from humane kind sever,
>   What numbers must strait away run?
> The beau pick his teeth must for ever,
>   The chatt'ring coquet be undone.
>
> The bards would have little to write on
>   The lawyers have little to say,
> The criticks would nought have to bite on,
>   The noncons not know how to pray.

Although the club which expressed itself thus had a name, it stands out no more clearly than the two nameless ones. The only evidence that it existed is contained in the title of the song.

CLUBS OF RAKES: MOHOCKS AND HELL-FIRES

Fortunately, not all the clubs of the period leave us so completely in the dark about their history. If little can be discovered about the informal "street clubs" described in *The Spectator*, No. 9, where men congregated with their neighbors of the same street to avoid braving the dangers

---

1. Page 20.
2. *The Gentleman's Magazine*, v (1735), 554.

of a night walk through London, there is some compensation in the more complete literary picture of the societies of rakes which made such caution necessary. For it is possible to trace the movements of these barbarous young gallants through a period of two centuries, an important part of which lies within the reigns of Anne and the first George.

The first group of rakes to be called a club was the Mohocks, who became a matter of general concern about London early in 1712. The activities in which they engaged were not new. The excitement of nocturnal marauding, and the accompanying danger of a possible encounter with the watch, had led bands of young bloods to prowl the streets at many different times since the window-breaking exploits of the Earl of Surrey in the fifteen-forties. Shadwell's play *The Scowrers* (1691) describes a group, remarkably like the Mohocks, which was headed by Sir William Rant, Wildfire, and Tope. In one of the speeches of Tope, who was a rake of the old school, there is a hint of the boldness of earlier street gangs.

> *Tope.* Puh this is nothing, why I knew the Hectors, and before them the *Muns* and the *Titire Tu's*, they were brave fellows indeed; in those days a man could not go from the *Rose Tavern* to the *Piazza* once, but he must venture his life twice.[1]

The history of such gangs in the seventeenth century has been written so completely[2] that it is not necessary to trace it here. But Shadwell's scourers were so nearly the contemporaries of the Mohocks that their misdemeanors are of more than common interest. In Act II Whachum tells how "we scowr'd the Market people, overthrew the Butter-women, defeated the Pippin-Merchants, wip'd out the

1. *The Complete Works of Thomas Shadwell*, ed. Montague Summers (1927), v, 89.
2. T. S. Graves, "Some Pre-Mohock Clansmen," *Studies in Philology*, xx (1923), 395–421.

Milk-scores, pull'd off the Door-knockers, Dawb'd the gilt Signs," until people actually thought it was Sir William Rant's followers. These pranks seem innocent enough compared to the atrocities of which the descendants of the scourers were accused some twenty years later.

With the outbreak of nocturnal barbarities which terrified London early in 1712 came the flood of occasional literature which immortalized the Mohocks. An objection may at once be raised to characterizing this group of rakes as a club, but the question may be ignored for the time being. Resting on the authority of *The Spectator*, No. 324, in which the band is referred to as a "nocturnal fraternity under the title of the Mohock Club," we may proceed to the more serious problem of the actuality of the Mohocks. More than one credible writer, Lord Chesterfield among others, has gone so far as to doubt their very existence. Maitland's account records the reports of the outrages, and then continues as follows:

However, it does not appear, that ever any Person was detected of any of the said Crimes; and notwithstanding I made all the Inquiry imaginable, in those Places where the Offences were said to have been chiefly committed, I never could learn of any one Person having received the least Hurt upon that Account.[1]

Maitland was not alone in adopting the view that "these idle and fictitious stories" were "artfully contrived to intimidate the people." It is worth while to run quickly over the evidence of the club's existence.

Swift was one of the first to record Mohock activities. On March 9, 1712, he wrote to Stella:

Young Davenant was telling us at court how he was set upon by the Mohocks, and how they ran his chair through with a sword. It is not safe being in the streets at night for them. The

1. William Maitland, *History and Survey of London* (1756), I, 510.

Bishop of Salisbury's son is said to be of the gang.[1] They are all Whigs; and a great lady sent to me, to speak to her father and to Lord-Treasurer, to have a care of them, and to be careful likewise of myself; for she heard they had malicious intentions against the ministers, and their friends. I know not whether there be any thing in this, though others are of the same opinion.[2]

Although Swift was not sure that the Mohocks had special designs on him, he realized that if the Whigs were staging the demonstrations to terrorize their enemies, he was as liable to persecution as anyone. Even after he learned that Davenant's assailant was merely "a drunken gentleman, none of that gang," Swift took a coach or chair when he found it necessary to go abroad after dark.[3] If, as the Whigs insisted, the whole affair was simply Tory political propaganda, it is strange to find a person as completely *au courant* as Swift thus imposed upon.

The night of Tuesday, March 11, 1712, was one of particular activity for the Mohock Club. Arrests followed the disorders, and publicity followed the arrests. An original manuscript [4] of what appears to be a set of memoranda made by a constable reveals that Richard Lord Hinchinbroke, among others, was released on heavy bail, having been taken up "for that the said Lord Hinchinbrook together with other persons did on the 11th of March instant between 1 & 2 a clock in the morning make a riot & assault upon Iohn Bouch Watchman in Essex street." On the following day two broadsides appeared. One, entitled "The Town Rakes: Or, The Frolicks of the Mohocks or Hawkubites," gives a sensational description of the brawl of the

---

1. Hearne's testimony (*Remarks and Collections*, III [1889], 327) on the membership of Tom Burnet is amusing. An entry in Hearne's journal, dated April 1, 1712, runs as follows: "Bp. Burnett's Son, who was lately either Commoner or Gent. Commoner of Merton-Coll. (and hath been always look'd upon as a Young, little impudent Brat) is said to be one of the principal of the Mohocks."

2. *Prose Works*, II, 351.

3. *Ibid.*, pp. 355, 356, 360, 362.

4. Now in the Ernest Gay Collection of the Harvard College Library.

night before, which terminated, according to the writer, in a wholesale incarceration of the offending rakes in various roundhouses. The other publishes the names of those taken up "Monday Night, Tuesday, and this Morning," listed under the various jails in which the malefactors were confined. Swift was among the first to read these broadside accounts of the affair. On the night of their publication he wrote to Stella:

Here is the d—— and all to do with these Mohocks. Grub Street papers about them fly like lightning, and a list printed of near eighty put into several prisons, and all a lie; and I begin almost to think there is no truth, or very little, in the whole story.[1]

As has already appeared, Swift's subsequent conduct belied this assertion of incredulity.

The excitement did not soon abate. Three days later (March 15) Thomas Burnet, who was mentioned by Swift and Hearne as a member of the gang, wrote a graphic account of it to his friend Duckett.

There have of late been about the Town a sett of young fellows that called themselves Mohocks and had chosen one Tim: Allyn to be their Emperour; these men used inspired by Potent Bacchus to run out at 12 a clock from Taverns and beat Watchmen, slit fellows noses and cut women's arms, stop coaches or chairs, and offer violence to Ladys even of Quality. Upon these accounts the Queen has issued out a Proclamation promising a hundred ll. to any one that can discover any of these men. The Town, because I have gone sometimes to Nando's Coffeehouse and have a sort of innate fierceness in my Looks, will have it that I am one of this gang.[2]

The final sentence is non-committal enough. In view of the liberties taken at this time with the mail of persons under suspicion, one wonders that Burnet did not declare his innocence outright, regardless of the facts of the case.

1. *Prose Works*, II, 352–353.   2. *Letters*, p. 2.

The royal edict to which Burnet referred was not issued officially until two days after the letter was written. After noting "the Great and Unusual Riots and Barbarities, which have lately been committed in the Night-time in the open Streets . . . by numbers of Evil-Disposed Persons, who have combined together to disturb the publick Peace," the proclamation offered the reward mentioned by Burnet and promised exemption from punishment to any Mohock who would inform upon his fellow-rakes. In addition a commission was instituted by Lord Harcourt at the queen's command for the purpose of investigating the disorders. On April 12 a report was presented. The only offenders who had actually been arrested, according to the commission, were those captured on the night of March 11, among whom were Lord Hinchinbroke, Sir Mark Cole, Thomas Fanshaw, Captain John Reading, and Captain Robert Bard. But the commissioners were able to report that the watch had been redoubled and was now on duty from nine at night till six in the morning.

The investigation did not stop here. Another proclamation, inserted in *The London Gazette* on April 19, declared that sufficient evidence had been gathered for the conviction of the leaders, and solicited further information to be used against the abettors of those already under prosecution. "To this Advertisement," as Boyer puts it,[1] "were subjoyn'd the Particulars of thirteen Assaults, committed on different Persons therein named, between the beginning of *February* and the latter end of *March*." Harcourt was doing a thorough piece of work.

When Sir Mark Cole and three of the other prisoners were brought to trial on June 6, 1712, their defense was most interesting. They alleged that they were not Mohocks but scourers, "who had gone out with a magistrate's warrant to scour the streets, arrest Mohocks and other offenders, and deliver them to justice." Pearson

---

1. *Annals*, XI (1713), 7.

says that this statement did not effect their acquittal, referring vaguely to "one of the papers of the day" as his
authority.[1] Abel Boyer's version of the case, or one exactly
like it, disagrees on this point. His *Annals* for 1712 puts
the matter thus:

A Young Lord and an Officer of the Army, who, at the Desire, and in the Company of a Constable of *Westminster*, went
out one Night in quest of the pretended *Mohocks*, in order to
suppress them; were afterwards arraign'd and try'd as if they
had themselves been Distrubers of the Publick Peace. But their
Innocence appearing manifest, the Notion of *Mohocks* and
Hawkubites was entirely exploded, to the Shame and Confusion
of those who broach'd and endeavour'd to support it.

In view of the official proclamations already mentioned,
some Mohocks seem to have been actually convicted. But
Boyer would hardly have dared to refer to the manifest
innocence of these particular gentlemen if they had been
adjudged guilty. That the whole "notion of Mohocks"
was exploded by the results of this one trial is highly
doubtful.

From these conflicting records of the Mohock disturb-
ances, a number of positive facts may be deduced. Between the first of February and the last of March there was
an extraordinary amount of violence in the streets, late at
night, which was not committed from the usual motives of
criminals. The residents of London, high and low alike,
were genuinely afraid to go out after dark. Official proclamations were made and men arrested. Some were almost
certainly convicted. Since at the time everyone attributed
the disorders to the Mohocks except a few writers who had
strong political motives for not doing so, there is little reason in denying their existence. It is not necessary to put
implicit faith in all the Grub-Street journalism connected
with the outbreak of March 11 in order to credit the deeds

1. Norman Pearson, *Society Sketches in the Eighteenth Century* (1911), p. 13.

of a band of rakes who were simply carrying on an old tradition. The true motives of the Mohocks were not unlike those of their seventeenth-century predecessors. It was the attempt of Queen Anne's subjects to find subtler reasons for the outrages that created the panic and led to the confusion.

Each political party had its own explanation. The Tory suspicions, already hinted at, are stated at some length by Swift in his *History of the Four Last Years of the Queen*.[1] According to his theory, the Mohock atrocities were designed to screen a plot, instigated by Prince Eugene while he was in England early in 1712, to assassinate the Earl of Oxford. The Whigs' version was given by the author of *The Observator*, who looked upon the Mohocks as "the Van or Forlorn Hope of the *French* and the *Pretender*'s Faction, who do all they can to involve the Nation in Disorders." [2] These counter-accusations are alike unconvincing. The Mohocks made up a club of rakes, not a club of Whigs or a club of Tories.[3]

As has already appeared, popular notions about the Mohocks agreed very ill with the facts. In order to observe what the people of London thought of the society, it is necessary to turn to the literature which dealt with this band of rakes. On March 12, 1712, the day after the great riot, Steele wrote for *The Spectator* a letter signed "Philanthropos," which gives one of the most interesting accounts of the society ever written. The letter purports to be a contribution to the materials which Mr. Spectator had been collecting "towards a general history of clubs." Ac-

---

1. *Prose Works*, x, 45. Compare Hearne's less definite but more violent charges against the Whigs in *Remarks and Collections*, iii (1889), 326–327.

2. *The Observator*, March 15, 1712. Compare John Oldmixon, *The History of England*, iii (1735), 494, where a similar charge is made.

3. The scourers had also been accused of affiliation with a party (*The Complete Works of Thomas Shadwell*, v, 102). Graves even notes (*Studies in Philology*, xx [1923], 399 ff.) a suggestion that the Tityre Tu's of 1623 were connected with a political plot.

cording to Steele, the name "Mohock" was borrowed "from a sort of cannibals in India, who subsist by plundering and devouring all the nations about them."

The President is styled Emperor of the Mohocks; and his arms are a Turkish crescent, which his Imperial Majesty bears at present in a very extraordinary manner engraven upon his forehead. Agreeable to their name, the avowed design of their institution is mischief; and upon this foundation all their rules and orders are framed.[1]

Steele makes the club-like organization clear enough; and if, as Addison calculated, *The Spectator* was at this time read by 60,000 people, the Mohocks were a genuine society in the popular mind. The name was suggested by the visit to London of four Iroquois chiefs in 1710, which had aroused much interest.[2] Whether the faulty ethnology was Steele's or not, it became traditional. Gay's farce pictures the emperor in oriental costume. The letter goes on to describe the cruel and indecent practises of the society, which Steele traces back to the scourers of the previous reign, and concludes with the hope that such conduct will soon meet with severe punishment.

Even more graphic is the letter signed "Jack Lightfoot" in Number 332, wherein Steele makes Jack recount an adventure with "that worthy society of brutes, the Mohocks." The letter describes a game called "sweating," in which the victim was surrounded by the drawn swords of the band and prodded from the rear to make him turn round. Jack Lightfoot was fortunate enough to escape by taking to his heels before the Mohocks could close in upon him. The danger is once more set forth, this time by Addison, in Number 335, the famous essay describing Sir Roger at the play. In order to convince skeptical country readers that the club was not a myth, Budgell devoted Number 347 to what purported to be a manifesto of the

1. *The Spectator*, No. 324.
2. See *The Tatler*, No. 171, and *The Spectator*, No. 50.

Mohock emperor, who desired its publication. This ironical edict, dated from "our Court at the Devil Tavern," generously offers to furnish surgical treatment to the club's victims and promises that the streets shall be safe until one in the morning. By enumerating the emperor's self-imposed restrictions, Budgell manages to reveal once more the methods by which innocent citizens were tormented.

These papers of *The Spectator* inspired an unknown writer to publish in 1712 *The Mohocks: A Poem, in Miltonic verse; Address'd to the Spectator*. The poem throws little light upon the club, because its author was more interested in his blank verse, his mock-heroic machinery, and the success of *The Spectator* in reforming manners, than in the Mohocks themselves. The style of the poem and particularly the account of the brush between the rakes and the constable's men seem to bear some relation to Gay's play, *The Mohocks*; but the mock-heroic does not approach the farce in cleverness.

One of the most curious publications called forth by the panic was a broadside, sometimes attributed to Gay, which bore the title, "An Argument Proving . . . that the Present Mohocks and Hawkubites are the Gog and Magog mention'd in the Revelations . . . Written by a Reverend Divine, who took it from the Mouth of the Spirit of a Person, who was lately slain by one of the Mohocks." The enunciations of this ghostly informer, which are rather prophetic than polemical, are rendered the more amusing by being couched in biblical language. The spirit predicts:

The Day shall come, when the *Junto* shall be overthrown, then shall GOG and MAGOG arise, and the MOHOCKS and HAWKUBITES shall possess the Streets, and dwell in their Quarters, they shall come from far at the Sound of the Cat-call - - - - Yea, they shall come from the furthermost Part of *America*.[1]

1. This is one of the few cases in which the Mohocks are referred to their proper hemisphere. Cf. Defoe, *The Review*, VIII (1712), 613.

The dead man continues to pour forth his prayers and prophecies, until weakness overcomes him and he is forced to conclude:

Half dead and speechless I sing the following ejaculation

> From MOHOCK and from HAWKUBITE,
>   Good Lord deliver me,
> Who wander through the Street by Night,
>   Committing Cruelty.

> They slash our Sons with bloody Knives,
>   And on our Daughters fall,
> And if they ravish not our Wives,
>   We have good Luck withal.

> Coaches and Chairs they overturn,
>   Nay Carts most easily,
> Therefore from GOG and eke MAGOG,
>   Good Lord deliver me.

Although the broadside seems too crude to have come from Gay's pen, his authorship is strongly indicated by the appearance fifteen years later in Motte's *Miscellanies* of a piece entitled "A wonderful Prophecy Taken from the Mouth of the Spirit of a Person who was barbarously slain by the Mohocks." This short essay has very little in common with the broadside except the title, as it has been completely rewritten. It is divided between a violent lamentation over the wickedness of the world, and a solemn demonstration of the connection between Gog and Magog and the Mohocks. The slain porter is still represented as the speaker; but so many journalistic touches have been omitted that the piece is much less topical than before and more purely a *jeu d'esprit*. The irony is greatly heightened, and the little essay was enough esteemed by the compilers of the *Miscellanies* to be given a place [1] just before Swift's "Meditation upon a Broomstick."

1. *Miscellanies in Prose and Verse*, II (1727), 260.

Gay's pen has given us the most vivid of all the contemporary pictures of the Mohocks' frolics. The lines in
Trivia have been quoted so often that it is only necessary
to allude to them as showing how inextricably the clubs of
rakes were bound up with London street life at this time.
One detail, however, is of special interest. Gay wrote:

> I pass their desp'rate deeds, and mischiefs done,
> Where from Snow-hill black steepy torrents run;
> How matrons, hoop'd within the hogshead's Womb,
> Were tumbled furious thence.[1]

Two years before the publication of *Trivia*, the author of
the broadside entitled "The Town Rakes" had informed
the horror-stricken public that "they likewise rowl'd a
Woman in a Tub down *Snow-hill* that was going to Market." The similarity of the two accounts speaks elo-
quently. Either the incident was common talk or Gay was
recalling this very broadside as he wrote.

In *The Mohocks*, published four years before *Trivia*, the
picture is even more lively. That the group represented in
the farce was considered a club is evident from the opening
scene, which represents the initiation of Cannibal into the
band. Before the candidate is admitted, his qualifications
are examined by the Emperor and Myrmidon.

> *Emp.*   Go, and introduce him:
> But search with care th'intentions of his heart,
> See he be not a superficial sinner,
> That talks of mischiefs which he ne'er perform'd:
> Those are mean villains, and unworthy us.

> *Mir.* I'll answer for him, for I've known him long,
> Know him a subject worthy such a prince;
> Sashes and casements felt his early rage,
> He has twisted knockers, broken drawers heads,
> And never flinch'd his glass, or baulk'd his wench.[2]

1. *Trivia* (1716), pp. 52–53.
2. *The Plays of John Gay* (1923), I, 8.

The rites which follow the entrance of Cannibal show that Gay had in mind no casually met band of street ruffians but a well-established and thoroughly organized society.

One part of Gay's plot is of particular interest in the light of the knowledge we have of Sir Mark Cole's trial. It will be remembered that Cole sought to defend himself by identifying his gang with the watch. In Gay's farce, the Mohocks meet the watch, change apparel with them, and impersonating them play many pranks, until they are at last apprehended, unmasked, and convicted. The parallelism is so striking that Gay may well have conceived the central idea of his play from reports of Sir Mark Cole's defense.

The Mohocks was not intended to reform the young rakes, satiric as it was. Their escapades are treated with much more frivolity than appears in the *Spectator* letters, and their activities were held up to ridicule, not to horror.[1] The actual atrocities with which the Mohocks were credited would have been difficult to stage. Accordingly, the reader's idea of the outrages must come from the rakes' own boasting and from the fear of them which other characters show, rather than from any frightful vindication of their reputation on the stage. If the piece had been acted, it would have done the Town a service by relieving its exaggerated dread.

The Mohock Club was not long in finding its way into the songs of the period. One collection of Mohockiana contains a leaf from a contemporary song-book on which are printed four stanzas of a Mohock song called "The Huzza." The first may well be quoted to show the spirit with which the rakes sang of their exploits:

> When the Streets are all clear,
> The Town is our Own;

---

1. This was the method of Prior in his brief attack on the Mohocks in the third canto of *Alma*.

We *manage* the Humour, and laugh at the Fear
Of all those we *Lay on*.
Down goes the *Bully*, the *Heck*, and *Night-walker*;
But oh! the Brisk Girl, we will never forsake her.
The Constable flies,
And his Clubmen withdraw,
When they hear the fierce Cries
Of the dreadful *Huzza, Huzza, Huzza!*

Another song, which bears the name of the club as its title, appeared in *Pills to Purge Melancholy*. Its author approached his subject with obvious timidity and did little more than enumerate the different theories about the origin of the society. The third stanza versifies one of the views which has already been noted.

Some count it a Plot,
And the Lord knows what,
Contriv'd by the *Whigs* out of Season;
But shou'd it be so,
By the *High-Church* or *Low*,
Rebellion was always high Treason.[1]

The last stanza warns the group to make an end of their foolishness before they are sent to the gibbet, and so concludes the song in a mood more in keeping with public sentiment than that of "The Huzza."

The career of the Mohocks seems to have ended almost as suddenly as it began. The panic subsided within a year, and practically all the published accounts of the club, besides the sundry references to it in private correspondence, are dated 1712. This by no means implies that the streets of London became at once as safe a place in which to walk about as my lady's drawing-room. It was the club that had ceased to exist, not the rakes.[2] For the next decade, however, their activity was disorganized and sporadic.

---

1. *Pills to Purge Melancholy*, vi (1720), 336.
2. See W. H. Irving, *John Gay's London* (Cambridge, Mass., 1928), pp. 247–250.

When their clubs next came into prominence, the rakes had partially given over physical violence in favor of blasphemy. At some time in 1720, or even a little earlier, three organizations known as Hell-Fire Clubs sprang up in London. The first record of their existence is the royal proclamation issued April 28, 1721, to suppress their atheistical ceremonies. This edict ordered an investigation of "certain scandalous Clubs or Societies of young Persons who meet together, and in the most impious and blasphemous Manner, insult the most sacred Principles of our Holy Religion . . . to the End that all proper Methods may be taken for the utter Suppression of all such detestable Practices." There is an implication that even some gentlemen of the court were involved, for the following paragraph is appended:

His Majesty hath been pleas'd to give Orders to the Principal Officers of his Houshold, to make strict and diligent Enquiry, whether any of his Majesty's Servants are guilty of the horrid Impieties mention'd in the Order of Council inserted above, and to make Report thereof to his Majesty.[1]

On the following Tuesday (May 2, 1721), there was a meeting of the justices of the peace, designed to secure united action against the Hell-Fire Clubs. Rigid instructions were delivered by the lord high chancellor "to make the most diligent and careful Enquiry" into the matter. There was to be a meeting of the constables on May 11 to pool what evidence had been gathered, and a broad hint was thrown out that anyone who would furnish information would be rewarded.

Oldmixon remarks that "these lewd young Rakes were branch'd out from the *Stowrers* [*sic*] and *Mohocks* before spoken of, and were guilty of the like Extravagancies" as well as of blasphemy. He adds that "several Persons of Quality, particularly the Duke of *Wharton*, were mark'd

1. *The Post-Boy*, May 2, 1721.

out as Members of the *Hell-Fire Club*." [1] This was the Wharton of whom Pope wrote:

> Though wond'ring senates hung on all he spoke,
> The club must hail him master of the joke.[2]

He was not only a member, but was even president of one of the societies.

When the impious secrets of the clubs began to be noised abroad, the interest of Grub Street was soon kindled. A broadside at once appeared (1721) which printed the names of a number of supposed members. In the same year was published *The Hell-Fire-Club: Kept by a Society of Blasphemers*. This satire was inscribed to Lord Macclesfield, who was carrying on the investigation. Certain passages are of peculiar interest in that they show how these rakes furnished an example for the group which assembled at Medmenham Abbey some forty years later. The following lines might have been written of the "monks" who gathered about the Earl of Sandwich:

> *Virtue's* discountenanced by these Beasts,
> Whose revelling at *Bacchanalian* Feasts,
> Makes them, when Fumes of Wine in Brains abound,
> Think, like *Copernicus*, the Earth turns round;
> Then, then how they the *Christian* Faith revile,
> And at their execrable Actions smile;
> But here their curst Profaneness do's not end,
> The Empire of the Devil to defend,
> They go upon the diabolick Theme
> Of striving who their God shall most blaspheme.[3]

The outspoken satirist shows clearly how the clubs of rakes turned to a new form of license and acquired a new kind of notoriety.

1. *The History of England*, III (1735), 718.
2. *The Works of Alexander Pope*, ed. W. Elwin and W. J. Courthope (1871–1886), III, 66. See also E. Beresford Chancellor, *Charteris and Wharton* (1926), p. 197.
3. *The Hell-Fire Club* (1721), pp. 19–20. Compare the warning sounded by "Aminadab" in a letter to *Applebee's Weekly Journal*, June 3, 1721.

THE HELL–FIRE CLUB

The Diabolical Maskquerade,
Or the Dragon's-Feast as Acted by the HELL–FIRE–CLUB,
at Somerset House in the Strand.
From a satiric engraving in the Collection of Prints
and Drawings in the British Museum

The hack-artist's graver did its share in exposing these rash young noblemen. The British Museum has a print entitled "The Diabolical Maskquerade, Or the Dragons-Feast as Acted by the Hell-Fire-Club, at Somerset House in the Strand," also of the year 1721, which represents a club debauch, the members being disguised as Pluto, Proserpine, and various animals and demons.[1] Some verses below the picture describe the blasphemous nature of the club and express the hope that it will soon be brought to justice.

Two letters printed in *Mist's Journal* gave the London public a clearer impression of what was going on than an engraver could do. On February 10, 1721, "Cato Addison" wrote to Mr. Mist, presenting for his correction "two Clubs, the BOLD BUCKS and the HELL FIRES, the former distinguished by its debauchery, the latter by its practice of deriding religion." Cato averred that one of the Hell-Fire men was abandoned enough to call for a "H—y G—t Pye at the Tavern," and commented on the shame with which the ancestors of these scoundrels must have viewed this conduct if they had been alive to witness it. A week later "Cordelia" wrote Mist that her lover, Florio, had become a member of the Bold Bucks and Hell-Fires, and had told her of a plot to assassinate the publisher in Paul's Churchyard. Out of admiration for Mr. Mist she took this occasion to warn him dramatically to go armed with pistols for a month or two and remember a churchyard.

Defoe must have been at work on *A Journal of the Plague Year* (published in 1722), when the excitement over the rakes was at its height. With this idea in mind it is of some interest to glance at his description of the blasphemers who met in 1665 at the Pie Tavern and mocked the

---

1. Reproduced facing page 120. See the *Catalogue of Prints and Drawings in the British Museum*, Division I, II, 588. The descriptive entry asserts that "upwards of forty persons of quality of both sexes" belonged to these clubs.

mourners as they passed by in the wake of the burial carts. "This Tavern, where they held their Club," he wrote, "being within View of the Church Door, they had the more particular Occasion for their Atheistical prophane Mirth."[1] It is very doubtful if this insensitive group of mockers would have appeared in Defoe's picture of plague-ridden London in 1665, had not his mind been running on the Hell-Fire men of 1721.

A vivid and amusing description of one of the societies occurs in *The Accomplished Rake: or, Modern Fine Gentleman*, a novel which deals with the wild-oats period in the life of Sir John Galliard, a typical young rake. Sir John goes blithely from one vice to another, until, at the lowest ebb of his morals, just before he reforms, he joins the Hell-Fire Club. His initiation makes a lively scene. In order to be admitted to membership, he is required to meet the club "in St. *Martin*'s Church-Yard about One o'Clock in the Morning, where, on a Tomb-stone were set Wine and Glasses, with no Light but a Bundle of Brimstone-Matches set on Fire: and if Sir *John* could Devoutly Drink, *A Health to the DEVIL*, without Hesitation, or being shock'd, he was from that time to be reckon'd one of them."[2]

The very nature of the societies has doubtless prevented the survival of many contemporary accounts of them. Such is also the case with another club of rakes to which Wharton belonged, called the Schemers. Lady Mary Wortley Montagu gave the following ironical account of this society to Lady Mar in 1724:

In general, gallantry never was in so elevated a figure as it is at present. Twenty very pretty fellows (the Duke of Wharton being president and chief director) have formed themselves into a committee of gallantry. They call themselves *Schemers*; and meet regularly three times a week, to consult on gallant schemes for the advantage and advancement of that branch of happi-

1. *A Journal of the Plague Year* (Oxford, 1928), p. 82.
2. *The Accomplish'd Rake* (1727), pp. 88–89.

ness. . . . I consider the duty of every Englishwoman is to do what honour she can do her native country; and that it would be a sin against the pious love I bear the land of my nativity to confine the renown due to the Schemers within the small extent of this little island.[1]

In this passage the excision following the word "happiness" is not mine but Lady Mary's editor's. If Lady Mary's account of the club's *raison d'être* is too indelicate for the general reader, the club must have been a very wicked one indeed.

The proclamation of 1721 had the effect of suppressing the clubs of rakes for a number of years. In deploring the scarcity of news a fictitious quidnunc of 1728 says that of late there has been

> No Frolick — nay, Men cease to sport on,
> His poor and merry Grace of *Wharton*.[2]

That the tradition did not entirely die out, however, is apparent from various numbers of *The Connoisseur*, the authors of which, Bonnell Thornton and George Colman, were much interested in the societies of rakes. The twenty-second number (June 27, 1754) informs the reader that "the present race of Bucks, Bloods, and Free-thinkers, are but the spawn of the *Mohocks* and the *Hell-Fire-Club*." Number 54 aims a rebuke at the so-called "frolics" of the Bucks and Bloods, the description of their violences bearing a marked resemblance to those of the Mohock barbarities of 1712. The essayist again gives the earlier group the doubtful honor of priority in crime when he writes:

The *Mohocks*, and the members of the *Hell-Fire-Club*, the heroes of the last generation, were the first, who introduced these elevated Frolicks, and struck out mighty good jokes from all kinds of violence and blasphemy.

1. *Letters and Works*, I, 476–477.
2. *Gulliveriana* (1728), p. 96.

Still another paper describes the life and remorseful death of Tom Dare-Devil, an atheistical rake of infamous character and president of an "abominable club, who met together every Sunday night to utter the most horrid blasphemies."[1] As in many other matters, *The Connoisseur* imitated *The Spectator* in its effort to discredit such misguided groups as these.

The name and traditions of the Hell-Fire Clubs of the 'twenties were carried on in the latter half of the century by a society which has left more complete records. This later group, founded about 1760 according to a contemporary biographer of Paul Whitehead,[2] was variously known as the Order of the Monks of St. Francis, the Medmenham Club, and the Hell-Fire Club. Besides Paul Whitehead, who was secretary, it numbered among its members the most notorious statesmen-rakes of the time, including John Wilkes, the Earl of Sandwich, and Sir Francis Dashwood, the founder of the society. In the literature and private correspondence of the decade in which it flourished are a number of horrified references to the lewd and impious rites which went on in the old abbey, and the yearly assemblies at Medmenham form a fitting climax to the story of the clubs of rakes which achieved so much notoriety during the course of the century.

QUIDNUNCS AND FREETHINKERS

Among the favorite objects of early eighteenth-century satire, the clubs of quidnuncs held a conspicuous place. Pope was but falling in step with his contemporaries when he used them for purposes of comparison in the passage in which he describes the temple of Dulness.

1. *The Connoisseur*, No. 28.
2. *The Poems and Miscellaneous Compositions of Paul Whitehead*, ed. E. Thompson (1777), p. xxxvii.

This the Great Mother dearer held than all
The Clubs of Quidnuncs, or her own Guildhall.[1]

The genus had been defined much earlier by Charles Davenant in his dialogue between Sir Thomas Double and Sir Richard Comover.

Sir *T. D.* If you please, I'll leave Orders to be deny'd; and then pray let us *Quid nunc* all this Morning over our Tea.

Sir *R. C.* *Quid nunc!* What's that?

Sir *T. D.* 'Tis the modish Word for talking with one another of Publick Matters.[2]

The quidnunc *par excellence* is Addison's political upholsterer, whom the essayist deftly sketched in *The Tatler*, No. 155; and the nature of the conversation at such clubs as Pope had in mind is revealed by the same pen in *The Spectator*, No. 403, where Mr. Spectator goes the rounds of the coffee-houses to make himself acquainted with the political opinions of his countrymen. A letter signed "Thomas Quidnunc," printed in a later number of the same periodical,[3] gives a lively description of the life of a frenzied news-hunter. Mr. Quidnunc's time was spent in driving madly in his swift coach between St. James's and the various coffee-houses in an effort to anticipate the newspapers with his tidings of great events without missing any choice items while out on his reporting rounds.

The Hebdomadal Meeting at Oxford, described by Steele in *The Spectator*, No. 43, was a typical club of these critics of news. A letter signed "Abraham Froth," and significantly dated "Four o'clock in the Morning," sets forth their program.

We think it our duty, as far as in us lies, . . . to censure doctrines or facts, persons or things, which we don't like; to settle the nation at home, and to carry on the war abroad,

1. *The Dunciad*, 1, 268–270.
2. *Sir Thomas Double at Court, and in High Preferments* (1710), pp. 5–6.
3. *The Spectator*, No. 625.

where and in what manner we see fit: if other people are not of our opinion, we can't help that. 'Twere better they were. Moreover, we now and then condescend to direct, in some measure, the little affairs of our own university.

As "Froth" proceeds to give the club's solution of various affairs of state, in the casual manner that dinner-table politicians are wont to use, the object of Steele's ridicule is sufficiently clear.

One of the most amusing satires on the societies of quidnuncs appeared in the "Last Volume" of Motte's *Miscellanies*, collected by Pope and Swift in 1727. The piece in question was called "The Quidnuncki's: a Tale. Occasion'd by the Death of the Duke Regent of France." In the introductory lines Master Trevors is shown haranguing a group of these lay politicians in the typical jargon.

> I do foresee (and for Fore-seeing
> He equals any Man in being)
> The Army ne'er can be disbanded.
> ----I wish the King were safely landed.
> Ah Friends! great Changes threat the Land!
> All *France* and *England* at a stand!
> There's *Meroweis*----mark! strange Work!
> And there's the *Czar*, and there's the *Turk*----
> The *Pope*---- An *India*-Merchant by,
> Cut short the Speech with this Reply.[1]

The India merchant's interruption took the form of a tale of the Ganges.

> There dwell the Nations of *Quidnuncki's*,
> (So *Monomotapa* called Monkies:)
> On either Bank, from Bough to Bough,
> They meet and chat (as we may now.)
> Whispers go round, they grin, they shrug,
> They bow, they snarl, they scratch, they hug;
> And, just as Chance, or Whim provoke them,
> They either bite their Friends, or stroke them.

---

1. *Miscellanies in Prose and Verse*, Last Volume (1727), 230.

The implied parallel with the quidnunc groups shows through with ridiculous clarity. *A Letter from the Quidnunc's at St. James's Coffee-house and the Mall, London, to their Brethren at Lucas's Coffee-house, in Dublin* (1728) is equally sarcastic. According to this epistle, London had become very dull for the quidnuncs because of the pall of peace which had settled over national affairs. Conversation had become reduced to predictions of the possible calamities of the future and discussions of the current society gossip. The conclusion is ingenious.

> When will *Miss* EUSTACE cease to Charm?
> And Crafty CLODIUS mean no Harm?
> But — *just arriv'd one* Holland *Mail*;
> And so, in haste, we Sign and Seal. —

Politic, Dabble, and Porer, in Fielding's comedy, *The Coffee-House Politicians* (1730), are typical quidnuncs. The scene in Act V in which Politic and Dabble run through the news from the journals of the day shows what the discussions at the clubs were like. The current preoccupation with affairs abroad is even more evident earlier in the play. In the third and fourth scenes of Act I, the three cronies are so much taken up with the international menace from Don Carlos in the west and the Turk in the east that when word is brought in of the disappearance of Politic's daughter Hilaret, they refuse to be diverted from the weighty questions under consideration; and while the girl wanders alone through the streets of London, they fall to arguing the question whether Tuscany is a nation somewhat larger than France, or merely a city, as Dabble firmly believes. It was an age of political obsession, and the clubs of quidnuncs were the clearing-houses for the news that kept alive the questions over which men were pleased to perplex themselves.

The societies of freethinkers also found a place in the London scene. The following which was quickly built up

by writers like Toland, Collins, and Mandeville began
early to form discussion clubs, where they could debate
without restraint the problems in which their disbeliefs involved them. The freethinker was a well-known type in
the reign of Queen Anne. Addison sketched one in his
character of Tom Puzzle, who had that fondness for turning all conversation into religious polemics which was
typical of his kind.[1] An early glimpse of a society of free-
thinkers is given in *The Drummer*, where Tinsel, having
shocked Lady Truman, explains that he is not an atheist
but a freethinker.

Tin. To tell you the Truth, I have not time to look into these
dry Matters my self, but I am convinc'd by four or five learned
Men, whom I sometimes over-hear at a Coffee-house I frequent,
that our Fore-fathers were a Pack of Asses, that the World has
been in an Error for some Thousands of Years, and that all the
People upon Earth, excepting those two or three worthy Gentlemen, are impos'd upon, cheated, bubbled, abus'd, bamboozl'd —[2]

This arrogance was more typical of such fashionable dab-
blers as Tinsel than of the leaders in free thought; but the
trait dominates the caricatures of many groups of free-
thinkers.

The gathering mentioned in the *Memoirs of Martinus
Scriblerus* was a full-fledged club. In the course of his in-
vestigations into the seat of the soul, Martin found occasion to correspond "with the Society of Free Thinkers, who
were then in their infancy in England." The descriptive
clause implies the progress which the clubs had been making since the beginning of the century. In the letter which
Martin receives from the society, the principles of the free-
thinkers are repeatedly held up to ridicule, particularly
their fallacious methods of reasoning. On reading the letter, Crambe, Martin's companion, "advised his master by

1. *The Spectator*, No. 476. See also Steele's attack in No. 234.
2. *The Miscellaneous Works of Joseph Addison*, ed. A. C. Guthkelch (1914),
I, 441–442.

no means to enter into their Society, unless they would give him sufficient security, to bear him harmless from anything that might happen after this present life." [1]

The most notorious freethinking club of the century was the Robin Hood Society. Although the period of its greatest activity came shortly after Swift's death, it cannot be passed over; for the accounts of the Robinhoodians form a more nearly complete picture than any of the earlier descriptions of such clubs. Even the society at the Robin Hood was maligned by satirists and lauded by defenders until its true nature is hard to define. But certain statements about it check well enough to give a fair idea of its purpose.

The Robin Hood Society, so called from the tavern in Butcher's Row where it met, appears to have been formed in 1747. It consisted of between forty and sixty citizens of London who met every Monday evening to debate any questions which the members chose to submit. Since there was no restriction on membership except the payment of sixpence on entering each meeting, the assembly was a heterogeneous one. The president was one Caleb Jeacocke, a wealthy baker of the City, who served for years because he had the ability to keep a semblance of order and because he enjoyed his prestige. The rest were obscure young writers, actors, and professional men, and prosperous tradesmen. Francis Gentleman, Foote, and Macklin were members. Derrick sometimes took Goldsmith there.[2] Tradition has it that Burke attended in his younger days. As a body, however, the company aroused little admiration except for the freedoms in which it indulged in the debates.

1. Pope, *Works*, x, 336.
2. In *The History of the Robinhood Society* (p. 193), "Mr. G ** D***TH" is listed among the "principal speaking Members for the Year 1764." He is described as "a Man of Learning and Judgment, Author of *An Inquiry into the modern State of Literature in* Europe, and many other ingenious Works; a good Orator, and a candid Disputant, with a clear Head, and an honest Heart. He comes but seldom to the Society."

It was the speeches that made the club notorious. The questions for discussion were chosen a week ahead from lists proposed by the members. Each man present had the right to speak for five minutes on any question, at the end of which time he was silenced by the rapping of Mr. Jeacocke's hammer on the table. Since complete freedom of utterance was encouraged and the questions frequently turned upon politics and religion, the casual visitor who went out of curiosity was often scandalized. The club developed a reputation for licentiousness, blasphemy, deism, atheism, and disloyalty to the crown that was bound to make it grist for the mills of Grub Street.

The History of the Robinhood Society (1764) was the latest and the least biased of these products. And a curious product it is. The author attempts to trace the club back to the time of James I, inventing a grandfather as founder and alleging manuscripts as authority. Some of the members of the original "Societie for Free and Candyd Enquirie," like Sir Hugh Myddelton and Dr. Richard Palmer, actually lived in the reign of King James. But faulty chronology proves that the documents, like the society itself, were a fiction.[1] The author goes on to tell how in his father's time, just after the restoration, the club became too large to meet at the houses of the members and changed its assembling place to the Essex-Head Tavern. There it remained until 1747, when it moved to the Robin Hood and became the Robin Hood Society.

The *History* achieves a semblance of veracity, in its treatment of these early periods, by giving characters of the members and reproducing their speeches at the club. There are also stories attached to different members which combine the character and the brief fictitious memoir, in the manner so commonly used by the periodical essayists. "Bob Scamper," for example, came to London from a re-

1. A contemporary reviewer of the *History* pointed out this fact with much glee. See *The Critical Review*, xviii (1764), 398.

spectable home in the country. He soon lost his money through overindulgence in the pleasures of the Town, and took to the road. As a highwayman he flourished, and he became a respected member of the Essex-Head Club. One night while he was speaking on the doctrine of repentance, in vindication of Christianity, he was recognized by a man whom he had lately robbed. His arrest soon followed, and he died upon the gallows too drunk to repent. In this story, in that of Tom Rakewell, and in a number of others, the author shows no little ability as a narrator.

The last two sections of the *History*, which deal with the society as it existed between 1747 and 1764, seem to agree with the facts well enough. The description of the debating, showing how the members spoke in turn and Mr. Jeacocke summarized at the end, the account of the club's charities, the remarks on the attacks from press and pulpit upon the freedom of the discussion, and the explanation of the club records are circumstantial in themselves, besides being generally supported by the other contributors to the literature of the Robin Hood. Most interesting of all is the set of memoirs of living members, with its remarks on Macklin, Foote, and Derrick, and its favorable notice of Goldsmith. Few of the memoirs are flattering. The author was not more tender of the characters of most of the members than were the satirists who attacked the club most violently. But the fact that he did distinguish between them gives this section of the book an air of impartiality. The *History* concludes with the story of Opsinous, which Hawkesworth had printed twelve years before in *The Adventurer*. A compilation of more assorted material is hard to imagine. The author was adept at mingling truth with fictions of his own and counted on the journalistic interest of the book to sell it. The contents, he knew, were readable, however amorphous the *History* was, taken as a whole. To a decade that delighted in magazines, miscellanies, and "histories" it may have been palatable enough, though references to it are uncommon.

From the first, the Robin Hood Society occasioned much talk and much writing. During the years 1751 and 1752, the discussion was at its height. An argument began in *The Whitehall Evening Post* for December 29, 1750, in which a letter to the editor inveighed bitterly against the society without mentioning its name. On January 15, 1751, in the columns of the same newspaper, a letter signed "Robin-Hood" sought to reply by means of ridicule and counter-accusation. The issue of January 31 contained a second attack by the original writer. In February Grub Street definitely joined the fray. An unknown writer produced a pamphlet entitled *An Apology for the Robin-Hood Society. Wherein the Cause of Liberty and Free Enquiry is Asserted, and all the Objections (particularly those in the Whitehall-Evening-Posts, of Dec. 29, and Jan. 31, 1750.) against that Society, are fully obviated.* The dedication is artfully directed to the Earl of Chesterfield, "the Zealous and Steady, the Distinguished and Justly Celebrated Assertor of his Country's Rights." The bulk of the pamphlet is devoted to an enumeration of the charges against the club, which the author answers *seriatim*. He replies to the criticisms of the society's enemies in a straightforward, if sarcastic, manner. The aim of the Robinhoodians, he protests more than once, is to get at the truth by "a free and candid Enquiry." [1] His stand is for freedom of conscience and freedom of speech. The pamphlet is of some interest as a document in the history of the growth of English liberty, even though the debates of the gentlemen at the Robin Hood may not have been as purely academic as the author of the *Apology* would have us believe.

This rather too favorable account of the society did not go long uncorrected. Another obscure Grub-Streeter took

1. This phrase may be the source of the name given by the author of the *History* to the fictitious society which he insists was formed in 1613.

his pen in hand forthwith, and published in the same year
(1751) the *Genuine and Authentick Memoirs of the Stated
Speakers of the Robin Hood Society*. For the only information about the authorship of this pamphlet, we are indebted to the author of the *History*, whose unflattering
characterization of him is as follows:

> Mr. H**H*M. Author of *Genuine and authentic Memoirs
> of the* ROBINHOOD *Society*, and an *Oration in Praise of the* LAW,
> pronounced there a few Years ago, by one PITTARD, a strolling
> Actor. He is a Person of some Sense, but not half so much as
> he thinks he has. He has not attended the Society for some
> Years, nor, indeed, is the Loss of him very great; for, as he is to
> be ranked in the middling Class as an Author; so, as an Orator,
> he is a very mean one, unfurnished with Ideas, and destitute of
> a graceful Delivery.[1]

The modesty of his accomplishments, however, was not
what made the author of the *Memoirs* hide behind the
pseudonym of "Timothy Scrubb"; for his dedication to
the "President in chief, Secretary in ordinary, sole Ham-
merer, Regulator, and sovereign Moderator of the Robin
Hood" is impudent to the last degree. He admits that he is
exposing the society in order to make money, dates the
dedication "From my Garret, in *Grub-Street*," and concludes with the impertinent postscript:

> Please to desire your Association of Bl-kh-ds not to expect
> that I should condescend to answer any Nonsense they may
> publish; for as the Town is filling, I shall have other Fish to fry.

The author addresses the *Genuine and Authentick Memoirs* to a friend who has just read the *Apology*, supposedly
with the design of correcting the exaggerated notion the
latter has formed of the club's dignity and morality. Far
from being intelligent searchers after the truth, Scrubb
insists, "this illustrious Assembly is composed of Bakers,
Shoemakers, Journeyman-Barbers, *Fleet* Parsons, Psalm-

---

1. *The History of the Robinhood Society* (1764), p. 170.

singing Clerks, and Apprentice Boys." After a brief introduction in this vein, the author proceeds to his memoirs of the Robinhoodians, beginning with Jeacocke, the president. These satiric pictures were doubtless drawn from life. Shallowell, "an infidel," was probably intended for Peter Annet, and Gallipot was the same physician that Richard Lewis was later to satirize as "Gargle" in *The Robin-Hood Society*. But the sketches are patently caricatures, done with more gusto than fairness.

The periodical essayists were not far behind the Grub-Street pamphleteers in finding material among the Robinhoodians. The cleverest attack on the group was carried on in *The Covent-Garden Journal*. In the eighth and ninth numbers (January 28 and February 1, 1752), Fielding used all his fertile wit to cover the society with shame and ridicule. He prepared the way in Number 6, in which he was discussing the transitory character of works of the pen as compared with works of art. At the close he cited as an example a curious manuscript which he had rescued from around two hot rolls sent him by his baker, and promised to transcribe its contents. In Number 8, where he takes up the trail again, the reader slowly becomes aware that the rolls must have come from Mr. Jeacocke himself, even though Fielding does not say so. For the papers which are transcribed prove to contain "*Importinent Questions cunsarning*, Relidgin *and* Gubermint, *handyled by the Robinhoodians*," together with speeches on those questions. The first subject for debate was "whether Relidgin was of any youse to a Sosyaty." Another summarized arguments on the question "whether infinite Power could make the World out of Nothing." The manuscript broke off just as it was coming to the question "Whether, in the Opinion of this Society, the Government did Right in — ." In his reproductions of the speeches Fielding is at his best. His dramatic skill lights up each sentence, until the whole scene becomes visual. In addition he shows satiric acumen

THE ROBIN HOOD.

From a satiric engraving in the Harry Elkins Widener Collection

by striking at the chief weakness of the society, — its propensity for discussing insoluble problems and matters about which the members knew nothing.

Another dramatist who was conducting a periodical at this time appears to have taken a cue from Fielding in launching a little attack on his own account. On February 10, 1752, Arthur Murphy devoted Number 17 of *The Gray's-Inn Journal* to "an account of a very extraordinary college, called the *Robin Hood*." Murphy actually uses the form of a play, in which the members make up the *dramatis personae*, and is thus able to give an excellent caricature of the club in session. His laughter is directed at the custom of cutting off the speakers with the hammer after five minutes, at the absurd questions which were discussed, and at the unruliness, ignorance, and inebriety of the members. Not all the essayists treated the club so lightly. Hawkesworth, in December, 1752, used four numbers of *The Adventurer* [1] for a serious discussion of the society as a menace to public and private morals. But *The Connoisseur* and *The Drury-Lane Journal*,[2] like the periodicals of Fielding and Murphy, paid most attention to the comic side of the club's activities.[3]

Remonstrance against the debates of the Robinhoodians was continued in 1756 by a mock-heroic entitled "The Robin-Hood Society: A Satire . . . by Peter Pounce, Esq." The dedication to the Reverend Mr. Romaine (himself an opponent of the club) is signed "Richard Lewis." Lewis seems to have attended the meetings, for he is listed as a member by the author of the *History*. But his attitude toward the Robin Hood is one of uncompromising hos-

1. Nos. 10, 12–14.
2. Nos. 5–13, *passim.*
3. The absurdity of some of the questions debated at the club was often the subject of ridicule. A comic engraving of the Robin Hood shows a sign on the president's desk bearing the announcement:
"Q. to be Debated next Thursday Eve. 'How Far is it from the 1st ot Aug. to the foot of Westminster Bridge.'"

tility. The preface renews the old charges of treason and blasphemy. The blank-verse satire itself reveals both by description of the members and by fictitious samples of their oratory an honest revulsion from what Lewis considered an abuse of British freedom.

Interest in the Robin Hood Society did not flag for a number of years. A letter written by Horace Walpole to the Earl of Hertford, November 9, 1764, indicates that a visit to the club was still one of the experiences which the London sight-seer must not miss. The pretentious *History*, which was published in the same year, is further evidence of its continued notoriety. It is a pity that no more was written about the club in connection with the principle of free speech in England; for in spite of the continued public remonstrance against the proceedings at the Robin Hood, no official action seems to have been taken to put an end to the debates. The conclusion of the society's career is wrapped in obscurity. It may have survived long enough to merge into one or the other of the clubs that were formed in sympathy with the French Revolution. In the sixties, however, its reputation was built upon its attitude toward religion rather than its political views. The unpopularity of such freethinking clubs is easy to understand. The time had not yet come when people realized that such gatherings could safely be ignored.

BEEFSTEAK SOCIETIES

Among the most famous of the purely social clubs of Swift's time were the beefsteak clubs. Four distinct societies, formed within a period of fifty years, took their names from the same substantial fare. One of the four, called the Rump-Steak Club, has already been discussed under its other name, the Patriots Club. Another, organized in Dublin by Thomas Sheridan in 1753,[1] was made up

1. See Benjamin Victor, *The History of the Theatres of London and Dublin* (1761), i, 153–154.

largely of Irish lords and members of Parliament, and was patterned after the Sublime Society of Beef Steaks. Engaging as the Dublin group is, with its tradition of Peg Woffington's presidency, it must be passed over in favor of the more widely known London clubs, the Beefsteak Club of Queen Anne's reign and the Sublime Society.

The former of these two was founded somewhat before 1705, if William King's undated *Miscellanies in Prose and Verse* is rightly assigned to that year; for the volume is dedicated "To the Right Honourable Lords and Gentlemen, Members of the Immortal Beef-Steak Clubb." The author of the *Miscellanies* promises the club material of all sorts.

In short it should contain such things as may satisfy the Mind when its Thoughts incline either to Instruction or Pleasure. . . . To whom then should the Author address sooner than to the noble *Beef-Steak-Club*, where every valuable Quality reigns differently, but are all cemented by the Ties of Good Nature and Good Humour.

King's testimony to the gentility of the members is substantiated by other contemporary comments. Their wit was never questioned.[1]

By 1709 the fame of the club was well established. In that year was published King's *Art of Cookery*, which contains a handsome tribute to the Beefsteak men.

He that of honour, wit, and mirth, partakes,
May be a fit companion o'er Beef-steaks,
His name may be to future times enroll'd
In Estcourt's Book, whose Gridiron's fram'd of Gold.[2]

The lines also give evidence of Dick Estcourt's early connection with the club. Without the vivacious personality

1. William Chetwood, *A General History of the Stage* (Dublin, 1749), p. 143. Chetwood characterized the members as the "chief Wits and great Men of the Nation."
2. *The Original Works of William King* (1776), III, 86.

of this clever Irish actor, the picture of the society would lose much of its charm. Steele wrote of him:

> The best man that I know of for heightening the revel-gaiety of a company, is Estcourt, whose jovial humour diffuses itself from the highest person at an entertainment to the meanest waiter. Merry tales, accompanied with apt gestures and lively representations of circumstances and persons, beguile the gravest mind into a consent to be as humorous as himself.[1]

It requires no great effort of the imagination to picture the delights of the club gatherings with such a personality dominating the scene.

The book of which King wrote is explained in Ned Ward's account of the club.[2] It served as a repository for the *jeux d'esprit* of the members, and it was the duty of Estcourt, as secretary, to make the entries. One can only regret that the book has not survived. As to the gridiron, Chetwood explained in his brief memoir of Estcourt that "he was made Providore of the *Beef-Stake-Club*, and for a Mark of Distinction, wore their Badge, which was a small Gridiron of Gold, hung about his Neck with a green Silk Ribbon."[3] Dr. William King, of St. Mary Hall, apostrophized the symbolic gridiron in the opening lines of *The Toast*.

> O resound the Utensil invented for Grilling!
> Let it henceforth be Splendid as *Philips* his Shilling!
> Tell how 'twas apply'd to confound Calculation,
> To enrich a great Artist, and beggar a Nation.[4]

This gridiron has fascinated every *raconteur* who has attempted to describe the society. Sometimes it is of silver instead of gold; sometimes its ribbon is red instead of green; sometimes it depends from a button of Dick's coat instead of from his neck; but never is it neglected. Its

1. *The Spectator*, No. 358.
2. *Satyrical Reflections on Clubs* (1710), pp. 378–392.
3. *General History*, p. 143.
4. *The Toast* (Dublin, 1732), pp. 22–23.

legitimate offspring, or perhaps even the original token, appeared twenty-five years later as an emblem of the new beefsteak society which was then formed.

On December 28, 1711, an advertisement in *The Spectator* announced that Richard Estcourt would on January 1 open the Bumper Tavern in James Street, Covent Garden. It seems likely that during the few remaining months of Estcourt's life the Bumper was the scene of the Beefsteak meetings. This inference is strengthened by *The Spectator*, No. 264, which contains a letter from Sir Roger de Coverley "to Mr. Estcourt, at his house in Covent Garden." Since the salutation is worded "Old Comical Ones," the whole club seems to be implied. The enterprise was probably sponsored by the wealthy members, much as Button's was by Addison, for the purpose of having control over their assembling place.

Thomas Davies was of the opinion that while the tavern enlarged Estcourt's acquaintance, it shortened his days. There is also a hint that the step was accompanied by a slight social degradation. That the player suffered no loss of prestige, however, is implied by Steele's eulogistic essay, which occupied *The Spectator*, No. 468, on the day of Estcourt's funeral.

Men of sense, who could taste his excellences, were well satisfied to let him lead the way in conversation, and play after his own manner; but fools, who provoked him to mimicry, found he had the indignation to let it be at their expense who called for it, and he would show the form of conceited heavy fellows as jests to the company at their own request, in revenge for interrupting him from being a companion to put on the character of a jester.

The intimate, even affectionate, tone of the eulogy, coupled with the fact that Steele wrote every *Spectator* in which Estcourt figures,[1] tempts one to the conclusion that Sir

1. Nos. 264, 358, 370, 468.

Richard was himself a member of the Beefsteak Club and was here voicing the grief of the whole society over the actor's death.

The hearty food on which the club habitually dined gave it a reputation for virility. *The Lay Monk*, No. 36, tells of an effeminate young man who was advised by a witty friend to learn to smoke and enter himself a member. There are also implications that the Beefsteak men were Whiggish in their sympathies, Ned Ward going so far as to suggest that they may have been connected with the Kit-Cat Club. "An Epilogue written for the late celebrated New Play, call'd, The Drummer" seems likewise to point to party affiliations in the lines:

> While these at *Wyburn's* in *October* riot,
> *Nanny* broils *Whigs* and Beef-stakes for her Diet.
> No Fare more luscious can your Hearts regale
> Than fat Rump-Stakes.[1]

A note on the word "Beef-stakes" explains that the reference is to "*A Beef-stake Club kept at* Nanny Roch[ar]d's"; but there is some doubt whether this was a survival or an imitation of the original club. Certainly the early society was loyal to the queen, for in 1710 they had a celebration in honor of her birthday. "From Dinner till Evening," says *The Daily Courant*, February 8, "a curious Collection of Musick was perform'd, and at Night a Firework illuminated Covent-Garden." If the members were actually Whigs, politics did not figure largely in their activities.

There remains to discuss the account of the Beefsteak group in Ward's *Satyrical Reflections on Clubs*, which appeared in 1710 as the fifth volume of his works. Having disposed of the Kit-Cats in the last chapter but one, Ward finished his book in a burst of scurrilous effrontery with an

---

1. *Pills to Purge State-Melancholy* (1718), part ii, p. 12. Also printed by Edmund Curll in *The Ladies Miscellany* (1718).

attempt to discredit the Beefsteak Club by relating it to the older society. He rambles barbarously along in his obvious fashion, pausing at one point to insert some coarse verses of his own, which he generously fathers on the Beef-steak wits, and keeping just close enough to the facts to lend face to his nastier inventions. Dick Estcourt is throughout the principal object of his ridicule. One feels that there may be an element of truth in Ward's hint that by means of his mimicry Dick "always preserves a full Community, for what-ever Member neglects to appear upon the Club Night, is assur'd in his Absence to be so comically represented by their officious Buffoon, that they are made the Jest and Laughing-stock, of the whole Company." [1] On the whole, however, Ward's facts are little more to be relied upon than the purity of his idiom.

The connection between this early club and the Sublime Society of Beef Steaks, which was founded in 1735, has been the source of much worry to antiquarians. The situation of the later club in Covent Garden, its relation to the theatre through some of its leading members, and its use of the gridiron bearing the motto "Beef and Liberty" as an emblem, all indicate the influence of Estcourt's renowned company. Yet actual evidence for inferring that the Sublime Society was simply a continuation of the earlier society is lacking; and the members of the second group insisted from the beginning on their originality and independence. No definite solution of the problem has been reached, though the gridiron alone is enough to show that the club of Queen Anne's day was still alive in the minds of the charter members of the Sublime Society.

Two stories of the founding of the later group are current, both of which involve John Rich, the harlequin-manager of the Covent Garden Theatre. It seems that Rich, when busy in his room at the top of the theatre, often avoided interrupting his work to dine at a tavern by

1. *Satyrical Reflections on Clubs* (1710), pp. 387–388.

grilling a beefsteak over his own fire. According to one tradition, the old Earl of Peterborough happened in upon one of these hasty repasts of beefsteak and wine, and being invited to partake found the fare so good that he used to bring a friend or two occasionally to share Rich's hospitality. It was not long before the meetings became periodic, Saturday being the day chosen for the assembly because it was on that day that Lord Peterborough first dined with Rich.[1]

But this pleasant story is not authenticated by the society itself, nor is the earl's name on the list of original members. When the club broke up in 1867 after a long and distinguished life, its secretary published an authoritative history of its career based upon actual records, which seem to have been kept from its earliest days. To this account we must look for the true story of the club's origin.

The Society was founded by Henry [*sic*][2] Rich, the celebrated harlequin and machinist of Covent Garden Theatre in 1735. . . . In his room at Covent Garden (probably the painting-room), many of the eminent men of the time connected with literature, fashion, and the drama, used to assemble to have a chat with the witty machinist and his fellow labourer and friend George Lambert, described in the archives of the Society as "Landscape Painter."[3]

There from time to time they partook, at two o'clock, of the hot steak dressed by Rich himself, accompanied by a "bottle of old port from the tavern hard by."[4]

1. F. S. Russell accepts the story in *The Earl of Peterborough* (1887), ii, 261. See also *The National Review*, iv (1857), 313–314.

2. A mistake for "John," that being the name of the manager of the theatre. In the list of the original members the name is "John Rich."

3. Edwards, in his *Anecdotes of Painters* (1808), asserts that Lambert, the "scene-painter to Covent Garden," was the original host and purveyor of the steaks. Edwards does not mention Rich and clearly considers Lambert responsible for founding the society.

4. Walter Arnold, *The Life and Death of the Sublime Society of Beef Steaks* (1871), p. 2.

The membership of the club is impressive. Along with Rich and Lambert, Hogarth appears among the original members; and as the eye runs down the list, it stops frequently at such names as Theophilus Cibber (elected in 1739), Paul Whitehead (1744), John Wilkes (1754), the Earl of Sandwich (1761), George Colman (1767), Samuel Johnson (1780), the Prince of Wales (1785), and Charles Morris (1785), whose good nature and knack of versifying won him the esteem of his fellow-members over a long period of years.[1] Arnold's history of the society forms an interesting study in the evolution of English *mores* during the one hundred thirty-two years of the club's existence. In that time the dining-hour shifted from two to eight, and the day eventually had to be changed from Saturday to Friday because of the increasing popularity of Saturday evening for London social events. The very termination of the society was conditioned, according to Arnold, by social difficulties and by a growing impatience with the eighteenth-century customs which had been maintained as a means of perpetuating the old flavor.

Distinguished as the group was, it cannot be said to have figured prominently in literature. Walpole's letters mention it occasionally, notably in connection with the Earl of Sandwich. "He has impeached Wilkes," wrote Walpole to George Montagu in 1763, "for a blasphemous poem [the *Essay on Woman*], and has been expelled for blasphemy himself by the Beef-steak Club at Covent Garden." [2] A few days before he had written to Sir Horace Mann:

The wicked even affirm, that very lately, at a club with Mr. Wilkes, held at the top of the playhouse in Drury Lane, Lord Sandwich talked so prophanely that he drove two harlequins out of company.[3]

1. See Richard Dexter, *Captain Charles Morris* (Cleveland, 1923).
2. *The Letters of Horace Walpole*, ed. Mrs. Paget Toynbee (Oxford, 1903–1905), v, 396.
3. *Ibid.*, p. 395.

Many verses were written to be read or sung at the club, but these were of a nature to be of interest chiefly to the members and do not appear to have circulated widely. One of the most delightful tributes to the society appeared in *The Connoisseur*, one of the editors of which later became a member. A letter in Number 19 laments the disrepute into which good English beef had fallen.

> Our only hopes are in the Clergy, and in the Beef-steak Club. . . . The latter, who are composed of the most ingenious artists in the kingdom, meet every saturday in a noble room at the top of *Covent-Garden* theatre, and never suffer any dish except Beef-steaks to appear. These, indeed, are most glorious examples: but what alas! are the weak endeavours of a few to oppose the daily inroads of fricassees and soup-maigres?

The letter concludes that soon "it will be absolutely necessary to enforce the love of Beef by act of parliament."

In one instance familiarity with the club was assumed to be a part of the reader's literary background, much as various societies had been in the days of Queen Anne. Smollett is said to have attended one of the dinners as a guest; and in *Sir Launcelot Greaves* he uses the inevitable gridiron in a discursive simile to describe the one with which Ferret armed himself against Mr. Clarke.

> The young lawyer seemed to be a little discomposed at the glancing of this extraordinary weapon of offence, which the fair hands of Dolly had scoured, until it had shone as bright as the shield of Achilles; or as the emblem of good old English fare, which hangs by a red ribbon round the neck of that thrice-honoured sage's head, in velvet bonnet cased, who presides by rotation at the genial board, distinguished by the title of the *Beef-steak Club:* where delicate rumps irresistibly attract the stranger's eye, and, while they seem to cry, "Come cut me — come cut me," constrain, by wondrous sympathy, each mouth to overflow. Where the obliging and humorous Jemmy B[en-craft]t, the gentle Billy H[owar]d, replete with human kindness, and the generous Johnny B[ear]d, respected and beloved

by all the world, attend as the priests and ministers of mirth, good cheer, and jollity, and assist with culinary art the raw, unpractised, awkward guest.[1]

Smollett's picture is one of the most pleasant ever drawn of an eighteenth-century club. In a sense, however, it is an anachronism. The rarity of such scenes in the literature of his time shows that the club was passing as literary material, and we have only to trace the history of White's to see how the change came about.

WHITE'S AND THE TRANSITION

The story of London's oldest surviving club is too well known to need retelling in detail. White's began as a chocolate-house, which was set up shortly before the turn of the old century.[2] Even before the days of the club, White's was the haunt of the gentleman of fashion. Farquhar's beaux, Archer and Aimwell, were habitués of the house. It was from White's that Steele directed those portions of his early *Tatlers* that dealt with affairs of gallantry; and in *The Spectator*, No. 88, he showed how well the quality of the house was recognized by his readers when he wrote:

You shall frequently meet with lovers and men of intrigue among the lackeys, as well as at White's or in the side boxes.

Farquhar hints at the nature of the conversation in this haunt of the beau in his "Song on a Trifle."

What Mortal Man wou'd be able
At WHITE's Half an Hour to sit?
Or who cou'd bear a *Tea-Table*,
Without talking *Trifles* for *Wit*?[3]

---

1. Chapter iv. Bencraft was elected to the society in 1748, Howard in 1745, and Beard in 1743.

2. See John Timbs, *Clubs and Club Life in London* (1872), pp. 92–93.

3. *The Ladies Miscellany* (1718), p. 28.

The prevalence of gaming, which for a time was almost a tradition of the club, was also frequently mentioned by writers on the chocolate-house. In an outcry against the "chocolate-coffee-gaming-houses," as the idling place of noblemen, Swift wrote in his *Essay on Modern Education* (1729):

I have heard, that the late Earl of Oxford, in the time of his ministry, never passed by White's chocolatehouse (the common rendezvous of infamous sharpers and noble cullies) without bestowing a curse upon that famous academy, as the bane of half the English nobility.[1]

Thus, even before 1714, unless Swift's memory was influenced by subsequent developments, White's had gained a reputation as a gaming center. By 1732, the year of Pope's epistle to Lord Bathurst, the stakes had become large. In describing the inconveniences which would result from a return to the ancient custom of barter, Pope wrote:

> His Grace will game: to White's a bull be led,
> With spurning heels and with a butting head.
> To White's be carried, as to ancient games,
> Fair coursers, vases, and alluring dames.[2]

The change in the traditions of White's between 1710 and 1750 is succinctly pointed out in Number 15 of *The Connoisseur*.

During the publication of the TATLER, Sir *Richard Steele* thought proper to date all his love-news from that quarter: But it would now be as absurd to pretend to gather any such intelligence from *White's*, as to send to *Batson's* for a lawyer, or to the *Rolls* coffee house for a man-midwife.

The transformation of the chocolate-house into a club took place partly because of a practical necessity for exclusiveness. In a public house, where by paying an inconsiderable sum at the bar upon entrance, any sharper could

---

1. *Prose Works*, XI, 53.   2. *Works*, III, 134.

practise upon unwary addicts of play,[1] the sport was often highly irregular and productive of quarrels. Then, too, it was desirable to exclude that perennial nuisance, the coffee-house bore. In order to keep out cheats and other undesirables and to assure the honorable character of the assembly, arrangements were made to take over the house for the exclusive use of the members of the club formed for that purpose. The exact steps by which the change was made cannot be followed, because the club records go back only as far as 1736, at which time the metamorphosis was complete.[2]

The membership was from the first distinguished. Among the early members were the Duke of Devonshire; the Earls of Cholmondeley, Chesterfield, and Rockingham; Sir John Cope, Major-General Churchill, Bubb Dodington, and Colley Cibber.[3] The number soon had to be limited to five hundred, and in 1743 a probationary group called the Young Club was formed, through which all members were required to pass before they might be admitted to the Old Club. The social prestige of both groups was enormous. White's soon assumed a sort of dictatorship of fashion, in matters as various as dress, food, play, and conversation.

Not long after the club was founded, a lady with keen and disillusioned eyes found herself in a position to catch intimate glimpses of life at White's. The result was the scattered descriptions of the club which appear in the *Memoirs of Mrs Letitia Pilkington*. Having left Ireland under somewhat trying circumstances, the dauntless little lady arrived in London about 1739, bent upon living by her pen as Mrs. Behn had done. In order "to make interest with the great," she took lodgings in St. James's Street exactly

1. James Puckle, *The Club* (1713), pp. 16–18.
2. For the method by which such changes were effected somewhat later, see *The Times Literary Supplement*, No. 1593 (August 11, 1932), p. 561.
3. *The National Review*, IV (1857), 323.

opposite White's. Thence she launched out on her disappointing career under the benevolent guidance of Colley Cibber, with whom she was already acquainted. One day Cibber waited upon her with the disquieting news that her reputation as a poet had been blasted at the club by an Irishman, who accused her of having stolen her verses from her husband.

'But (said he [Cibber]) to set that right, you must take some subject that has never yet been touched upon, dress it poetically, and send the lines to White's.' [1]

Although the verses to Cibber which resulted from this hint are in no way distinguished, their author asserts that many of the club subscribed for the forthcoming volume of her poems.

Mrs. Pilkington gradually became acquainted with a number of the gentlemen from over the way, including an old colonel of the foot-guards for whom she wrote love letters, Lord Weymouth, Lord Fitzroy, and others, all of whom took an interest in her verses. She tells how Colonel Duncombe, the Duke of Bolton, and the Earl of Winchilsea sent over a bottle of Burgundy to cheer her spirits, on seeing her watering the flowers in her window. The gentlemen at White's amused themselves by observing the arrival and departure of her guests, and they used to rally her on her curious visitors. Thus her plan for making interest with the great was, in a sense, successful. She even records preventing Robert Nugent's election to White's by telling the story of how he had insulted her. "Their way of election," she notes, "is by ballotting and one black bean is sufficient to overturn any man's pretension to that honour." [2] She also describes a poetical intrigue with Lord Middlesex to discredit Lord Raymond, his rival, the scene of the action being laid in the club itself.

1. *Memoirs of Mrs Letitia Pilkington*, p. 178.
2. *Ibid.*, p. 253.

It is impossible to read her vivacious pictures of club life at White's without regretting the literary neglect which it suffered.

Colley Cibber's relations with the aristocratic society were a source of much satisfaction to him. He occupied a unique position as being the only professional man of letters on the club roster. Pope mentions Cibber's connections there in a line of the 1743 edition of *The Dunciad*:

> Familiar White's, "God save King Colley!" cries.[1]

Pope's editors record the tradition that Cibber "was received there simply in the capacity of a buffoon." However this may be, the amiable Mrs. Pilkington's account of the laureate at White's shows that he was not unpopular. And Bramston intimates that true men of fashion

> In *Fig* the Prize-fighter by day delight,
> And sup with *Colly Cibber* ev'ry night.[2]

The literary treatment of the club was largely satiric. One essay in *The Connoisseur* (No. 19) was directed against the members' luxurious tastes in food. Most of the attacks were based on the passion for gaming which pervaded the rooms. The popular conception of White's as a gambling resort was built, of course, largely upon hearsay. The good London citizens could not drop in and see for themselves, and consequently their ideas of what went on were exaggerated. The sentiment against the club was sufficient in 1750 to call forth a sixpenny pamphlet entitled *A Letter to the Club at White's. In which are set forth The great Expediency of Repealing the Laws now in Force against Excessive Gaming*. As the title suggests, the tone of this prose attack is predominantly ironic. The author's alarm arose from the influential position in which the club stood. In this connection he wrote:

1. I, 321.
2. *The Man of Taste* (1733), p. 17.

The Pertinency of my Address to You, *my Lords and Gentlemen*, on this Occasion, must be evident to every one that knows any thing of your history; as that you are a Club of about *Five Hundred*, much the greatest Part of you P[ee]rs and M[em]b[e]rs of P[ar]l[iame]nt, who meet every Day at a celebrated Chocolate House near *St. James's*, with much greater Assiduity than you meet in the Court of Requests; and there, all Party Quarrels being laid aside, all State Questions dropp'd, Whigs and Tories, Placemen and Patriots, Courtiers and Country-Gentlemen, you all agree for the Good of the Public, in the salutary Measures of Ex[cessi]ve G[a]m[bl]ing.[1]

The pamphleteer remarked bitterly that membership at White's should be considered essential to election to Parliament, and then broke through his irony to propose "that a List of your club, which might be called the Bl - - ph - -ing Club, in contradistinction to the Hell-Fire Club, of famous Memory, should be hung up in every Alehouse in *Great-Britain*, to direct the Honest Electors whom they are not to chuse." In spite of extravagances of this sort, parts of the tract, such as the passage in which the author reviews Mr. Bickerstaff's humorous exposé of the gamester's brain,[2] are skillfully written.

Although such pamphleteering had little effect upon White's, the attacks continued. In the initial number of *The Connoisseur*, the club was referred to as an expensive place of amusement where the great entertained themselves by playing whist "for the trifle of a thousand pounds the rubber, or by making bets on the lye of the day." Number 15 of the same periodical is devoted entirely to gaming, which, the author says, "is now become rather the business than amusement of our persons of quality." The two clubs at White's came in for a special reprimand. The essayist described the curious wagers, recorded in the betting-book, on such matters as the color of a horse, the

1. Erasmus Mumford, *A Letter to the Club at White's* (1750), pp. 4–5.
2. *Ibid.*, pp. 21–24. See *The Tatler*, No. 13.

weather, and the longevity of various members. The custom of pitting one man's life against another's — that is, of laying a wager upon which of two men would outlive the other [1] — came in for a particular rebuke.

It would be pointless to collect from the memoirs of the last half of the century all the available testimony about the high stakes for which the members played. A letter from Mrs. Delany to Mrs. Dewes, written in 1755, gives an illustrative incident.

Sir John Bland lost to Capt. O'Brien, who married Lord Inchiquin's deaf and dumb daughter, £32,000. Mr. O'Brien honourably gave him his chance of winning it back again, and he reduced it to £9000. What a curse to nations is such a pit of destruction as *White's!* It is a sad thing that in a Xtian country it should continue undemolished.[2]

Although not everyone viewed the situation with Mrs. Delany's moral indignation, there is little difference of opinion on the actual prevalence of gaming at White's. When one imagines the sparkling conversation which must have gone on in a club that boasted the membership of the Earl of Chesterfield, George Selwyn, and Horace Walpole, one regretfully wonders that the contemporary references confine themselves so exclusively to its most picturesque vice.

White's and the Sublime Society of Beefsteaks were the two clubs formed before 1740 that survived longest. They were the most like the social clubs of to-day. And of all the more distinguished groups of the first half of the eighteenth century, they were the least written about. In this peculiarity they were rivaled later only by the societies which most resembled them, Almack's, Arthur's, Boodle's, and

1. Colley Cibber, who died in 1757 at the age of eighty-six, caused much money to change hands in wagers of this sort. The betting-book records, for example, that "Lord Mountford bets Sir John Bland twenty guineas that Nash outlives Cibber." Both wagerers died before either Cibber or Nash.

2. *The Autobiography and Correspondence of . . . Mrs. Delany,* ed. Lady Llanover (1861), iii, 336.

the rest. The renown of all these has survived, but not through literary monuments. Why this was true will be explained in the concluding chapter by a consideration of the changes that came about in the nature of the clubs themselves, in literary fashions, and in the position of the author as a clubman.

The literary importance of club life in Swift's day did not arise from the number of societies of gentlemen then in existence. There were not as many clubs in London in 1710 as there were in 1780. It was the fact that gentlemen of fashion in London and the reading-public of the whole kingdom were extremely interested in the new social institution that made it prominent in contemporary literature. The great clubs had not yet become so exclusive that the public knew nothing about them. The small ones were not so commonplace that the public cared nothing about them. For years they were the scene of the making of epigrams, political schemes, critical decrees, and religious heresies. To their own gregarious age, they were an important step in the social evolution — a step toward that highly valued Augustan quality, urbanity.

These were the clubs that Addison and Swift visited and read about and wrote about. The foregoing attempt to describe them cannot but reveal their great variety and their hold upon the interest of the Town. It gives, however, no fair idea of the prominence of the society of gentlemen in the literature of the time. That can be done only by considering the myriads of fictitious descriptions which were fabricated by writers for the amusement of their club-loving readers.

CHAPTER III

The Fictitious Club

EARLY EXPERIMENTS

THE success of eighteenth-century writers in turning the current preoccupation with clubs to their own account is no small tribute to their ingenuity. Not content with frequent references to the existing societies, they produced purely imaginary ones. Indeed, it became almost a rhetorical fashion to introduce fictitious clubs, whether to preserve anonymity by fathering the production on a society of gentlemen, or to draw satiric portraits of members representing social types, or to lend a general air of dramatic verisimilitude to the project in hand.

One of the first experiments tried with the fictitious club was that of making it responsible for the authorship of a publication. As early as 1692, a book was ingeniously contrived by John Dunton, with the help of Charles Gildon, which bore over Dunton's imprint the title, *The Post-boy rob'd of his Mail: or, the Pacquet Broke Open. Consisting of Five Hundred Letters, To Persons of several Qualities and Conditions. With Observations Upon each Letter. Publish'd by a Gentleman concern'd in the Frolick.* The book is made up, as its title partly suggests, of letters supposed to have been stolen by the members of a club from the packet of a post-boy. Both Gildon's dedicatory epistle to Mr. George Porter and Dunton's preface to the reader shift what blame there was in the affair to the club members, who had the excuse of intoxication. Dunton further palliates the theft by insisting that "all the Letters which they found, which had an *honest end in the speed*, they took care to send as directed." [1] Since they retained the rest for publication, it is not surprising to find the letters somewhat sensational in their contents.

The introductory letter, which did not come from the packet, describes the club. The group was made up of ten young wits, who had chosen that number to represent Apollo and the Muses. Apollo, the president of the club, was elected anew at each meeting. The organization and members having been described, the author proceeds to relate the story of the escapade itself. As the club was considering, one stormy night, what manner of adventure it might best undertake, one of the members drew from his pocket a misdirected letter which he had opened and read by mistake. It revealed an act of astonishing perfidy on the part of an old and respected acquaintance of the company. After an airy discussion of the merits of the case, the club decided that since the weather was very bad for deeds of knighthood, the wrongs of the old man's victim would have to go unrighted; but one idea led to another until a member suggested that they take horse in pairs and sally forth to rob the post, returning afterwards to the Bull-Head with what spoils they could take, to divert themselves "with the Scene of *Hypocrisy uncas'd*." This suggestion was forthwith carried out; and, after changing their wet garments, they met to recount their adventures, which proved highly entertaining. On the same night they journeyed on to Putney, where the next day at the house of Summer, one of the members, they opened and read the stolen letters.

The bulk of the volume is made up of selected letters from the pillaged mails. After each is read, the various members indulge their wit at the expense of the correspondents or discuss the moral values of the case in question. The framework is sustained at the end of Book I by

1. *The Post-boy rob'd of his Mail* (1692), sig. A6ᵛ.

attributing the interruption to a summons to dinner. In the afternoon, four of the members, including the supposed author, steal away from the rest and continue with the mail, nor are they joined by the other six until a score of new letters have been discussed. So the business of the club proceeds, until by the end of the volume one hundred twenty-nine letters have been opened.

The book must have enjoyed some popularity; for in 1693 a second volume was added, almost as large as the first. The club framework was sustained, with the explanation that the stock of stolen letters had not been entirely exhausted by the preceding meetings. Gildon varied the contents of the new volume by introducing a whole packet of letters that describe an oriental journey. These have a certain continuity, and the longer ones have a considerable narrative interest. The series as a whole seems, in certain respects, to look forward toward the epistolary novel. Both volumes were reprinted, with some excisions and additions, in 1706.

The Post-boy rob'd of his Mail is particularly significant for the care with which the trick of the fictitious club is carried out. Not only is the book ascribed to a member of the society, but the group is consistently kept in sight and has much intrinsic interest. The body of narrative and satiric material which the author has to present is poured into his artificial mold with a good deal of originality. Although Gildon neglected an opportunity to heighten the interest in his clubmen by making their remarks on the letters individualize them, his development of a fictitious society of gentlemen credited with authorship is more complete than any attempt of this sort before the device reached its highest form in the essay periodicals.

William Paterson used the same method, in a less carefully evolved form, for lending authority to some of his political tracts. The financier had been associated early in the sixteen nineties with a society which had been instrumental in the founding of the Bank of England.[1] He may have had this club in mind when he published a pamphlet entitled *An Inquiry into the Reasonableness and Consequences of an Union with Scotland* (1706), detailing the "Proceedings of the Wednesday's Club in Friday Street." Eleven years later appeared the same author's *Inquiry into the State of the Union of Great Britain and the Past and Present State of the Trade and Public Revenues Thereof. By the Wednesday's Club in Friday Street.* Each tract is made up of a number of papers dated on various Wednesdays over a period of months, so that at first sight it seems reasonable to suppose that the pamphlets were transcriptions of actual club debates. Writing under the pseudonym of Lewis Medway, Paterson sought in the introductory epistle to the earlier pamphlet to foster this illusion by such statements as the following:

After having omitted the trivial and frothy parts of the occurrences, and corrected the different dialects, our society have thought fit to transmit those inquiries in their native habit, and without any dress, that thus not only the matter, but likewise the manner, might the better appear, and that the characters of the persons speaking, as well as the things spoken, might be more easily seen.[2]

Saxe Bannister, however, gives convincing evidence that the Wednesday's Club was a pure fiction as far as these papers are concerned, conceived by Paterson for the lively expression of his own theories and opinions;[3] and one cannot but wonder at the ingenuity with which the hoax was perpetrated in order to engage the reader's interest.

1. See Saxe Bannister, *William Paterson* (Edinburgh, 1858), p. 93; also p. 83, where the following passage is quoted from Paterson's *A Brief Account of the Intended Bank of England* (1694): "But no sooner was this proposal stated by A SOCIETY of considerable persons, than the notion of *currency* was started."

2. *The Writings of William Paterson*, ed. Saxe Bannister (1858), I, 167.

3. *Ibid.*, I, 163; II, 5.

Occasionally a piece was published anonymously as the work of a club without any hint at the nature of the group. Such was the comedy entitled *The Roving Husband Reclaim'd.* . . . *Writ by a Club of Ladies, in Vindication of Virtuous Plays* (1706), which shows how Fidelia won back her philandering husband, Thoughtless, through her undeviating constancy. Equally elusive is the club connected with *The Diverting Muse, or, the Universal Medley* (1707), which purported to have been "written by a society of merry gentlemen, for the entertainment of the town." This anthology of verse was evidently intended to be carried farther, as the title-page labels it "The First Part"; but no additions seem to have followed. After the last poem, in the position of a colophon, is a paragraph inviting contributions and concluding as follows:

If they please to communicate their Instructions to the Persons concern'd in this Miscellany, which will be continued Monthly, by a Society of Merry Gentlemen, they have it done gratis, and inserted herein; also if they have anything of their own, that they are willing to make publick, if it be judg'd proper for our present undertaking, it shall be carefully admitted, as aforesaid: if they please to direct for Mr. George Dagonstaff, to be left at Mr. Hogarth's Coffee-house in St. John's Gate.

The foregoing passage contains all the information given to the public concerning the "society of merry gentlemen" who were responsible for *The Diverting Muse*. Still less is revealed about the "society of gentlemen" who, according to another title-page, are alleged to have written the miscellany entitled *The Honey-Suckle; Consisting of Original Poems, Epigrams, Songs, Tales, Odes, and Translations* (1734).

Where the information about the clubs is as scanty as in these last three cases, the only objects of the authors in inventing the fictions were to profit by the popularity of the club as an institution and to preserve complete anonymity. In some instances, especially in the case of the miscellanies, there may have been an actual plurality of authorship. Even if this was true, however, the authors need not have composed a genuine club; and it is much more likely that a single writer was responsible for each piece, the society being, as it seems now, a somewhat gratuitous fiction. It was the periodical essayists who perfected the device; and their handling of it was of such interest as to demand separate treatment.

SATIRIC PORTRAITS OF FICTITIOUS CLUBMEN

The fictitious club was employed even more widely as a framework for satiric characterizations of actual or typical men, who were represented as members. One of the early examples of such procedure has a special interest because of its tentative assignment to Swift.[1] The piece in question is a satire, nearly three hundred couplets in length, which was first published anonymously in Dublin (1706) under the following title:

The Swan Tripe Club in Dublin. A Satire: Dedicated to all those who are true friends to her present Majesty and her Government, to the Church of England and to the Succession as by Law establish'd; and who gratefully acknowledge the preservation of their Religion, Rights, and Liberties, due to the late King William, of ever glorious and immortal Memory.[2]

A London edition of the poem was printed by Tonson in the same year with the title, *The Tripe Club, A Satire. . . . By the Author of the Tale of a Tub.* It reappeared in Lon-

1. Temple Scott (*The Prose Works of Jonathan Swift*, XII, 197–198) places *The Swan Tripe Club* among the supposititious works. John Nichols implies, in a note to John Barret's *Essay on the Earlier Part of the Life of Swift* (p. 107), that he accepts it as Swift's. The only evidence that I can see for this ascription is the title-page of Tonson's first edition, which means very little in the light of contemporary publishing practises.

2. Reprinted by John Nichols in John Barret's *Essay on the Earlier Part of the Life of Swift* (1808), pp. 107–123.

don in 1710 as *The Swan Tripe-Club: A Satire, on the High-Flyers; In the Year 1705.*

The poem begins with a description of the peaceful days in Ireland before faction raised its head and the Tories became violent. The haunt of the militant high-fliers of Dublin was a "modern dome," which, a note in Tonson's edition informs us, was generally known as the Swan Tavern and was situated near Lucas's Coffee-house.

> Here gravely meet the worthy *Sons* of *Zeal,*
> To wet their pious Clay, and decently to Rail;
> Immortal Courage from the Claret Springs,
> To censure Heroes, and the Acts of Kings:
> Young *Doctors* of the *Gown,* here shrewdly show,
> How *Grace-Divine* can Ebb, and *Spleen* can Flow;
> The Pious *Red-coat,* most devoutly Swears,
> Drinks to the *Church,* but Ticks on his *Arrears*;
> The gentle *Beau* too, Joyns in wise Debate,
> *Adjusts* his Cravat, and *Reforms* the State.[1]

Such was the society of Tories that gathered at the Swan to incite all malcontents to action.

After this general description the satirist launches his personal attack on the leaders of the faction by showing them gathered at the club. A number of the objects of the onslaught have been identified.[2] Borachio is intended for Dr. Higgins, "the Irish Sacheverell"; Magpye represents Archdeacon Percival; and Nutbrain, Mr. Nutley, a lawyer. There is a difference of opinion about the others, but their portraits too were without question drawn from the life. The caricature of "Parson Percival" is fairly typical.

> Egregious *Magpye,* charms the list'ning throng,
> Whilst in-offensive *Satyr* tips his Tongue;
> Grey *Polliticks* adorn the Beardless *Chit,*
> Of foreign Manners, but of Native *Wit*;
> Scarce wain'd from *Diddy,* of his *Alma Mater,*
> The cocking *Thing* steps forth the Churches *Erra Pater*;

---

1. *The Tripe Club* (1706), pp. 5–6.
2. John Barret, *Essay,* p. 142.

> High flying Thoughts, his Moderate Size supply,
> And wing the Tow'ring *Puppet* to the Sky;
> On brazen Wings, beat out from Native stock,
> He mounts, and Rides upon the Weather-cock.[1]

His gallery complete, the satirist shows the club in session. As they sit drinking, Faction enters in the form of old Grimberd, one of the members, and after some egregious compliments to the society, proceeds to depict the sad state in which the church finds herself. After assailing the memory of King William and the Whiggish infection of Queen Anne's reign, Grimberd sounds the call to action. The best proselytes, he asserts, are to be gained among the "beardless boys" of the land.

> "Shew them the *Lure*, which *never* fails to *Hit*,
> "*Approve* their *Briskness*, and *Admire* their *Wit*;
> "*Youth* against *Flattery* has no Defence,
> "*Fools* still are Cheated with the *Bait* of *Sense*; . . .
> "'Tis *Fools* we *want*, and of the *Largest* size,
> "Twou'd spoil our *Cause* to practise on the *Wise*.[2]

Just as the members of the club are applauding Grimberd's suggestion, Religion enters and rebukes them for their neglect of her and for their failure to realize the greatness of King William and Queen Anne. She concludes by urging that the factionists help to better the state of Britain instead of aggravating national difficulties by their unpatriotic caballing. The satire ends with the lines:

> Frowning, the *Goddess* spoke, and Strait withdrew,
> Scatt'ring *Ambrosial* Odours as She flew;
> Her *Trembling Sons Immoderately* Scar'd,
> *Fled* from th'uneasie *Truths*, which *sullenly* they heard.[3]

The fictitious nature of the group here presented has been questioned. The meeting-place is authentic enough, as Dublin is known to have had a Swan Tavern, and Lucas's Coffee-house, near which the Swan stood, occupied

1. *The Tripe Club* (1706), p. 7.   2. *Ibid.*, p. 15.
3. *Ibid.*, p. 20.

the site of the present City Hall;[1] but there is no evidence that the Tripe Club itself ever existed. It must rather be looked upon as a device of the satirist for bringing together the individual high-fliers whom he wished to attack, so that he could expose their common principles as well as their personal delinquencies. Since a club was the natural place for such men to gather, it was well suited to the author's method.

The Irish fortune-hunter and his quarry were among the favorite objects of early eighteenth-century satire. The machinations of both the hunter and the hunted appear in all their absurdity in *The Spectator*, No. 561, for which Addison furnished a letter from an experienced but unsuccessful pursuer of widows. The supposed correspondent writes to inform Mr. Spectator of the "mysteries of a certain female cabal . . . who call themselves the Widow Club. This club consists of nine experienced dames who take their places once a week round a large oval table." Beginning with the president, who has just determined to marry for the seventh time, the writer gives a short character of each member, revealing her matrimonial experience and her qualifications for membership. According to the rules of the club, each lady was obliged to inform the others of any new suit that had developed; and if the affair met with the approval of the group, suggestions were freely offered about the best method of closing the venture satisfactorily. The society also discussed the management of husbands, laying down a set of rules therefor, the publication of which must necessarily have brought forebodings to the undiscriminating hunter after fortunes.

If the object of Addison's essay was to expose the calculating nature of both the widows and their suitors, as it

---

1. Lucas's is referred to in *A Letter from the Quidnuncs at St. James's Coffee-house . . . to their Brethren at Lucas's Coffee-house, in Dublin* (1728). A lively scene at Lucas's in 1753 is described in Arthur Murphy's *Gray's-Inn Journal*, No. 24.

seems to have been, he could not have chosen a more lively way of accomplishing his end than by the little cabinet of characters with which he presented the public. His use of the device was very different from that of the satirist of the Tripe Club. Instead of using vague names to represent actual individuals, Addison merged many offenders under each type figure, the attack being directed upon the groups thus represented.

This satiric scheme was not new. James Puckle had worked it out very thoroughly in his strangely popular little book entitled *The Club. In a Dialogue Between Father and Son* (1711). The extraordinary history of Puckle's book has been pleasantly recounted by Austin Dobson.[1] It is enough here to note the use which the author made of his happily chosen method of satirizing contemporary manners.

The dialogue begins somewhat abruptly:

Father. *What made you out so late last Night?*
Son. Mr. *** invited me to his Club at the *Noah*'s Ark; where, in a low Room that stunk like a Drunkard's Morning-Breath, several sat round the Fire complaining of *Gouts, Dropsies, Consumptions, Pleurisies, Palsies, Rheumatisms, Catarrhs, &c.* 'till more Company coming in, cry'd, *To the Table, To the Table*, where one began his Right-hand Man's Good-health (over the Left Thumb), which having gone round, the next was begun, and so they drank on 'till each had pledg'd every Man's Health in the Room.[2]

At this point the father interrupts characteristically to insert a proverb and a moralization on the subject of drinking healths, and then inquires about the nature of the conversation.

Father. *What was't they said?*
Son. E'en what came uppermost; for, as Wine laid Reason a-sleep, each gave the Reins to his Vanity, and Folly.

1. *Eighteenth Century Vignettes* (Oxford, 1923), III, 270–292.
2. *The Club* (1713), p. 7.

The son proceeds to characterize each of the members, "not only individually," as Austin Dobson happily puts it, "but alphabetically . . . the twenty-four letters ending, as in duty bound, with Zany, the Vintner or landlord." [1]

As a picture of club life the book is by no means notable. Occasionally, it is true, we get a momentary glimpse of the meeting itself, as in the passage where Wiseman rebukes Detractor.

At length *Wiseman* ask'd the Difference between smiting with the Sword, and a killing Tongue; whereat *Detractor* being dumb-founded, threw down his Club, and left the Room. [2]

In the practises of Gamester and Knave upon Buffoon and Critic at the "whisk" table, we see the havoc that was sometimes wrought in clubs through card-sharpers; and the Xantippe incident recalls the sage rule for the Two-penny Club, set down by Addison in *The Spectator*, No. 9, that "if any member's wife comes to fetch him home from the club, she shall speak to him without the door." In general, however, the picture of the group in session is by no means all that could be desired. The author is so exclusively concerned with the son's characters of the members and the father's allusive moral comments on them that the artificiality of the device is always apparent. Nevertheless, the adoption of the form is significant. The book showed its popularity by demanding a new edition in 1711, two further editions in 1713, and others in 1721, 1723, 1733, and 1743, besides an undated "fifth edition." [3] No more editions were published until 1817, by which time the book had acquired an antiquarian interest. Its popularity

1. The fact that the landlord is named Zany inevitably suggests Dick Est-court and the Beefsteak Club. Puckle even gives (p. 43) an instance of his mimicry. The hint may have been taken from Ward's *Satyrical Reflections*. See above, p. 141.
2. *The Club*, (1713) p. 13.
3. See G. W. Kohlmetz, *Bibliographical Notes on "Puckle's Club"* (Cleveland, 1899).

parallels in a striking manner the vogue of the club as
literary material.

A double attack was launched in a curious essay that
was printed in a continuation of *The Spectator*. The whole
of the eighth number (August 1, 1716) was devoted to de-
nouncing clubs as "seminaries and nurseries of faction."
The author was probably masking his disapproval of the
riots caused by the Mug-House Clubs and their Jacobite
opponents. Not content with condemning clubs in general,
the author attempts to expose the factionists who attended them. He describes the members of a society
known to a friend of his. The president was a broken army
officer who drank off bumper after bumper to the government in the hope of getting a better commission. The vice-
president was a non-juring divine whom poverty had compelled to offer allegiance to the crown in order to secure a
living. Another member was a *valet de chambre* who wanted
to be a gentleman of the bed chamber to a duke. An Oxford student had been in a riot and was attending the club
to avoid suspicion. And one gentleman came only for the
purpose of drinking. When the author has finished the
fifteen brief sketches of the various members, it is evident
that their highly articulate loyalty was purely mercenary.
Every man had his own ax to grind. The author of this
Spectator liked neither clubs nor those who attended them,
and he found his imaginary society an excellent method of
saying so.

A fictitious club was used as an excuse for another set of
satiric characters in *The Grub-street Journal* some years
later. Number 176 of that periodical, dated May 10, 1733,
begins with a letter from a society of ladies called the Fid-
dle-Faddle Club, who protest that their sex is not sufficiently esteemed.

We meet twice a week to settle fashions, and talk over the
beaux, and all the pretty things that have been sayed to any

of us. Our employment, when we are not at the club, is to dress in the whims invented there; and to endeavour to get our fashions follow'd; and to make new conquests.

These ladies are thoroughly disgusted with the current political talk of the excise, and desire Mr. Bavius to preserve the *beau monde* from such an annoying obsession. In order that he may form some impression of his correspondents, characters of the members are given in the letter. Since each lady has some particular foible, collectively the portraits form a very fair composite of the feminine affectations which the author of the essay wished to satirize. The imaginary society is sketched in so deftly that in addition to furnishing the material for the satiric characters the members take on a good deal of intrinsic interest.

A few years later, in a prose satire entitled *The World Turn'd Inside-Out; or, Humankind Unmask'd* (1737), appeared a section directed against clubs. In entering upon a discussion of "The Abuse of Clubs, especially of such as reckon themselves Virtuosos to countenance their Pretence," the essay produces a very shrewd impeachment.

Your greatest Sticklers for Clubs always alledge, *The Good of Society*, or *the Benefit of Conversation*. On this Basis they pretend to erect their Fabrick; but rarely, very rarely, shew Skill enough to make the Building answerable to the Model.[1]

The author describes, by way of example, a club of connoisseurs or virtuosos,[2] first characterizing the members separately and then repeating their conversation, to show how the group missed both the aims commonly set up by clubs. He seems to be particularly scandalized by the brutishness of such men as he has described, and they are

---

1. *The World Turn'd Inside-Out* (1737), I, 169.
2. Compare the club of virtuosos in *The Rambler*, No. 177, of each of whom there is a lively character. The club of virtuosos in *Peregrine Pickle* and the club of originals in the debtor's prison in *Ferdinand Count Fathom* are somewhat similar.

not spared in the vision which follows the essay. Thus the device is here turned not only against a social type, but also against the club as an institution.

The depth to which the fictitious club penetrated the literature of our period is evident from its use in David Fordyce's *Dialogues Concerning Education* (1745). This group of moral essays deals with an academy in the country, whither Simplicius goes to improve his understanding. Upon his arrival the young scholar finds that in order to provide socially attractive scenes for the discussion of their studies, the young academicians have formed a number of societies.

One is called the *Poetical* Club; another, the *Mathematical;* a third, the Club of *Politicians;* a fourth, the *Virtuoso* Club; and several more, who are denominated from those Arts and Sciences, about which they chiefly converse.[1]

Simplicius's friend Sophron was a member of the Philosophical Club, of which there is an excellent description in Dialogue III. Sophron draws characters of the various members: Eugenio, the good-natured, sprightly young beau; Constant, the blunt, plain-dealing republican; and Hiero, the grave, metaphysical young man. These with Sophron and Philander, who drifts in occasionally as a visitor, make up the club. Aided by the good offices of Sophron, Simplicius soon becomes a member; and it is chiefly through the conversation of the group that Fordyce presents his own principles.

The club's rules, though informal, are well established, and its meetings are intrinsically interesting. The reader of the *Dialogues* soon feels almost as intimate with the members as the devotee of *The Spectator* does with the Templar and Sir Andrew Freeport; and, forgetting that they are merely points of view, follows their arguments with a keen personal interest. Thus a lively narrative

1. *Dialogues Concerning Education* (1745), I, 70.

element is introduced through the fictitious circle, which makes Fordyce's ideas much more palatable than they would otherwise have been. A few of the dialogues, it is true,[1] show no introductory effort to suggest the club setting; and when the book ends at Dialogue XX with a speech of one of the members, there is no attempt to account for the later history of the society. Indeed, the club is subordinated throughout to the expository purposes of the author and must, consequently, be looked upon as a trick of composition rather than as an end in itself. Nevertheless, the book shows in a highly evolved form the type of fictitious club in which the imaginary members are individualized by separate characterization.

An impressive number of fictitious clubs found their way into the literature of the early eighteenth century in a much more haphazard fashion than those which constituted a more or less sustained device of form. There is, for example, the society of baronets described by Lady Scandal to Mrs. Crackenthorpe, in *The Female Tatler*, No. 5, as a satiric thrust at the effeminacy of the London beaux. The group is represented as meeting at "the Smyrna and other Coffee-Houses" to work elaborate embroidery.

These *Baronets* it seems, have a Sweet-meat Club at a Confectioners in *York Buildings*, where they meet three times a Week, to work a fine *Wastcoat* for a Brother *Beau's* Wedding, — Sir *Formal* did the *Border*, Sir *Tawdry* a *Sun-Flower*, Sir *Finical* a *Tulip*, Sir *Plump* an *Artichoke*, and Sir *Dapper* a *Primrose*.

The essayist goes on to describe the laughably innocent refreshments of which the fops partook, and then relates how their eccentricities were revealed to an amused world.

They hugg'd themselves two Months with this mighty Secret, and thought themselves very Happy in making Business a Pleasure; but an odious Thing, as ugly as the Devil, bolting

1. *E.g.*, Dialogue XII.

unawares into the Room, the Matter was blown up, and the Ill bred Creature instead of begging Pardon for her Rudeness, tir'd six pair of Horses to carry the Jest about Town.

The method in this bit of satire on manners was, obviously, to group certain representatives of the objectionable social type in a fictitious club, where their foibles could be revealed with all the vivacity of a comedy of manners. This satiric contrivance reached its highest perfection in the essays of *The Spectator*. Parallel to the Sweetmeat Club is Steele's "set of sighers" at Oxford, who met under the name of the Amorous Club.

> These gentlemen are of that sort of inamoratos, who are not so very much lost to common sense, but that they understand the folly they are guilty of; and for that reason separate themselves from all other company, because they will enjoy the pleasure of talking incoherently, without being ridiculous to any but each other.[1]

Steele describes the tokens of their mistresses' affection with which the languishing gallants were invariably provided, and gives an amusing account of their behavior and conversation. The essay concludes with a letter from one of their number, which reveals still further the tender mysteries of the society. Since the Oxford group reminded the author of the Fringe-Glove Club in London, he briefly summarizes its career as well. Its members, "who dressed like lovers . . . were persons of such moderate intellects, even before they were impaired by their passion, that their irregularities could not furnish sufficient variety of folly to afford daily new impertinences, by which means that institution dropped." Steele's sympathy with the objects of his exposé precluded any malicious delight on his part in revealing the weaknesses of the lovers; and his Amorous Club represents the kindliest satiric manner in which a fictitious society was used.

1. *The Spectator*, No. 30.

The Duellists' Club of *The Spectator*, No. 9, is devised much less ingeniously. By describing its membership, meetings, and ambitions, however, Addison manages in three sentences to depict the barbarities of a practise against which his periodical persistently waged war. Through the Rattling Clubs of Number 630, an attack was launched against the unimaginative sets of men who interrupted church services, when any unwelcome sentiment was voiced from the pulpit, by a concerted outbreak of conversation.

These gay fellows, from humble lay professions, set up for critics without any tincture of letters or reading, and have the vanity to think they can lay hold of something from the parson, which may be formed into ridicule.

When their activities have been described, the clubs appear eminently deserving of the severe rebuke of Mr. Spectator's correspondent.

It is comforting to the student of early eighteenth-century clubs to learn that the problem of the actuality of certain societies was sometimes as troublesome to writers of that time as to himself. The difficulty is implied by Budgell in *The Spectator*, No. 217, where a communication concerning a club of "she-romps" is printed, along with several other letters. Budgell writes:

The first of them is the description of a club, whether real or imaginary I cannot determine; but am apt to fancy that the writer of it, whoever she is, has formed a kind of nocturnal orgie out of her own fancy.

Regardless of his suspicions, Mr. Spectator inserts the letter of Kitty Termagant, in which is described her boisterous society of romps, in order to reveal to the world the inelegance of their weekly riots. The description of their blithe dismantling of a prude perturbs Mr. Spectator so much that he finds himself little inclined to accept their invitation to attend, for fear of sharing the fate of the prude.

The trick of satirizing a social type by means of a fictitious club was not confined to the pages of *The Spectator*. "The Art of Political Lying," as published in Motte's *Miscellanies* (1727), also used the device with telling effect. In the prospectus of Chapter VIII of this important work, the reader is promised an account of "a Project for Uniting the several smaller Corporations of Lyars into one Society."

This Society ought to consist of the hopeful Genius's about the Town (of which there are great plenty to be pick'd up in the several Coffee-houses) Travellers, Virtuoso's, Fox-hunters, Jockeys, Attorneys, Old Seamen and Soldiers out of the Hospitals of *Greenwich* and *Chelsea*.[1]

The leaders of each political party were to be members, and were to judge which lies should pass current. An outer room was always to be provided with a number of persons of unquestioned credulity to spread the lies for absolute truth. The project even lays down a set of rules for the society, providing, among other things, that no member should blush while telling a lie and that spies be employed to collect hints for new falsities. The whole account is an elaborate attack on the professional circulators of political propaganda.

A Trip through London (1728), attributed to Erasmus Jones, shows two satiric clubs. The account of one is directed at a profession. The society in question was composed of undertakers, who feasted sumptuously at a tavern and drank toasts "to *Lead and Velvet*, *The New Distemper*, &c." During the meeting, "the Healths of certain Physicians . . . went frequently round, as being great *Benefactors* to the *Company*."[2] The group patronized a periodical called the "*Sick-List*," and gleaned all possible information

---

1. *Miscellanies in Prose and Verse*, II (1727), 313.
2. *A Trip through London* (1728), p. 31.

about business prospects from the coachmen of the greatest physicians. The other club described in *A Trip through London* is an Irish society of fortune-hunters, who held their monthly meetings at a tavern in the Strand. The author asserts that he happened one day "into the Company of some of the Members of that *Honourable* Body" and "obtain'd a true Copy of their Votes, Schemes and Designs, for the ensuing Year," which he proceeds to reproduce at length "for the Benefit of the Ladies, Trades-People and others."[1] The orders and resolutions which follow are designed to reveal the dishonest practises of fortune-hunting Irishmen. Most of their deceits were calculated to give social prestige to the members, thereby assuring the success of their schemes. Such is the case in the following item, which is fairly typical:

ORDER'D that *Philip O Finikin*, according to the Prayer of his Petition, have Leave to put himself into *deep Mourning*, as for the Death of some near Relation; and that Care be taken to have it incerted in some of the Publick News-Papers, that he is thereby become possess'd of a very considerable Estate.[2]

The use of the club device for exposing fortune hunting[3] forms a striking parallel to that of Addison in his account of the Widow Club.

The devastating possibilities of the imaginary club are fully displayed in Swift's "Character, Panegyric, and Description of the Legion Club." His virulent attack on the Irish Parliament was occasioned in 1736 by the introduction of a bill for exempting from church taxes the pasture lands of Ireland. It is not surprising to find the dean, who had spent some of the best years of his life in fostering the financial interests of the Irish church, enraged at this en-

1. *Ibid.*, p. 23.
2. *Ibid.*, p. 24.
3. Benjamin Victor mentions (*The History of the Theatres of London and Dublin* [1761], II, 120) a play entitled "Club of Fortune Hunters, or *Widow bewitch'd*, by Mr. *Macklin*," as performed in 1747.

croachment on its revenues. Swift pictures the Irish House of Commons as a club of demoniacs, taking his title from the reply of the unclean spirit of St. Mark's Gospel. The idea of representing Parliament as a club was not new, and Swift may have borrowed the scheme from the author of the Crown Inn pamphlets.[1] But the relentlessness of the device, in Swift's hands, is unparalleled in the satire of the time. Grimly the aging dean offered his opinion concerning the fate which the members of Parliament deserved.

> Since the house is like to last,
> Let the royal grant be pass'd,
> That the club have right to dwell
> Each within his proper cell,
> With a passage left to creep in
> And a hole above for peeping.[2]

The ensuing picture of the Legion Club is painfully vivid. A few members are singled out for special revilement; but despairing of reaching his enemies individually, Swift abandons personalities toward the end of the poem and concludes with a general curse upon the whole group. The change in the dean's mental state since the days when he went with pleasure to Lord Bolingbroke's Society of Brothers is nowhere more apparent than in this poem. Here he uses a social institution which once delighted him as a machine for hurling contumely upon his political enemies.

In 1740 Henry Fielding invented a society called the Scull Club for the purpose of satirizing his journalistic enemies. *The Champion* for June 17 of that year (No. 93) contained the following postscript to the news-section, addressed to the president and secretary of the Scull Club:

---

1. *The History of Crown Inn* (1714). In the allegorical account of the political strife on the peace question, of the fall of Oxford, and of the death of Queen Anne, the tavern represents the Court, and the club which met there is equated with Parliament. Another allegorical use of the club appears in Philip Horneck's *High-German Doctor*, No. 32, where the Jacobites are represented as the Snake Club.
2. *The Poems of Jonathan Swift*, ed. W. E. Browning (1910), II, 265.

It has been thought proper to give this public Notice, that we did not *bribe* the said Mr. *Lead*, or the said Mr. *Barren-Brains*, to do us that *Honour* by way of *Puff*, but that 'tis purely an *Act of Grace* on their Side, and what we shall never fail to *acknowledge* on ours as it deserves.

In Number 94 Fielding noted that the Scull Club had been casting reflection on the accuracy of his news. He showed his scorn by adding, "N. B. This Article should have been placed among the Puffs."

The satiric fictions persisted in the last half of the century. *The Connoisseur* (1755) gives a vivid account of a society of "broken gamesters and desperate young rakes" who called themselves the Last Guinea Club and were pledged to die like gentlemen when their common fund of resources was exhausted.[1] The passage which deals with the club forms the introduction to an attack on gaming, in which White's occupies a prominent position. A later number of the same paper (No. 87) exposes the contemporary extravagance in the matter of diet by depicting an eating club, whose members were chosen for their ability to provide delicacies for the club feasts. Similar bits of satire appear in *The World*[2] and in Goldsmith's *Citizen of the World*.[3] Another fictitious group, called the Blackleg Club, was used in a parody of a newspaper controversy between the Jockey Club and a certain Major Brereton, who asserted that he had detected members cheating at cards.[4] It may be said in general, however, that the flourishing days of the club as a satiric device were over some years before the midpoint of the century.

If we may credit the biased history of John Oldmixon, a strange fictitious club was connected with the plot to bring in the Pretender in 1723. The phantom society seems to

1. *The Connoisseur*, No. 50.
2. *The World*, No. 90, September 19, 1754.
3. Letters XXIX and XXX.
4. *The New Foundling Hospital for Wit* (1786), III, 246–248.

have been invented as a blind for the real activities of the plotters. Oldmixon's statement is as follows:

The Earl of *Orrery* was so active in this Matter, according to *Pancier*'s Information, that he was Chairman of the *Burford* Club, which *Plunket* told *Pancier* consisted of *Tory* Lords and others, and as it is very justly observ'd in the *Report*, the *Matter asserted of that Club in* Plunket's *Letters, seems inconsistent with the known Character of some of those Persons.*[1]

Oldmixon lists the fifteen who composed the "pretended" club, Orrery being set down as chairman, and Strafford, Shippen, and Bathurst as among the members. The deceit was discovered through the error of the plotters in listing as members certain men like Strafford who were not in sympathy with the scheme and promptly disclaimed all connection with the group. The exposure was the signal for a deluge of declarations from the press, in which the alleged members sought to exonerate themselves. There are many questions one would like to ask Oldmixon; but if his account is based upon fact, it shows a peculiar relation between club fictions and English politics.

PICTURES OF CLUB LIFE

By the time *The Tatler* and *The Spectator* came into being, the London club had so insinuated itself into the good graces of the reading public that writers needed no ulterior motives for introducing imaginary societies into their writing. Accordingly the fictitious groups began to appear, without any very serious satiric intent behind them, merely because they were the fashion of the day. The club was found to have enough intrinsic interest to be worth treatment on its own account. In the descriptions of many imaginary companies of men, the satire, if it was present at all, was on the institution itself.

1. *The History of England*, III (1735), 739.

The Society of Upholders was introduced into *The Tatler* by Steele and Hughes for reasons only partly satiric. The society[1] devoted itself to seeing after the interment of deceased persons, who, like Partridge the almanac-maker, refused to be decently buried. In *The Tatler*, No. 110, Hughes shows the club taking the necessary steps in the case of the young beau who could not survive the loss of his snuff-box; and Number 113 contains the famous description of the deceased beau's property, which was put up for sale by the society to defray the expenses of his funeral. Among other offenders who were sentenced to a speedy burial were the authors of still-born literary works, "superannuated benchers of the inns of court, senior fellows of the colleges, and defunct statesmen." Thus satire does creep into the essays wherein the Upholders figure. As a cleverly devised fiction, however, the society was popular on its own merits, independent of its function as a means to a satiric end.

The case is clearer for many of the fictitious clubs of *The Spectator*. The interest shown throughout *The Spectator* in the club *per se* is freely admitted, as has already appeared, in a letter from an imaginary correspondent on the Mohock Club. The opening lines of his letter may well be requoted.

Mr. Spectator, — The materials you have collected together towards a general history of clubs, make so bright a part of your speculations that I think it is but a justice we all owe the learned world to furnish you with such assistances as may promote that useful work.[2]

Indeed, if the sections dealing with clubs were collected from *The Spectator*, the result would be a book nearly as large as Ward's *Satyrical Reflections on Clubs* and vastly more readable. A number of these societies have already

1. Introduced in *The Tatler*, No. 99.
2. *The Spectator*, No. 324.

been discussed elsewhere; but several remain to be treated as illustrative of the extraordinary interest which Addison and Steele took in the club as an institution.

Although hints of this phase of Mr. Spectator's observation appeared somewhat earlier, Number 9 gives the first definite indication of the degree to which clubs attracted him. In that number Addison not only explains how human nature prompts men to come together in social groups, but he also describes, by way of illustration, a round dozen of the societies which he claims to have known. In order to show how a common interest or characteristic draws men together, he contrasts the corpulent club of "a considerable market town" with a society of meagre individuals who sprang up in opposition; he mentions the clubs of Georges and of Kings, which were unified, respectively, by the identity of Christian names and surnames among their members; and he shows how such matters as locality of residence, a predilection for dueling, and a fondness for eating and drinking formed the basis for certain companies. The essayist did not scorn to manufacture a set of nine amusing laws for "a knot of artisans and mechanics, who used to meet every night" under the name of the Twopenny Club. Thus in one short essay Addison gave an admirable view of that manifestation of human gregariousness which was to play so prominent a rôle in enlivening the later issues of the periodical.

The Spectator, No. 17, contributes notable additions to the picture in the account of the Ugly Club of Oxford. Alexander Carbuncle, through whose pen Steele describes this merry group, tells of the societies which had lately sprung up at the university under the names of the Punning Club, the Witty Club, and the Handsome Club. As a burlesque on this last society, the Ugly Club had been formed, the qualifications for membership having been rigorously laid down to assure the selection of the most ill-favored gentlemen available. On a similar basis were selected the favorite authors of the group, as well as its toasts. It was probably through the influence of this imaginary club that Mr. Spectator came to be known for his round face; for it was on the basis of this peculiarity of physiognomy, possessed in a remarkable degree by Steele himself, that the worthy observer of manners gained admittance to the society of ugly faces. Steele's *Spectator*, No. 32, gives an account of the meeting at which Mr. Spectator was elected to membership; and in Number 78, by the same hand, a correspondent traces the history of the group in order to claim the honor of its founding for Cambridge.[1]

Another unusual assembly which laid claim to some antiquity was the Everlasting Club described by Addison in Number 72. It had been instituted during the Civil Wars and had continued without interruption, except for a few weeks at the time of the Great Fire, having resolved in 1700 "to sit out the other century." The method by which the sessions were made continuous is explained as follows:

The Everlasting Club consists of an hundred members, who divide the whole twenty-four hours among them in such a manner that the club sits day and night from one end of the year to another; no party presuming to rise till they are relieved by those who are in course to succeed them. By this means a member of the Everlasting Club never wants company.

After summarizing the history of the society, Addison describes the singing, drinking, smoking, and conversation which made up its diversions. In introducing this perpetual body to his readers, the essayist says that he has decided to "communicate it to the public as one of the greatest curiosities in its kind." Here is the explanation of

1. For evidence that the essay on the Ugly Club had its admirers, see *The Ugly Club: A Dramatic Caricature in One Act. Performed on the 6th of June, 1798, at the Theatre-Royal, Drury Lane. Founded on the Seventeenth Number of the Spectator. By Edmund Spenser, the Younger* (1798).

a number of the bizarre fictitious clubs with which the Town was entertained during the early years of the century.

One of the most perplexing social problems of every club is the member who from time to time becomes temperamentally difficult. An ingenious solution of the problem is offered in the numbers of *The Spectator* dealing with a nameless society in the country, where headquarters had been found for the summer in the house of an absent nobleman. In the first of these papers (No. 424), Steele tells by means of a letter how the group disposed of any member who suffered from a momentary attack of temperament. They merely sent him off to a separate wing of the house designated as the "infirmary."

Whoever says a peevish thing, or acts anything which betrays a sourness or indisposition to company, is immediately to be conveyed to his chambers in the infirmary, from whence he is not to be relieved until by his manner of submission, and the sentiments expressed in his petition for that purpose, he appears to the majority of the company to be again fit for society.

The group of essays which deal with this original club in the country is not designed to improve the reader so much as to entertain him with an amusing account of how an imaginary group overcame one of the greatest difficulties of club life.

An additional instance of the thoroughness with which the fictitious club worked itself into the fabric of *The Spectator* is to be found in Number 560. When the periodical was revived on June 18, 1714, with Number 556, Addison announced that Mr. Spectator had abandoned his habitual taciturnity and had formed a new club at which he might talk his fill. Ten days later Mr. Spectator received the following letter, which Addison printed without comment:

Dear Mr Prate-apace, — I am a member of a female society who call ourselves the Chit-Chat Club, and am ordered by the whole sisterhood to congratulate you upon the use of your tongue. We have all of us a mighty mind to hear you talk, and if you will take your place among us for an evening, we have unanimously agreed to allow you one minute in ten, without interruption.

I am, Sir,
Your humble Servant,
S. T.

Such sketches as this, which would mean nothing out of their context, show what an integral and important part of the periodical the clubs formed. Some twenty-seven societies, a few real but most imaginary, are mentioned in *The Spectator*, their treatment presenting an amazing variety of purpose. Nor does that number include the inimitable club involved in the framework of the periodical, which has been reserved for discussion in another place.

The popularity of these curious societies led to their being introduced into *The Guardian*. Pope gave a droll account of one of them in Numbers 91 and 92, where Bob Short writes to inform Mr. Ironside that a Short Club has been organized for men who are less than five feet tall and are not ashamed to own it.[1] "The day of our institution," remarks the sprightly secretary, "was the tenth of December, being the shortest of the year, on which we are to hold an annual feast over a dish of shrimps." Their motto was "Dare to be short," and the rules expressly forbade any subterfuge calculated to increase the apparent height of a member. Number 92 is of special interest because in Dick Distich Pope drew a caricature of himself.

The first of these, Dick Distich by name, we have elected president, not only as he is the shortest of us all, but because he has entertained so just a sense of the stature, as to go generally in black, that he may appear yet less. Nay, to that perfection

1. Compare *A Collection of Miscellany Letters, Selected out of Mist's Weekly Journal* (1722), I, 51–54. Letters XXI and XXII, which describe a Pigmy Club, show that their author made very free with *The Guardian*, No. 91.

is he arrived that he stoops as he walks. The figure of the man is odd enough; he is a lively little creature, with long arms and legs: A spider is no ill emblem of him. He has been taken at a distance for a small windmill. But indeed what principally moved us in his favour was his talent in poetry, for he hath promised to undertake a long work in short verse to celebrate the heroes of our size.

Descriptions of the other members follow, and there is some account of their conversation, its theme being prominent men of the past who were noted for their small stature. The secretary concludes his letter with a promise to keep *The Guardian* informed of the society's activities.

It was not long before an exasperated beau, six and a half feet in height, wrote a letter to Mr. Ironside, protesting against the rising popularity of the Short Club. The airs which the *homunculi* gave themselves seem to have been endangering the prestige of men of height. To obviate the menace, some thirty gallants had formed a Tall Club, and now issued the following defiance:

> I know the short club value themselves very much upon Mr. Distich, who may possibly play some of his Pentameters upon us, but if he does he shall certainly be answered in Alexandrines.[1]

The Tall Club also threatened to "bring away their whole club in a pair of panniers and imprison them in a cupboard," unless they should desist from their arrogance.

For Number 121 of *The Guardian* the lion's head produced a letter from Ned Mum, which describes a Silent Club composed largely of "married men, and such whose wives are remarkably loud at home." The president having been deaf and dumb since his birth, their debates were carried on silently by means of their fingers. Thus no one had the advantage of an argument because of the loudness of his voice. The letter cites the literary favorites of the

1. *The Guardian*, No. 108.

group, Jonson's *Silent Woman* being held in particular esteem. Some days after Ned Mum's communication had been published, a protest against the Silent Club was registered by the wife of a member. Her illuminating letter [1] complains that her husband used to abuse her in violent terms upon his return from the meetings of the taciturn brotherhood.

An equally diverting society is described by "Abraham Standfast" in *The Senator* (1728), a bi-weekly designed to recount the progress of parliamentary affairs to a gentleman in the country. Standfast tells (No. 22) of finding in his chamber "a blotted scrawl, very ill spelt," which his servant Jeffery had dropped there. The document proves to be the journal of a club of footmen. For the amusement of his readers, Standfast translates the writing into "common English." The enactments of the club are highly amusing, and the author of the periodical makes the most of his opportunity to burlesque parliamentary procedure. At the same time he lays bare the tendency among the socially inferior classes in London to form cheap imitations of the more distinguished clubs — a practise that is suggested more definitely by Ward's *Satyrical Reflections*.

The small, informal club appears to its best advantage in Thomas Gordon's *Humourist*. A short essay "Of a Club of Authors" tells of the writer's friendship with a satirist of a modest, almost surly, but fundamentally pleasant disposition. This friend was accustomed to escape his more dismal meditations by attending a club which met two or three times a week. He introduces the writer of the essay as a candidate for membership. Gordon's description of the group is short and general; but a fairly complete impression can be pieced out from the details given about rules, penalties, and time of meeting. The most surprising characteristic of this club of authors was the harmony which

1. *Ibid.*, No. 132.

prevailed among them. Upon entering, the members were required to lay aside their personal differences, and literary antagonists were accustomed to "sit together in a peaceable Confederacy, and light their Pipes friendly at the same Candle!" [1] Gordon's picture is in every way remarkable; for when essayists contrived imaginary clubs, it was not generally for the purpose of glorifying the institution in so idealistic a manner.

Club life did not run quite so smoothly for James Heywood's Amicable Club. In a letter "To the Author of the Freethinker," [2] Heywood describes a pleasant company of twelve members, who meet with no other end than "to be soberly chearful" in their conversation. In the course of the letter it transpires that the club meets "during the two Winter-Quarters" every Monday and Friday evening; that *The Freethinker* is read aloud at their meetings; that their hours are from seven to ten o'clock; and that they are all between twenty-four and thirty-four years of age. The harmony of the society had been disrupted by a disagreement over one of the rules which Heywood had sought to introduce, namely, "That every Member shall spend One Shilling, and no more." Six members voted in favor of the provision, and six held out for a full bottle of wine to each man. *The Freethinker* is requested to break the deadlock by stating what amount of wine it was proper to drink at such meetings. The reply commends the society's program, and moderately advises against the full bottle.

Henry Carey has left to posterity one description of club life that shows how little human nature has changed in the last two hundred years. His poem entitled "The Spunger" portrays in the character of Toby Swill the perennial nuisance who allows his friends to pay his way. Toby, in Carey's verses, drinks from morning till night, but generally manages to be absent when the reckoning is called.

1. Thomas Gordon, *The Humourist* (1725), II, 169.
2. *Letters and Poems on Several Subjects* (1726), pp. 188–191.

The only thing that can damp his buoyant spirits is the appearance of the bill.

> Pay but his Shot,
> 'Tis all forgot,
> And he again is gay;
> He'll stand the Rub
> Of a whole Club
> To drink and not to pay.[1]

The influence of the fictitious clubs of Addison and Steele is admirably illustrated in the essay on "A Blundering Club," reprinted from *Fog's Journal* in *The Gentleman's Magazine* for March, 1732. The author begins by acknowledging the precedent of "some essay writers" who had concerned themselves with the history of the clubs. The reference is made unmistakable by the mention of the Mohock Club and the Female Romp Club of *The Spectator*, and of the Little and Tall Clubs of *The Guardian*. The Blundering Club was made up of a group of men who had formerly pretended to various branches of wisdom, among others the power "to foretell things past, present, and to come." Their contradictions and errors had led them to abandon prophecy and to form a club dedicated to inaccuracy. Each member was sworn "*to Act . . . contrary to Truth, Reason, and Demonstration, and to endeavour to improve the Art of Blundering.*"[2] The satire on people who are careless about facts is well submerged in the humorous description of the club's meetings. It comes to the surface, however, in the closing sentence.

They eat voraciously; and by a modest Computation, this Club, which does not consist of 300 Persons, destroy as much as would serve a whole Army; nay above a Million of People dine every Day the worse for what they devour.[3]

1. *Poems on Several Occasions* (1729), p. 203.
2. *The Gentleman's Magazine*, ii (1732), 647.
3. *Ibid.*, p. 648.

The sketch is drawn with a good deal of skill and is not on the whole unworthy of the pattern admittedly followed by its author.

WARD'S *SATYRICAL REFLECTIONS*

No discussion of the fictitious club can be complete without some recognition of a singular book by Edward Ward which was published from time to time under various titles during the first half of the eighteenth century. It appeared first in 1709 in two eight-page octavo pamphlets, the first being called *The History of the London Clubs, or, the Citizens Pastime*, and the second bearing the title, *The Second Part of the London Clubs*. These slender pamphlets were little more than a sample of the completed work, which was doubtless already in preparation in 1709. The title-pages list the clubs treated and ascribe the pamphlets to "the Author of the London Spy." Taken together they furnish descriptions of eleven imaginary societies, with verses and anecdotes interspersed through the expository matter.

In the following year (1710), a fifth volume was added to Ward's *Works* by the publisher John Phillips. The volume bore the title, *Satyrical Reflections on Clubs: In xxix Chapters. . . . By the Author of the London-Spy*. That it grew out of the brief *History* of 1709 is clear from the fact that the descriptions of the original eleven clubs are included, with additions, in the *Satyrical Reflections*. The title-page lists headings for twenty-nine chapters, but omits three chapters actually to be found in the book,[1] and the numbering is incorrect after the fifth chapter. The total number of chapters comes to thirty-two. The *Satyrical Reflections* furnished the basis of a number of subsequent editions which appeared from time to time between 1710 and 1756, most of which are inaccessible. In

1. *I.e.*, Chapters V, XXI, XXVIII.

1756, twenty-five years after Ward's death, a "seventh edition" was published with the title, *A Compleat and Humourous Account of all the Remarkable Clubs and Societies in the Cities of London and Westminster, from the R[oya]l S[ociet]y down to the Lumber-Troop*. This volume is reprinted from the *Satyrical Reflections* without important variations of any sort.

Ward's account of London clubs has been the source of certain misapprehensions on the part of writers on club life in the eighteenth century, because of their general failure to appreciate his purpose in writing the book. His ostensible intention is stated plainly enough in the opening chapter. He has observed that the clubs of London are noxious to the public weal, because they foster drunkenness and the spread of seditious doctrines.

> Therefore, all that I shall promise is, *A Merry History of the divers Clubs, and Societies, both Famous and Infamous, that for Sixty Years, and upwards, have been publickly Noted about* London, *for advancing and encouraging all those Vices, Immoralities, Follies, and Indecencies, that they ought to be asham'd of: The same being Imbellish'd with abundance of pleasant Stories, Jests, Poems, and comical Transactions, pertinent thereto, that the World may see herein, the old Proverb verefi'd, viz.* That Birds of a feather flock together.[1]

Thus Ward insists upon his reformative motive, but promises to make his book humorous. In order to see that he did not take the work seriously, we have only to look as far as the dedication "To that Luciferous and Sublime Lunatick, the Emperor of the Moon," where he writes:

> Besides, as I have principally treated of the Madness of Mankind in the following Sheets so I thought the Lunacies of this World a proper Subject to entertain your Highness, that you might discover thereby, what a wonderful Influence your glittering Pomp has upon all sublunary Mortals.

1. *Satyrical Reflections on Clubs* (1710), p. 10.

To look for sober facts after such prefatory facetiousness is absurd.

The clubs described in the book are made up for the most part of people from the lowest strata of London society. The Virtuoso's Club and the Knights of the Golden Fleece are composed of laborers and tradesmen who ludicrously ape the clubs of their social superiors. The seventh chapter describes the Surly Club, at which porters, watermen, and carmen gather to make contributions to the vernacular of Billingsgate. Each club is celebrated in some sort of verse, which is generally as scurrilous as the expository prose that introduces it. Occasionally, as in the accounts of the Atheistical Club and the Lying Club, Ward succeeds in being entertaining. For the most part, however, the book is not worthy of the literary historian's notice except as an example of the pruriency of its author's imagination, which is abundantly illustrated elsewhere.

The unwarranted assumption that these clubs really existed hardly needs exploding. It is utterly inconceivable that they used the designations ascribed to them. Even the existence of parallel clubs is in some cases incredible, though we grant the prevalence of the vices in which Ward shows them to have engaged. His clubs are devices for revealing debauchery rather than pictures of club life. The accounts of the Kit-Cat and Beefsteak Clubs, — societies which, as has already been shown, are grossly misrepresented, — seem to have been introduced at the end of the book as an afterthought, largely to lend an air of actuality to the whole performance. Ward did not need to fear that the public for whom he was writing would detect the inaccuracy of these two final chapters.

On the whole, then, it seems to have been Ward's purpose to amuse a group of readers whose stomachs were strong enough for anything by administering certain perfunctory thrusts at the depravities of low life, rather than to depict genuine London brotherhoods. Such a conclusion is in no way startling in view of the parallel use of the fictitious clubs in *The Spectator* a year after the publication of the *Satyrical Reflections*. To see how much more subtly Steele used the device than Ward, it is only necessary to compare the two authors' descriptions of an Ugly Club.[1] The book of the brewer-satirist, with its seven editions, is merely one more bit of evidence as to the vogue of club fictions in the early years of the century.

No attempt has been made to record all the imaginary societies created during this period. It seems sufficient to present the most successful fabrications, with an eye to showing how the author adapted them to the predilections of his readers and his own artistic ends. That the fashion persisted in the latter half of the century, along with others of Swift's time, is clear from such inventions as the clubs described by Goldsmith in *The Busy Body* for October 13, 1759. In spite of their frequent reappearance, however, the later fictitious societies were clearly derivative. They were the product of a past age rather than an expression of their own.

1. *The Spectator*, Nos. 17, 32, 78, and *Satyrical Reflections*, pp. 79–84.

CHAPTER IV

The Club Framework in the Essay Periodicals

FORESHADOWINGS

THE popularity of the club fiction is nowhere better exemplified than in the periodical literature of the time. Such early successes as *The Postboy rob'd of his Mail* taught the device to journalists as different as Ward and Addison. Mr. Spectator's club was so much a part of his papers that his imitators could seldom bring themselves to do without a society of some kind that served to bind together their essays. Although the early history of the club device has been traced through the more important precursors of *The Spectator* in the process of source-hunting,[1] no attempt has been made to follow the fortunes and misfortunes of the device *per se* from beginning to end.

The Athenian Mercury, John Dunton's question-and-answer periodical, which began its influential career on March 17, 1691, was the first to allege a club as its sponsor. At the outset, the answering of "all *ingenious and curious Enquirers* into *Speculations*, Divine, Moral and Natural, &c." was undertaken by Dunton with the help of only Richard Sault, a mathematician, who was the husband of the publisher's half-sister. The project soon became too

---

1. See Professor Graham's excellent account of the origins of the club idea in *The Beginnings of the English Literary Periodicals* (New York, 1926). G. S. Marr comments on some of the advantages of the method in *The Periodical Essayists of the Eighteenth Century* (1924), p. 16.

much for them, however, and Samuel Wesley's assistance was enlisted. These three, with the aid of a Dr. John Norris, formed the only actual basis for the Athenian Society which was supposed to answer the inquiries.[1]

The society was at first kept much in the background. Except for the use of the plural "we," there was nothing to indicate its existence until May 5, when an advertisement in Number 13 made the following announcement:

We have now taken into our Society *a Civilian, a Doctor in Physick, and a Chyrurgeon, on purpose to be more serviceable to the Age.*

Accordingly, questions relating to the sciences of these new men were cordially solicited. On June 16, an advertisement directed against an imitator of *The Athenian Mercury* was "*Publish'd by Order of the whole* ATHENIAN SOCIETY." [2] The preface to the second volume, besides giving sundry directions to questioners, remarked bluntly:

We have yet further to tell the World, that we have now fix'd our Society, *both as to* Number and Privacy, *and desire (notwithstanding many importunities to the contrary) to continue so in both.*

Another undertaking of the society was announced in the supplement to the third volume under the heading, "Proposals for Printing a Book Entitled, The young Students Library . . . Written by the Athenian Society." It was from such haphazard statements as these that the early readers of *The Athenian Mercury* gleaned their meager information about the club which purported to answer their questions.

The widespread curiosity concerning the authorship of the periodical is easy to understand. Many of the questions were singularly recondite, and the value of the

1. Walter Graham, *The Beginnings of the English Literary Periodicals*, p. 17.
2. Vol. ii, No. 7.

answers depended largely upon the ability of the exposi-
tors. If the unrevealed society were large and learned, the
querists could not but be satisfied. It was probably with
this in view that Dunton created the club myth. He realized, no doubt, that if the names of the actual authors
were set to the work, it would lose greatly in prestige.

On the first day of April, 1693, there was issued from the
press of James Dowley a publication designed to reassure
the readers of *The Athenian Mercury* about the authoritative nature of the society's *dicta*. An advertisement appeared on May 10 of that year,[1] announcing the publication of *The History of the Athenian Society, for the Resolving
all Nice and Curious Questions. By a Gentleman, who got
Secret Intelligence of their Whole Proceedings*. Although the
History was written by Charles Gildon and published by
another bookseller, Dunton's connection with it is clear.
The *History* was printed in such a way that it could be conveniently bound with the half-sheet folio pages of the periodical. It was advertised by Dunton. And it was written
by a friend of the publisher who was soon to collaborate
with him on *The Post-boy rob'd of his Mail*. Besides, the
History itself was obviously designed both to increase and
to capitalize the vogue of *The Athenian Mercury*.

It is from Gildon's folio pamphlet that Dunton's
readers first learned the nature of the hypothetical Athenian Society. The society's historian states definitely that
it was Mr. John Dunton who conceived the idea of publishing the periodical. The work was begun by the mathematical member, whose knowledge and acumen were
unbounded.

But as this Undertaking was too great for any one man to go
through with . . . it was thought fit, both for Ease, Dispatch,
and the fuller Satisfaction of all men, to receive in several Members to the composing a just number, for compleating the Under-

1. Vol. vii, No. 13.

taking, by having men qualified with all sorts of Learning, that so all sorts of Questions might receive just Answers.[1]

Accordingly, twelve became the number of members. The group consisted of a divine, a philosopher, a physician, a poet, a mathematician, a lawyer, a civilian, a chirurgeon, an Italian, a Spaniard, a Frenchman, and a Dutchman, the last four being merely interpreters in their respective languages and not connected with the expository business of the group. Although the historian admitted that he did not know all eight of the savants well enough to describe them, he gave glowing eulogies of the divine, the physician, and the mathematician. These accounts were designed, however, to show their erudition rather than their personal characters.

The Athenian Society is unique among the fictitious clubs of the early periodicals in that it was survived by an engraving which shows it in session. The frontispiece to the *History* [2] reveals the twelve members seated behind a long table with papers before them and engaged in answering queries. Various emblematic devices surround the central group, and below are explanatory verses which begin:

> Behind the Scenes, sit mighty we
> Nor are we known, nor will we be
> The World, and we exchanging thus
> While we find chat for them, they Work for us.[3]

As in the case of the descriptions of the members, the intention is to render the group authoritative and not to give it a personal interest.

Gildon's *History of the Athenian Society* does little beyond establishing the credibility of *The Athenian Mercury* and promoting its circulation by indiscriminate puffing. The club, as in the separate issues of the paper, is a very

1. *The History of the Athenian Society* (1693), p. 12.
2. Used also in *The Athenian Oracle*, vol. IV.
3. *The History of the Athenian Society*, p. 31.

nebulous organization. There was no such necessity for revealing the personality of the members as there was in the essay periodicals which interested themselves in the reformation of manners, nor did the club ever intrude into the main section of the paper, where the questions were answered. Dunton met fairly the charge that the paper "is a Mercenary Design to get a Peny" by answering:

And I'd fain know what even the whole Company's Design *is in printing the* Holy Bible, *don't they expect to* get *by it.*[1]

Clearly the authors were not interested in the club except as a bit of mechanics; its artistic possibilities never fully occurred to them. Nevertheless, *The Athenian Mercury* played an important part in the history of the device in the periodicals. It furnished a precedent for the use of a society of gentlemen as the framework of a number of later publications; it showed how useful the plan could be in producing credence in the author's work; and it revealed the value of a diversified *dramatis personae*.

It was not until Defoe began *The Review* in 1704, seven years after the cessation of *The Athenian Mercury*, that the imaginary club was used in connection with the reformation of contemporary manners. Defoe's periodical had, during its first two years, two separate departments. With the main section, which dealt with matters of trade, foreign relations, and domestic politics, this discussion has no particular concern, interesting as it is to the student of Defoe's economic theories and his place in Queen Anne politics. Appended to this editorial section was a department called "Advice from the Scandalous Club," the aim of which is fully stated by the author in the preface to his first collected volume. When Defoe undertook *The Review*, he feared that the substantial, profitable nature of his essays would not be sufficient to recommend them to a pleasure-loving society.

1. Preface to vol. 1.

To get over this Difficulty that secret hand, I make no Doubt that directed this [The Review's] Birth into the World, Dictated to make some sort of Entertainment, or Amusement at the end of every Paper upon the immediate Subject, then on the Tongues of the Town, which Innocent Diversion, would hand on the more weighty and Serious Part of the Design, into the heads and Thoughts of those, to whom it might be useful.

Defoe's method of entertaining his public was to devise a fictitious society of gentlemen, the Scandalous Club, whose opinions were to form the diverting part of the paper.

And whether Friend or Foe, one Party or another, if any thing happens so scandalous, as to require an open Reproof, the World may meet with it there.[1]

This openly stated reformative purpose is one of Defoe's greatest contributions to the development of the club device and to the essay periodical in general, as it forms a distinct departure from the avowed aim of *The Athenian Mercury*.

The amusing part of *The Review* appeared first in Number 2 on February 26, 1704, its heading being, "*Mercure Scandale:* OR, ADVICE from the Scandalous CLUB. Translated out of *French*." Although he tells the reader that the group was "long since established in *Paris*" and that a report of its meetings forms a necessary part of his account of the affairs of France, the author at once disregards his extraordinary apology and begins to introduce English matters into the department. The introductory announcement insists upon the impartiality of the club and its intention of avoiding personalities.

They who would not be censur'd by this Assembly, are desired to act with caution enough, not to fall under their Hands; for they resolve to treat Vice, and Villanous Actions, with the utmost Severity.

1. *The Review*, I, 4.

In the early numbers of *The Review*, the Scandalous Club [1] devoted a large share of its attention to the errors and misrepresentations of newspapers. Defoe attacked them with the utmost vigor as creating false impressions in the mind of the public through ignorance or downright dishonesty. The society soon turned to contemporary manners, however; and in Number 8 action was taken against the blasphemous practise of drinking the health of the church. Tales of private wrongs were often introduced at the meetings, such as that of the Newcastle coal merchant who forged letters to make his product increase in value, and that of the son who refused to aid his father in time of need. [2] These and countless other exposures of vicious behavior, like the remarks on dueling in Number 14, had much the same purpose as the essays of *The Tatler*.

The use of the fictitious letter to tell a story and give a moral was also managed through the club. In Number 53 a rake wrote for advice, reporting that he had seduced the young woman whom he was to marry. The society analyzed his crime very thoroughly and gave him the following directions:

1. That he immediately apply himself to the Father, and offer to Marry the young Woman, *if she be Fool enough to have him.*

2. That he agree to tell all the World *his Name*, that no other weak Sister may venture upon him.

3. That since he has declar'd himself such a Villain, as not to be fit for Human Society, he would please to dispose himself into her Majesty's Service, where he may Expiate his Crime by the Service of his Country, and perhaps stop a Bullet from killing an honester Man.

---

1. The name of the club called forth many epistolary objections (1, 115, 151, 156, 168). Eventually (1, 199) Defoe compromised by writing "The Scandal. Club" at the head of his department, but he showed that he always considered "Scandal." an abbreviation.

2. Vol. 1, No. 11.

4. There is another Method to rid his Native Country of such a Betrayer of Secrets, and that is, to *hang himself out of the way*; but they Advise him to let that be the last Remedy he takes, when all other means fail.

It is not difficult here to distinguish the pen of Defoe from the pen of Steele. But the moral position involved is strikingly like that of some of the epistolary essays in *The Tatler* and *The Spectator*.

It has been customary to relate *The Review* to *The Athenian Mercury* by asserting that Defoe was imitating Dunton in introducing the answers to queries in his paper. The theory is not easy to maintain. In the first place, Defoe did not at the beginning invite questions, nor even correspondence. The inquiries in the first volume are of no great bulk, and a number of them are requests for explanations of the faulty passages in certain newspapers. It is likely that Defoe wrote these himself, beside many of the questions on morals. The precedent of Dunton's paper seems to have affected *The Review*'s readers sooner than its author. In Number 79 there is a typical request for pure information in the query about "Whether Glass is a Body or Quality." Defoe shows some surprise at the question and in answering it lacks the confidence of the Athenian Society. *The Review*, No. 80, shows a marked impatience on Defoe's part with those who trouble him with metaphysical questions. He prints two very abstruse queries on the immortality of the soul with the introductory comment:

We think there never was a plainer Proof, that one Man may ask more Questions; than all the World can Answer; than in the following Case.

In spite of the journalist's attitude the questions kept on coming. When he produced the September supplement to the first volume, Defoe noted the peculiar turn of his

Scandalous Club papers by implying in the introduction that "answering Questions and deciding Controversies" were "absolutely remote and foreign to their first Design." He was so hard put to it that he was forced to make the following admission:

> And as, perhaps, the Hand that operates in this Work, being *allegorically* rather than *significantly* call'd a *Society*; may be for sundry Reasons uncapable of Performance in so vast a Variety as is like to come before him: So he thinks no Injury to the Undertaking, to let the World know, they must be content to be answered in the best manner he can.
>
> He assures the World, here is not, as was pretended in the *Athenian Mercury*, a Professor in all the Heads, which the Inquisitive World can propose.

After such a statement, no further evidence need be produced to show that the use of the club to answer questions was not part of an original design to imitate *The Athenian Mercury*.

Although the Scandalous Club papers purport to describe actual sessions of the group, the picture is somewhat indistinct. Occasionally we get a glimpse of some concrete detail of organization. In Number 3 of the first volume, for example, the director is mentioned as being ordered by the society to rebuke a news-writer of *The London Gazette* for an inaccuracy. Number 14 implies that a clerk and a doorkeeper were in attendance at the meetings. There are also a few instances in which particular members are singled out.[1] In the second of the supplements,[2] which came to be issued monthly when the department threatened to become too bulky, there was called to the attention of the club a letter protesting against the abuses of the privileges of burying grounds.

1. *E.g.*, I, 184.
2. Pages 25–26.

What a hard World is this, said a Member of the Society, that when a Man is so Civil as to Dye among his Neighbours, he can't have leave to be buryed among 'em!

Such individualizing of members is rare, however, and in several numbers Defoe writes in his own person, without constructing the club background at all. On the whole, the Scandalous Club acts rather as an impersonal, undifferentiated unit than as several real men.

The incompleteness of Defoe's revelation of his imaginary senate aroused some curiosity among his readers. In the fourth supplement, for December, 1704, he printed a letter from a correspondent who asked directly whether one man or a society was responsible for the lucubrations of the Scandalous Club. Defoe's answer implied that the doubt arose only from the obtuseness of the querist.

And therefore so far he is plainly in the Wrong, and his Observations was order'd to be enter'd in their Books among *Groundless Scruples* rais'd at the Society, *Fol.* 12. No. 2750. and left for him to make out at his Leisure.

On May 15, 1705, however, Defoe threw some interesting light on the question by announcing "*That* the Scandal. Club, *who* are now *as really a Society, as before* they were not, *will Publish their Proceedings in a Paper by it self, every* Wednesday *and* Friday; *in which, perhaps, the Readers may be more oblig'd both as to Profit and Delight, than they were before.*" [1] The new publication, entitled *The Little Review; or, an Inquisition of Scandal,* carried on the proceedings of the Scandalous Club much as they had been before until it was finally dropped with Number 23 on August 22, 1705. The task of maintaining the popular department seems to have been too exacting for the busy journalist, and it is not difficult to believe that he actually turned the

1. II, 124. See *The Little Review* (Nos. 1, 21) for other implications of plurality of authorship.

work over to a group of friends for the remainder of its
existence.[1]

The fictitious society, as managed by Defoe, shows a
number of marked advances over the obscure figment of
Dunton's imagination, the debt of *The Review* being a very
general one. Although in the later periodical individual
members are not characterized at all and are rarely singled
out, they at least appear before us in session. The reader
is constantly reminded that he is receiving the judgment
of a society instead of the dogmas of a single man. The
group serves as a high court of justice, a function quite
different from that of Mr. Spectator's club and the clubs
of his imitators; and it is the old aim of providing authority
which precludes any dramatic intent that Defoe may have
had. The avowed reformative purpose of the Scandalous
Club papers is what links them with the later periodicals,
and explains the introduction of the fictitious letter,[2] which
was used with such success in *The Tatler* and *The Spectator*.

After the beginning of *The Review*, the fictitious club
developed rapidly as a piece of periodical machinery. In
the first number of *The Rehearsal*, which appeared August
5, 1704, there is a suggestion that a club is behind the
paper which Leslie was attacking. Countryman remarks:

> And there is another *hard* word in what you quoted out of
> *Cassandra*, that is *principles*. It is some *outlandish* word. I
> never heard it, master *Observator*, from *you*, or any of our *club*.

Nothing was made of this society, however, and the paper
continued to follow the dialogue form.

1. Compare the preface to Charles Leslie's *Rehearsal* (rep. 1750), I, iii,
which says "that the *author* undertook not this task to make diversion for the
town, nor would let himself down to kick and cuff with *Tutchin*, *De Foe*, and the
rest of the *scandalous club* (as they were not ashamed to call themselves)." For
a similar reference, see *The Bagford Ballads*, ed. J. W. Ebsworth (1878), II, 830.

2. It is perhaps worth noting that Defoe regularly prints replies to the letters which his club receives. Steele and Addison often accomplished the same
end by allowing the letters to speak for themselves.

The value of a fictitious group of gentlemen was more fully appreciated by Ned Ward when he undertook, in 1707, *The Weekly Comedy: or, the Humours of a Coffee-House*. On the first page of each number was printed a list of the eighteen men who were to take part from time to time in the coffee-house conversation which made up the various issues.[1] The initial number, which appeared on August 13, announces the plan of the paper by means of a prologue spoken by Bohee, the coffee-man:

> *The* Soldier, Gamester, Sharper, *and the* Beau,
> *Shall in true Colours all their Vices show:*
> *The* Miser, Lawyer, Conjurer *and* Quack,
> *The* Merchant, *and the* Knave *that Jobs in Stock,*
> *Shall open each the Mistries of their Trade,*
> *And how their subtile Wiles and Snares are laid:*
> *The wav'ring* Fox *that changes with the Times;*
> *The Jingling* Poet, *stuff'd with Songs and Rhimes;*
> *The Frothy* Punster, *and the Downright* Dealer;
> *The* News-hound; *the* Projector; *and the* Sailer;
> *The Merry Roaring* Rake *that lives apace,*
> *And Values nothing but his Friend and Glass,*
> *All on our Stage agree to play their Parts,*
> *And shew their sundry Vanities and Arts.*
> *But e'er we draw the Curtain, let me see*
> *Who wants fresh* Coffee, Chocolate, *or* Tea.
> *Drink, Gentlemen, for that's the only way*
> *To save poor* Bohee, *tho' you damn our* Play.

The plan is carried out with not a little success. As the different characters sit about tables and talk over the news of the day, each reveals in his remarks the foibles of a social type. Although Ward's satiric position is everywhere evident, his particular spokesmen are Bohee, the coffee-man, and Blunt, the plain-dealer. In Number 2 the latter rebukes Nice, the beau, for his foppery and loose living,[2] and

1. Another *Weekly Comedy* much like this one ran for at least ten numbers beginning May 10, 1699. See Walter Graham, *The Beginnings of the English Literary Periodicals*, p. 40.
2. Compare No. 6.

remonstrates to Bays against the servile tricks of the poet's trade. Except in the case of his two favorites, Ward shows no mercy to the characters whom he has created, but looses his irony upon them at every turn. Thus Harlem, the news-writer, remarks to the company:

Ah Gentlemen! we that Live in this Religious Town, little think how busie the Devil may be in the Country.[1]

Even in their conversations on current events, the men are obviously satiric puppets, — straw men for Ward to knock down.

The resemblance of the *dramatis personae* of *The Weekly Comedy* to a fictitious club is marked. There is a definite coffee-house, at which Bohee is a fixture, where the group regularly assembles for conversation. The characters are always the same, no random visitors being admitted; and although the whole number never convenes at one time, the exclusiveness of the group suggests club membership. Although Ward observed the dramatic form of arrangement, his purpose was obviously not to publish a play in instalments, but to present news and comments on contemporary manners in a novel fashion. The method is simple and on the whole effective, since the reader soon becomes acquainted with the various characters and accepts the morals revealed in their speeches more readily than if the author's didacticism were immediate. As coffee-house talk the papers are unconvincing, it being everywhere apparent that Ward is behind the curtain pulling the wires. Nevertheless, *The Weekly Comedy* of 1707 anticipates the practise of a number of later periodicals in that it satirizes manners from several points of view, each represented by a person of a distinct social type.

Of much less significance in the development of the device is *The British Apollo, or, Curious Amusements for the Ingenious . . . Perform'd by a Society of Gentlemen,* which

1. No. 8.

enjoyed a considerable degree of popularity from 1708 to 1711. Although the preface uses the plural pronoun "we," the nature of the club which was responsible for the paper is not revealed. The appearance of "society" on the title-page, if not in direct imitation of *The Athenian Mercury*, is at least to be explained in the same manner as Dunton's fictitious club. It lent authority to the replies to the querists. The club was in no sense a framework, nor had it any influence upon the later developments of the device.

THE TATLER, THE FEMALE TATLER, AND THE SPECTATOR

In spite of the fact that *The Tatler* had no club for a framework, Steele's first periodical venture plays such an important part in the evolution of the device that it cannot here go unnoticed. For clubless though it is in the early numbers, it gradually builds up a *dramatis personae* with whom the reader becomes familiarly acquainted. First of all there is Isaac Bickerstaff himself, whose character Swift had begun for Steele in *Predictions for the Year 1708*. The worthy old gentleman gradually reveals himself, ostensibly through his own pen, in his reflections on such scenes as the Easter walk with Colonel Ramble, or the five-hour encounter with the "three Merry, and two Honest Fellows," [1] until he becomes as genuine a person as Steele's readers had ever had an opportunity of meeting in literature. At Number 10 it suddenly transpires that Mr. Bickerstaff has a half-sister, Mrs. Jenny Distaff, who performs his editorial duties while he is away in the country. The vivacious lady shows in this essay, as in her later contributions to *The Tatler*,[2] the influence of Mr. Bickerstaff. Having invented a half-sister, Steele became interested in the game, and in Number 11 printed a letter from D. Distaff which traces the history of the ancient

1. *The Tatler*, No. 45.
2. Nos. 33, 36–38, 247, in all of which Steele had a hand.

family of Staff back to one Jacobstaff, an astronomer, who flourished some time before the reign of Henry II. The essayist amuses himself by inventing various collateral branches of the family and carries on the joke in several subsequent numbers,[1] until the reader ends by feeling on rather friendly terms with anyone in "-staff." It was this family introduced in *The Tatler* that furnished the precedent for those used in the place of clubs as the framework for such periodicals as *The Guardian*, *The Grumbler*, and *The Champion*.

Another vital part of the *dramatis personae* of *The Tatler* is introduced in Number 58 in the little group of poetical friends who used to gather at Will's Coffee-house. During their conversations in this and subsequent numbers,[2] Will Dactyle, Jack Comma, Nick Crossgrain, Martius, Harry Spondee, and the rest characterize themselves until one knows what to expect from each of the different wits. They form an excellent vehicle for Steele's opinions as to true and false wit; but after arousing interest in the group, the essayist loses them among other frequenters of Will's and eventually forgets them altogether.

Besides the curious Society of Upholders, which has already been discussed, one other important club entered *The Tatler*. After the periodical had run more than half its course, its readers were introduced to the little society which gathered every evening at the Trumpet in Shire Lane. "Our club," writes Mr. Bickerstaff, "consisted originally of fifteen; but partly by the severity of the law in arbitrary times, and partly by the natural effects of old age, we are at present reduced to a third part of that number: in which however we have this consolation, that the best company is said to consist of five persons." Steele proceeds with his vivid characterizations of Sir Jeffrey Notch, the country gentleman; Major Matchlock, the retired

1. Nos. 14, 45, 75, 79. Compare the family in "-trix" in No. 35.
2. Nos. 60, 62, 63.

veteran; Dick Reptile, the good-natured old beau; and the bencher, who sets up for a wit. In addition to these remarkable portraits, Steele gives us a graphic account of the club in session.

Our club meets precisely at six o'clock in the evening; but I did not come last night till half an hour after seven, by which means I escaped the battle of Naseby, which the Major usually begins at about three-quarters after six; I found also, that my good friend, the bencher, had already spent three of his distichs, and only waiting an opportunity to hear a sermon spoken of, that he might introduce the couplet where "a stick" rhymes to "ecclesiastic." [1]

In the account of the ensuing conversation, the essay throws further light on the characters of the members and the manner in which they amused themselves.

It is precisely this intimacy of portraiture that constituted Steele's greatest contribution to the development of the fictitious club as a framework for the periodicals. Compared to the Trumpet Club, Dunton's Athenian Society and Defoe's Scandalous Club are mere names. Steele's Shire-Lane group is composed of men as authentic and genuine as the characters in *Humphrey Clinker*, and the earlier periodicals furnish no precedent for this feature of the club's treatment. In fact, the Trumpet Club is hardly foreshadowed anywhere except in Gildon's *Post-boy rob'd of his Mail*, of which, it will be remembered, there was a new edition in 1706, three years before Steele began *The Tatler*. Gildon's society of gentlemen was much more a means to an end than Steele's, and his characterization was noticeably less complete. But he gave names to his clubmen, showed them in actual conversation, and built up an intrinsic interest in his imaginary group in a way strikingly parallel to Steele's.

The Trumpet Club fits well into its author's program for

1. No. 132.

reforming manners. Since all the members are advanced in years, they furnish an excellent opportunity for remarks on growing old gracefully. Their gray hairs lend weight to their utterances, and we listen with some respect to the strictures of Mr. Bickerstaff and Dick Reptile on redundant language.[1] Steele evidently considered the intrinsic interest of the group a sufficient reason for introducing them, for aside from passing references [2] little is made of them after their first appearance, and they are not connected in any way with the publication of the periodical, their introduction being late. The Trumpet Club was only one of four social groups introduced in *The Tatler*, any one of which might have served Steele as a framework for his paper. The family device suggested in the "-staff" essays was brought into play, probably for the sake of variety, in *The Guardian*. But when Steele and Addison undertook *The Spectator* two months after the demise of *The Tatler* it was with a well-sustained club framework; and the imaginary society serving as a model was Steele's genial group which met at the Trumpet in Shire Lane.

Before examining the contributions of *The Spectator* to the evolution of the club fiction, it is well to consider an imitation of *The Tatler* which survived through one hundred eleven numbers, from July 8, 1709, to March 31, 1710. *The Female Tatler*, begun by Mrs. Manley,[3] pretended to be a subsidiary, not a competitor, to Steele's paper. In the opening number, Mrs. Crackenthorpe, the counterpart of Mr. Bickerstaff, remarks:

My Design is not to Rival his Performance, or in the least prejudice the Reputation he has deservedly gain'd: But as more Ridiculous Things are done every Day than ten such Papers can relate, I desire leave to prate a little to the Town, and try what Diversion my Intelligence can give 'em.

1. No. 137.   2. Nos. 196, 202, 208.
3. See P. B. Anderson, "The History and Authorship of Mrs. Crackenthorpe's *Female Tatler*," *Modern Philology*, XXVIII (1930–31), 354–360.

In spite of this avowal, *The Female Tatler* watched every move of its original and continually showed its dependence. Mrs. Manley imitates even *The Tatler*'s objects of satire, and does not hesitate to discuss affectation in dress, dueling, the relations between husband and wife, and other favorite topics of the essayists of her model.

At the end of Number 51, however, comes a sudden announcement which shows unexpected originality.[1]

> Mrs. Crackenthorpe *resenting the Affront offer'd to her by some rude Citizens, altogether unacquainted with her Person, gives Notice, that she has resign'd her Pretentions of Writing the* Female Tatler *to a Society of Modest Ladies, who in their turns will oblige the Publick with whatever they shall meet with, that will be Diverting, Innocent, or Instructive.*

Accordingly, the subsequent numbers have such headings as "Lucinda's Day" or "Emilia's Day," the six members of the invented society being made responsible from time to time, though not in exact rotation, for the essay of the day. There is no perceptible organization, and the club is a very informal one. Nevertheless, the device is often dramatic, many numbers [2] recounting the conversation which ensues when three or four of the ladies call upon another. The nature of the group precludes the coffee-house conviviality which flavors the gatherings at Will's and the Trumpet described in *The Tatler*. There is also remarkably little effort on the author's part to individualize the ladies. Any name might have been put to a given paper as well as any other. Thus it is always obvious that the method is simply a method, and the personal interest aroused by the group comes to practically nothing because the machinery is so ill concealed.[3] Nevertheless, this use of

---

1. According to Dr. Anderson the paper passed at this point out of Mrs. Manley's hands.   2. *E.g.*, Nos. 52, 53, 54, 62.

3. This society of ladies is used in a manner which makes it resemble more closely the society of gentlemen in *The Post-boy rob'd of his Mail* than either Defoe's club or the *Spectator* group.

the device is significant; for it makes a long stride from the Scandalous Club in the direction of the immortal club of *The Spectator*.

Although *The Spectator* was undoubtedly the most successful periodical with a club framework, its method, as we have seen, was not entirely original. By *The Review* it had been anticipated in the use of the device for the reformation of manners. By *The Weekly Comedy* and *The Tatler* it had been shown the way to a dramatization of contemporary foibles through an imaginary society, and *The Female Tatler* may be considered an actual experiment in this direction. There are, however, a number of advances, even innovations, in *The Spectator*, which became traditional in the essay periodicals.

In the first place, the club device was never before consistently sustained. It is true that many of the essays in *The Spectator*, like Addison's two series on Milton and on the pleasures of the imagination, are independent of the club framework; but there is rarely a sequence of more than half a dozen numbers into which the club does not somehow enter, and Mr. Spectator is always in the background. Number 1 informs the reader that the plan of the paper was "laid and concerted in a club" and goes on to explain:

I must further acquaint the reader, that though our club meets only on Tuesdays and Thursdays, we have appointed a committee to sit every night, for the inspection of all such papers as may contribute to the advancement of the public weal.

The club is kept in view until the conclusion of the original enterprise on December 6, 1712, with Number 555. The authors are careful to lead up to the dissolution of the society with the death of Sir Roger (No. 517), the marriage of Will Honeycomb (No. 530), the Templar's farewell to his poetical studies (No. 541), Captain Sentry's withdrawal to the country (No. 544), and Sir Andrew Freeport's renunciation of town life in favor of a meditative, philanthropic existence on his estate (No. 549). The tentative plans of Mr. Spectator for forming a new society [1] never appear serious; and the periodical ends logically with the passing of the original club. This intimate relationship between fictitious club and periodical is distinctly an innovation of *The Spectator*.

Equally original is the variety of uses which the club members are made to serve. Sir Roger de Coverley is portrayed as an embodiment of right-heartedness and sound virtue. By holding him up for admiration, his creators instruct their readers in the ideal relationship between master and servant, in enlightened charity, and in true hospitality. Will Honeycomb, on the other hand, is the object of gentle satire on the elderly fop and his obsession with fashion. When the essayists needed a mouthpiece for their own ideas, there was always Mr. Spectator ready to their hands; and the Templar could be called in to speak for them on things dramatic [2] or Sir Andrew Freeport on economic matters.[3] Steele appreciated the usefulness of the *dramatis personae* most concretely when in the farewell number of *The Spectator* he stepped out of his assumed character and addressed the world as plain Richard Steele. A certain bluntness not familiar in Mr. Spectator creeps into his style as he writes:

It is much more difficult to converse with the world in a real than a personated character. That might pass for humour, in the Spectator, which would look like arrogance in a writer who sets his name to his work. The fictitious person might contemn those who disapproved him, and extol his own performances, without giving offence. He might assume a mock authority without being looked upon as vain and conceited.

The whole plan on which the periodical was built furnished its authors with a freedom and a basis for imaginative

1. Nos. 549, 550, 553.   2. No. 541.   3. No. 232.

creation which led to the composition of some of the finest essays in our language. Another device might have done as well. Since the authors were writing in the reign of Queen Anne, it was a club.

Finally, *The Spectator* contributed to the evolution of the fictitious society of gentlemen in that it demonstrated to an unprecedented extent the dramatic value of the method. "The club," as Addison ingenuously remarked in Number 34, "is very luckily composed of such persons as are engaged in different ways of life, and deputed, as it were, out of the most conspicuous classes of mankind." The members were hence well suited to the portrayal of almost any social foible which the authors wished to expose. The dramatization does not consist simply of conversations between Mr. Spectator and individual members. In certain papers we see the whole group, assembled and in action. Thus in Number 34 when Mr. Spectator is receiving each member's advice on the "proper subjects for raillery," Addison shows the gentlemen delivering themselves in turn of arguments to prove that their particular social types should be spared. Number 174 recounts a good-natured, if unsuccessful, attempt on the part of Captain Sentry to settle a dispute between Sir Andrew and Sir Roger; and an admirable impression of the desultory conversation of the society is given in Number 359. Although there are not so many of these scenes as we could wish, *The Spectator* easily outstrips all its predecessors in its development of the dramatic values of the imaginary club.

Imitations

In planning *The Guardian*, the first number of which appeared March 12, 1713, a little more than three months after the suspension of *The Spectator*, Steele developed a new method of introducing his set of characters. The scheme of using for a framework a family instead of a club

THE LION'S HEAD AT BUTTON'S COFFEE-HOUSE

From the frontispiece of Charles Richardson's Notices
and Extracts Relating to the Lion's Head

This Head is to open a most wide and voracious Mouth, which shall take in such Letters and Papers as are conveyed to me by my Correspondents, it being my Resolution to have a particular Regard to all such Matters as come to my Hands through the Mouth of the Lion. There will be under it a Box, of which the Key will be in my own Custody, to receive such Papers as are dropped into it. Whatever the Lion swallows I shall digest for the Use of the Publick. This Head requires some Time to finish, the Workman being resolved to give it several Masterly Touches, and to represent it as Ravenous as possible. It will be set up in *Button's* Coffee-house in *Covent-Garden*, who is directed to shew the Way to the Lion's Head, and to instruct any young Author how to convey his Works into the Mouth of it with Safety and Secrecy. — *The Guardian.*

appears to have been the logical outgrowth of Steele's experiments with the "-staffs" in *The Tatler*. After outlining in Number 1 the aim of the paper, which does not differ materially from that of *The Tatler* and *The Spectator*,[1] Steele proceeded in Number 2 to intrench himself further in the character of Nestor Ironside and to describe the family around which the periodical was built. Mr. Ironside tells of his friendship with old Sir Harry Lizard and his son Sir Marmaduke, both deceased, and expresses his warm admiration for Lady Lizard, Sir Marmaduke's widow. "The members of this family," we are informed, "their cares, passions, interests, and diversions shall be represented from time to time, as news from the tea-table of so accomplished a woman as the intelligent and discreet Lady Lizard." The relation between this type of framework and the club method is obvious. *The Guardian* did not, however, show the sustained attention to its fictitious background that characterized *The Spectator*, and it cannot be said to have made any important contributions to the evolution of the structure of the periodicals beyond introducing for the sake of variety an alternative offshoot of the imaginary club.

On October 6, 1713, John Hughes, who had written a number of essays and letters for *The Spectator* and *The Guardian*, wrote to Addison to express his regret at Steele's sudden abandonment of *The Guardian* for *The Englishman*.[2] Apparently Hughes's stock of essay material was by no means exhausted; for his letter suggested that he would gladly undertake another periodical if he might count on Addison's assistance. He enclosed a prospectus of the work, together with part of the second number, that Addi-

1. See *The Guardian*, No. 98, in which Nestor Ironside asserts that he is a close friend of Isaac Bickerstaff, who "was succeeded by a gentleman of the same family, very memorable for the shortness of his face and of his speeches."
2. The final number of *The Guardian* appeared October 1, 1713. *The Englishman*, which had no club framework, was begun October 6.

son might "see an offer in it of a new invented character, with a cast of oddness in it, to draw attention, and to lay a foundation for a great variety of matter, and of adventures." Hughes gave the following explanation of the submitted fragment:

I must acquaint you that what I send is a sequel of a Paper which is to open the plan, and which describes a Society of learned men of various characters, who meet together to carry on a conversation on all kinds of subjects, and who empower the Secretary to draw up any of their discourses, or publish any of their writings under the title of *the Register*. By this means, I think, the Town might be sometimes entertained with dialogue, which would be a new way of writing, either related or set down in form, under the names of different speakers; and sometimes with Essays, or with Discourses in the person of the writer of the paper.[1]

As to form, at least, Hughes's project showed some ingenuity; but Addison was not to be inveigled into sharing the responsibility of the enterprise. On October 12, Hughes received a reply, which began as follows:

I am very much obliged to you for your kind letter and the specimen, which I read over with great pleasure. I think the title of *the Register* would be less assuming than that of *the Humanity Club*; but to tell you truly, I have been so taken up with thoughts of that nature for these two or three years last past, that I must now take some time *pour me délasser*, and lay in fuel for future work.[2]

Addison's pardonable weariness with the inexorable demands of a daily periodical did not prevent his encouraging Hughes to undertake it on his own account; but no paper appeared with either of the titles mentioned in the letter.

Hughes was not long discouraged by the rejection of his

1. *The Works of Joseph Addison* (1856), v, 411.
2. *Ibid.*, 412.

plan. He merely looked elsewhere for a collaborator. A month after he had received Addison's letter, he had formed an alliance with the prolific Sir Richard Blackmore and was hard at work on a new periodical called *The Lay Monk*, the first number of which was published November 16, 1713. *The Lay Monk*, though it ran for only forty numbers and expired on the fifteenth of the following February, is one of the most interesting of all the imitations of *The Spectator*, in that its fictitious club was more prominent than that of any other periodical of the time. The preface to the reprint of 1714 acknowledges the debt of the paper thus:

The Form, into which the best Writer among the Romans *generally chose to cast his Thoughts, was that of Dialogue, or Conversations related, in which the Persons introduc'd were all Philosophers, and the Discourses wholly serious; yet this he borrow'd from* Plato, *and others of the* Greeks, *whom he profess'd to imitate. But the introducing a Sett of Persons of different Humours and Characters, acting on some imaginary Occasion which might draw out a variety of Incidents and Discourses, and in which every Paper shou'd be an intire Piece, at the same Time that it is a Part of the whole, is the Invention of the Writer already mention'd, who seems at once to have introduc'd it, and carried it to Perfection.*

One other remark on the method is significant.

Some of the Essays in the following Sheets . . . had perhaps never appear'd at all, or not in this Manner, if the prevailing Taste of the Town had not seem'd to prescribe this Fashion of publishing them.

Here is ample evidence that the device was consciously introduced because periodical writers appreciated both its effectiveness and its popularity.

The first number of the paper informs the reader that a society of gentlemen had been meeting informally for about three years, when Sir Eustace Locker, "a Gentleman much esteem'd by the rest," proposed forming a monastic society, "that being separated from the Crowd, and de-liver'd from the Noise and Strife of the Busy, we may with greater Success pursue our Improvements, and enjoy the elegant Satisfaction of Friendship in Retirement." Ac-cordingly, rules were drawn up which provided for two meetings a week, the members being responsible in turn for papers on subjects of their own selection. Politics were strictly taboo at the club's discussions. Although vows of celibacy were not exacted, the marriage of a member auto-matically created a vacancy on the roster. The publication of *The Lay Monk* was undertaken by Mr. Ravenscroft, the secretary, at the suggestion of Sir Eustace Locker, who felt that the public should have the benefit of the club's specu-lations.

Number 2 parallels the corresponding number of *The Spectator* by giving characters of the members. The so-ciety is made up of Mr. Johnson, a critic; Dr. Lacon, a physician; Sir Eustace Locker, a philosopher; Sir Arthur Wimbleton, a middle-aged country gentleman; Ned Free-man, a young beau with a penchant for scholarly pursuits; and Mr. Ravenscroft himself, to whom we are indebted for this account of the others. After the secretary has given his own history in Number 3, the periodical becomes an ac-count of the transactions of the lay monastery. The fifth number is fairly typical in its material. The body of it is composed of a scientific essay, easily traceable to Black-more, which is introduced by the following remark:

The Reader of this Discourse will not, I imagine, want to be inform'd that the Author of it is Dr. Lacon, a Member of our Fraternity.

At the close of the paper, Mr. Ravenscroft invites corre-spondence from "all Gentlemen who will be pleas'd to communicate their Thoughts for Promoting our Design. . . . Note, Mr. Freeman makes the same Invitation to the Ladies."

It is the intrinsic interest of the club that makes the papers readable. Both the personalities of the members and the vicissitudes of the organization are skillfully disclosed. In Number 6 it appears that the name of the society had created suspicions of papacy, and the whole issue is devoted to a humorous description of the assault made upon the monastery by a mob of angry citizens. The destruction of the building was averted only through the sagacity of Sir Arthur Wimbleton, whose spirited harangue persuaded the attackers that the members of the club were all good protestants like themselves. Ned Freeman's discovery of a newly founded lay nunnery,[1] reported in Number 15, adds a new narrative interest to the account of the fraternity. The beau's adventures among the lay sisters caused much merriment at the club, especially since the escapade provoked a letter from the secretary of the sisterhood disclosing the whole incident. The rival society of ladies is kept in view by such means as the letter at the end of Number 21, which runs as follows:

Sir EUSTACE:
Look to your Fraternity. I have heard of a certain Creature, that by imitating the Voices of other Animals, draws them into its Reach, and then preys upon them. The *Lay-Nunnery* is a Decoy, and the *Sisters* have a Design on the *Lay-Brothers*. Be vigilant, and especially have an Eye upon NED FREEMAN.
Your Humble Servant,
Ralph Warnwell.

No misadventure occurred, however; and when at Number 40 the society decided to suspend publication, the original membership was still intact, even to Ned Freeman.

On the whole, the club device is better sustained in *The Lay Monk* than in any other periodical of the time. The connection between the society and the publication is fully

1. Probably suggested by *The Tatler*, No. 32, which describes the campaign of Rake against Madonella's protestant nunnery.

accounted for in the detailed introductory papers. Each essay fits naturally and easily into the form, those which are not made up of actual club proceedings being explained as the contributions of the secretary to the common undertaking. Characterization of the members penetrates a large number of the essays, and the periodical tends to deal with the club, its members, and its fate to the consistent subordination of satire on manners. What started as a mere trick of form became in *The Lay Monk* an end in itself.

Early in 1714, Steele returned to the essay periodical in *The Lover*, which ran through forty numbers between February 25 and May 27. His avowed aim was stated thus:

> After mature Deliberation with my self upon this Subject, I have thought, that if I could trace the Passion or Affection of Love, through all its Joys and Inquietudes, through all the Stages and Circumstances of Life, in both Sexes, with strict respect to Virtue and Innocence, I should, by a just Representation and History of that one Passion, steal into the Bosom of my Reader, and build upon it all the Sentiments aud Resolutions which incline and qualify us for every thing that is truly Excellent, Great, and Noble.[1]

A glance at a few of the essays reveals that Sir Richard was more concerned with stealing into the bosom of his reader than with moral inspiration; for the latter end is decidedly incidental.

The fictitious group whom Steele invented as his assistants are introduced in the first number. Most important is Mr. Severn, a highly eligible young bachelor, who has discovered the value of addressing his gallantries to mothers as well as daughters. The others are Mr. Oswald, a lonely widower; Mr. Mullet, a wealthy gentleman of fifty, whose life has been blighted by the loss of his lady and whose illusions have been shattered by repeated discoveries

1. *The Lover*, No. 1.

of the designs of match-making mothers; Mr. Johnson, a happily married gentleman; Mr. Wildgoose, a crotchety bachelor of fifty-three, who had been disappointed in love thirty years before; and finally Mr. Marmaduke Myrtle, in which character Steele writes.

This promising club of lovers suffered a great neglect as the successive issues of the paper followed one another. No connection is made between the society and the publication; nor do the members appear except in such random papers as Number 27, in which Mr. Severn receives a letter, and Number 29, which describes a mournful visit to Mr. Oswald. Mr. Myrtle's character is preserved through his comments on the letters he receives;[1] but even he seems only the shadow of a man, when compared to Mr. Spectator or Nestor Ironside. When *The Lover* came to a conclusion with Number 40, the club was left high and dry with no explanation of its further history. Indeed, Steele's tri-weekly readers had doubtless forgotten the society, so little was made of it in the later numbers.

The club device in *The Lover* appears to have been a perfunctory bit of mechanism, inserted as an easy, and by this time natural, way to introduce the paper to the public. Its neglect in the later numbers may ultimately be traced to the nature of Steele's material. The project was restricted to a defense of the tender passion against the glazed hardness of the Restoration attitude, an end not so friendly to the club method as the criticism of manners undertaken in *The Spectator*. The most significant feature of Steele's use of the device is the evidence therein presented of the logical connection between club and essay periodical which had built itself up in the mind of the author.

A letter from Thomas Burnet to his friend George Duckett, dated December 25, 1714, shows that at the time of his writing Burnet was preparing to publish a new periodical with a fictitious framework. The letter runs thus:

1. See Nos. 7, 9, 11, 12, 14, 17, etc.

I have writ three Grumblers, which I here send you; the first I think is a compleat piece; the second wants a little re-touching, which I expect from you. The Reason I make these Characters of my Brothers, rather than a Club, is because I would avoid imitation, and the *Spectator* has surfeited the world with Clubs.[1]

As will shortly appear, Burnet's family of Gizzards is so closely parallel to the Lizard clan of *The Guardian* that he cannot validly claim much originality. Nevertheless, his testimony as to the origin of the alternative device is valuable.

Burnet's *Grumbler* did not appear until February 24, 1715, on which day Number 1 greeted the world with the heading: "The Grumbler. By Squire Gizzard. To be con-tinued Weekly. *Non amo te, Sabidi . . .*" et cetera. Mar-tial's epigram has here some significance as a motto, for the grumbling feature of the paper was reasonably well sus-tained. The opening number presents a humorous account of Squire Anthony Gizzard's pedigree by tracing his an-cestry back as far as "*Humphry Gizzard*, who was killed in the left *Wing* of King *Richard* the Third's Army in *Bos-worth-Field.*" The Squire attributes his present undertak-ing to a necessity for giving vent to his grumbles, an afflic-tion that had long been recognized as hereditary in the Gizzard family.

The second number gives characters of Squire Gizzard's seven brothers and sisters, all of whom are constitutional grumblers except Tom, an illegitimate half-brother, who has his bar sinister to thank for abundant good spirits and a tolerant disposition toward the rest of the family. Tom Gizzard is obviously Burnet's favorite, and in the family arguments habitually speaks for the author. This is par-ticularly apparent in Number 4, which shows the Giz-zards "*grumbling* out their Censures on the New *Farce,*

1. *The Letters of Thomas Burnet to George Duckett*, ed. D. Nichol Smith (Oxford, 1914), pp. 76–77.

intitled the *What-d'ye-call it*." The criticism is humorous and trivial, but Burnet's genuine disapproval of the play shows in Tom's censure of it. To see the extent of Burnet's debt to *The Guardian* we have only to compare the fourth number of *The Grumbler* with Number 43 of the earlier periodical, in which Nestor Ironside visits the Lizard family on the morning after they have witnessed a performance of *Cato*. In *The Grumbler* Squire Gizzard goes to visit his family and finds them giving in character their judgments on a play, just as Lady Lizard and her family had done.

In one particular, Burnet's use of his fictitious framework was original. The author had little concern with serious matters, nor had he any sincere intention of reforming manners. He was young and witty, and wrote to amuse himself and the Town. The group which he chose as the *dramatis personae* served his ends admirably; but in securing his humorous effects, Burnet did not hesitate to turn his unsympathetic ridicule upon his imaginary people, a thing which the earlier experimenters with the form had generally eschewed.

It might be noted here that certain connections were suspected between the periodicals and actual clubs. Gay wrote, in *The Present State of Wit* (1711), that when Steele abandoned *The Tatler*, "immediately some of our Wits were for forming themselves into a Club, headed by one Mr. *Harrison*, and trying how they could shoot in this Bow of *Ulysses*."[1] Apropos of the newly begun *Spectator*, Gay remarked, a little later in the same essay:

Most People Fancy, from their frequency, that they must be compos'd by a Society; I, with all, Assign the first Places to Mr. *Steele* and *His Friend*.

There is an interesting hint of a similar nature in connection with Ambrose Philips's *Freethinker* in a letter which

1. This revival of *The Tatler* was actually carried on by Harrison, with the aid of Swift, Congreve, and others, until May, 1711.

Thomas Burnet wrote to George Duckett on April 6, 1718. The significant part reads as follows:

And now that I have mentioned the *Freethinkers*, I must tell you that there comes out twice a week a *Paper* of that Name, which is pretty well written; as you will see by the two that I send you in the Trunk. If any good whimsicall turn should come into your head, you may now and then work up a *Paper* and send it me; for though I am not the Author, yet I am one of a Club that revise every one before they go to the Press. And sometimes we quite work up a new Paper, when we do not like what is brought to us.[1]

It is only by interpreting the word "club" as a group of contributors to a joint enterprise that we can apply it to such collaborators as these. Although the plurality of authorship is common knowledge in the case of all three of these periodicals, there is no evidence that any organization bound the contributors together.

In the later imitations of *The Tatler* and *The Spectator*, the club framework was often present, though in many cases the device was used somewhat perfunctorily. *Town-Talk*, undertaken by Steele from December 17, 1715, to February 13, 1716, as a "series of letters to a lady in the country," has a recurring set of characters which tend to add life to the author's criticisms of dress, manners, and the theatre; but there is no true club. In *The Theatre* (1720), Steele produced a variation of the tea-table idea employed in *The Guardian*. The essays purport to be written by Sir John Edgar, whose son Harry is so much interested in the drama that the old gentleman recaptures some of his early enthusiasm for play-going. Harry has introduced his father to a society of virtuous ladies, the leader of whom, called Sophronia, knows many great actors. "It is therefore from the generous concern of Sophronia,"

1. *The Letters of Thomas Burnet*, p. 148.

writes Sir John Edgar, "that I am prevailed upon to undertake (in this public manner) the preservation and improvement of the English Theatre." [1] This looks like a
new purpose for an imaginary society. The members are
admirably characterized, and the reader is prepared for accounts of their meetings in the ensuing pages.

The third number of the periodical proposes a representative body "to approve, condemn, or rectify, whatever
shall be exhibited in the English Theatre." The group is
to consist of two players, one dramatic poet, three ladies
to represent the front boxes, two gentlemen of wit and
pleasure for the side boxes, three substantial citizens for the
pit, one lawyer's clerk and one *valet de chambre* for the first
gallery, and one journeyman baker for the upper gallery.
Steele tells of the election of these members and describes
the successful candidates. Thus he has admirably presented two club-like groups, either of which might serve as a
medium for his ideas on reforming the English stage. Having introduced them, however, he proceeds to ignore them
throughout the remainder of the paper. In the course of
the ensuing twenty-five numbers his interest veers from
the theatre to the South Sea Bubble, even his original purpose having been apparently forgotten. One is tempted to
infer that the two groups were introduced because they
gave an opportunity for character writing, a *genre* at which
Steele excelled.

The little knot of characters which enliven *The Plain
Dealer* (1724-1725) are a club in all but name. The clergyman, the critic, Major Stedfast, Ned Volatile, and the
Plain Dealer himself are the direct descendants of Mr.
Spectator's friends. Although they rarely, as in Number
101, appear all together, they figure prominently in the
papers from beginning to end. The vivacious Patty Amble,
of whom the Plain Dealer becomes more and more en-

1. *The Theatre*, No. 1.

amored as the periodical proceeds, is a most forgivable obstruction to her admirer's friendships and journalistic endeavors. One suspects that had it not been for the early intrusion of Patty, the club-like group of gentlemen might have received even more of the authors' attention.

The tenacity of the club tradition is curiously evident in *The Intelligencer*, which Swift and Thomas Sheridan undertook for twenty numbers in Dublin. The first paper, by Swift,[1] was published on May 11, 1728. In it is the following statement:

> But, because there are many effects of folly and vice among us, whereof some are general, others confined to smaller numbers, and others again, perhaps to a few individuals; there is a society lately established, who at great expense, have erected an office of Intelligence, from which they are to receive weekly information of all important events and singularities, which this famous metropolis can furnish.[2]

The remainder of the periodical is devoted largely to literary criticism and attacks on the enemies of the two authors. The society here mentioned is apparently forgotten, nor does it function at all except as a somewhat sketchy explanation of the title. Yet the opening number introduces it as a definite part of the reportorial machinery and seems to promise a certain prominence to the group by putting it in the title rôle. These circumstances can only indicate what a complete victory the club had gained over the traditions of the essay periodical.

If further evidence of the conquest were necessary, it would be available in another Dublin periodical, attributed to Patrick Delany and published, presumably, in 1729.[3]

1. For Swift's statement about the authorship of *The Intelligencer*, see his *Correspondence*, IV, 307–308.

2. *The Prose Works of Jonathan Swift*, ed. Temple Scott (1897–1908), IX, 314.

3. So it is listed by R. S. Crane and F. B. Kaye in *A Census of British News-*

The Tribune, which ran for only twenty-one numbers, was designed to improve the relations between Ireland and England by showing to each the point of view of the other. The second number, as usual, gives "the Characters of those Persons who are associated with me as my Colleagues." There is a retired merchant, Sir Humphrey Thorowgood, who has a country estate. There is Mr. Edward Thorowgood, his son, who has studied at the Temple and has traveled. There are a benevolent physician, a country squire of small property, and two other well-drawn members, who complete the "Tribunes-Club." Their conversations and individual remarks on Irish social and political conditions form the most lively part of *The Tribune*.

The device also occupied an important position in the early numbers of *The Grub-street Journal*, which was published under the editorship of Alexander Russell and John Martyn from 1730 to 1737. The handling of the fictitious society may be studied from the more accessible *Memoirs of the Society of Grub-street*, which is an authorized reprint of selections from the original *Journal*. The ostensible purpose of the paper was to carry on a systematic war against the Grub-Street hack and his "false confused histories, weak Treatises on any subject, low creeping Poetry, and groveling Prose." After describing the state of Grub Street and the necessity for repressing "the exorbitances of Authors, Book-sellers, Printers, and Publishers," the preface to the *Memoirs* continues:

This was the end and design of setting up *The Grub-street Journal*, by some Gentlemen; who, in order to carrie it on with the greater propriety, formed themselves into an imaginary Society, as meeting once a week at the Pegasus, which is a real house in Grub-street.[1]

---

papers and Periodicals, 1620–1800. I have seen only a London reprint in which the numbers are not separately dated.

1. *Memoirs of the Society of Grub-street* (1737), I, iv–v.

This attempt to connect the actual contributors to the paper with the fictitious group presented in Number 1 is made in strange terms. The meaning, however, is sufficiently clear; and it is regrettable that the author of the passage gave no more exact account of the function which the society was expected to perform.

The *dramatis personae* were selected for their susceptibility to ridicule. In Number 1 Mr. Bavius, the secretary of the club, describes some of the members whose literary output is to make up the paper. The leading spirits are Mr. Quidnunc, the scholiast, news critic for the group; Mr. Poppy, the poet, who is "ready to compose Panegyrics or Satires, Copies of verses from friends of Authors, Odes, Epithalamiums, Funeral Elegies, Anagrams and Acrostics, and annual Salutations from the City Bell-men to their worthy masters and mistresses, — at reasonable rates"; and Giles Blunderbuss, Esquire, historiographer to the society. Mr. Noodle and Mr. Numbscull are later elected to membership. Of this remarkable group Mr. Bavius is the only member who develops any personality. The others are obviously satiric puppets, not flesh-and-blood people. Although in several numbers [1] they are presented dramatically in club meetings with some effect, they are too often only the victims of the author's irony. A success with the device comparable to that of *The Spectator* was not possible when the imaginary group was so consistently the object of bitter attack. As issue followed issue, the importance of the society steadily decreased, until the group finally became as purely a matter of form as Defoe's Scandalous Club had been.

Two Edinburgh periodicals which appeared about this time show a closer relation to *The Spectator* in their treatment of the fictitious club. The earlier of these, *The Reveur* (1737–1738), begins with a vision essay, and gives no indi-

1. Nos. 3, 6, 15, etc.

cation that a society of gentlemen is intended until the fourteenth number.   Marr discusses the group thus:

> A number of characters are described. *Sir John Wischert* and his son, whom Wallace sets forth as examples to others; *Mr Jonathan Medley*, a bachelor of forty; *Mr Freeman*, a man of fortune; and, lastly, a clergyman. These Club members (if we may call them so) go walks through the town and have chats together in each other's houses. For example, at one of these meetings a sermon of the parson's (No. 27) is discussed.[1]

Although the imaginary society is managed with the same eye to dramatic effect that made Mr. Spectator's club so telling, its late introduction shows that it was by no means indispensable to the publication and, hence, that it must not be considered as a framework.

Such was not the case with the *Letters of the Critical Club*, which were published monthly in Edinburgh from January to June, 1738. The initial letter, dated January 2, is an ingeniously conceived reply of Jack Plyant, president of the Critical Club, to Ned Rhymer, who has written seeking admission. Jack Plyant's letter explains that the group was not in the habit of talking scandal, but was concerned with reforming manners.

> But, as you desired to be informed in the characters of the Members of our Society, I shall conclude this Letter with a description of them. Our Body, then, consists of five Members, and a Head, or President, that Place I have just now the Honour to possess; their Names are as follows, *Will Portly*, *Dick Crochet*, *Tom Meanwell*, the *Old Lady Courtly*, her Daughter *Miss Jeanie*, and your humble Servant, and you, since your Admission make the seventh.[2]

---

1. G. S. Marr, *The Periodical Essayists of the Eighteenth Century* (1924), p. 102.

2. *Letters of the Critical Club* (Edinburgh, 1738), pp. 8–9. The frontispiece of the collected edition shows five men and two women seated about a table.

The traditional characters of the members follow, and by the end of the letter, the club has been graphically introduced. The members here occupy a position comparable to that of John Hughes's lay monks; for each in turn contributes a letter to the periodical much as the monks had furnished papers for their meetings. In the *Letters of the Critical Club*, the fictitious society is used almost exclusively as a frame. Certain letters contain references to members,[1] but in the main the issues are devoted strictly to criticisms of literature and manners, with the occasional insertion of letters contributed by readers of the periodical. Although the dramatic possibilities of the method are thus neglected, the author takes his trick of structure seriously; and in the concluding letter, signed by Tom Meanwell, the reader is conscientiously informed that the club is to be dismissed until the coming winter.

One of the most striking instances of the widespread influence of Mr. Spectator's club is to be found in *The London Magazine*. Beginning with the issue of May, 1738, a fictitious political club was introduced, in a special department which survived for nearly twenty years. The purpose of the society was to satisfy a public desire for news of the state which could not with impunity be published in the form of parliamentary proceedings. The writer of the introductory letter, as secretary to the club, offers to submit "from Time to Time, Extracts of some of those political and other Debates that happen amongst us; because we think it may be useful as well as entertaining to the People of this Island; especially to such of them as live at a Distance, and cannot otherwise have an Account of the Disputes that happen in this great City." Far as this aim is from that of *The Spectator*, the author seems to have been indebted to Steele and Addison for his plan, as the following passage testifies:

1. *E.g.*, Letters IV, VI.

I know it will be expected, that upon this my first Appearance, I should give an Account of myself and the Club I belong to. This is a Sort of Curiosity that has always prevailed; for no sooner does a Man begin to appear as an Author, but People begin to ask, What is he? What Sort of Man is he? Is he a tall, or a little Man; a fat or a lean Man; of a swarthy or a fair Complexion? With twenty such Questions, that in their Opinion, very much contribute to the right Understanding of what he writes.[1]

Remembering that the club is not the important feature of the department, the author refuses to give details of this nature and furnishes only a general account of the society. "About *six* or *seven* years since," he writes, "a few young Gentlemen belonging to the Inns of Court, (of whom I was one) formed themselves into a Club, for their mutual Improvement in Knowledge, and the Art of Speaking or Debating." Since all the members designed to sit in Parliament one day, the rules of that body were observed in the club debates, and actual parliamentary bills were often the subject of discussion. Impartiality was encouraged by the requirement that each gentleman was to come prepared to uphold either side of the question of the day. By the time at which the author was writing, the club had become "very numerous." The tri-weekly meetings lasted from two until nearly ten o'clock, beginning with "a good, substantial old English Dinner" and continuing after supper.

As for myself, tho' I think it no small Honour to have been chosen Secretary to such a Club, yet I am apt to ascribe that Honour to the Regard the Gentlemen had for my *Unkle*, whose Chambers I now possess, and who is well known in the World by his having been one of the *Spectator*'s Club. The old Gentleman is now retired to the Country, but is himself a Member of our Club, and never fails attending when he is in Town.[2]

1. *The London Magazine*, VII (1738), 237. Compare the opening sentence of *The Spectator*, No. 1, from which the passage is obviously borrowed.
2. *The London Magazine*, VII (1738), 239.

Here is another connection with *The Spectator*, the secretary being conceived as the nephew of the very Templar who had been immortalized in his youth by Addison and Steele.

Since the purpose of the essays in which this political club appeared was rather to inform than to amuse, the society was handled, once it was introduced, in a very businesslike manner. The debates are recounted in due form in order to present the political issues before Parliament at the time, the various members, under classical names, speaking in turn. The Whiggish leanings of the author are apparent in the discussion of such questions as the nature of government and the desirability of maintaining a large standing army. By December the department devoted to the club's proceedings occupied three-fifths of the whole magazine, and its popularity needs no other proof than its survival till August, 1757. Although its success was due to the content of the papers rather than to public interest in the club itself, the idea of turning the fictitious society of gentlemen to a purpose of this sort was strikingly original. The significance of the experiment lies in its eloquent testimony to the conquest of the fictitious club over the periodical.

DECLINE

Two more imitations of *The Spectator* may be cited to illustrate the disintegration of the club method. In Eliza Haywood's *Female Spectator* (1744–1746), the device had become noticeably half-hearted. The author seems to have thought it necessary to have a fictitious society, for she sets about inventing one very methodically. It consists of herself and three other ladies, of whom the traditional descriptions appear near the beginning of the first monthly issue. Early in Book II there is a brief statement concerning the meetings of the little group, which occurred twice a week, once to "communicate to each other what intelligence we receive, and consider on what topics we shall proceed," and again to "lay our several productions on the table, which being read over, everyone has the liberty of excepting against, or censuring whatever she disapproves." [1]

To realize the author's attitude toward her club, we have only to return for a moment to Book I. There Mrs. Haywood makes the following remark on her supposed collaborators:

These *three* approved my design, assured me of all the help they could afford, and soon gave a proof of it in bringing their several essays; but as the reader, provided the entertainment be agreeable, will not be interested from which quarter it comes, whatever productions I shall be favoured with from these ladies, or any others I may hereafter correspond with, will be exhibited under the general title of *The Female Spectator*. [2]

The statement shows the fundamental difference between the imitation and the original. Mrs. Haywood's club is shadowy in its outlines; it is not intrinsically interesting; and it does not dramatize the author's ideas. Only occasionally, at widely scattered points, is the society or some member of it mentioned. [3] The material with which *The Female Spectator* deals contributes to the hollowness of the club device. The essays are largely narrative, the stories being related ostensibly for the purpose of illustrating a moral principle. Although Mrs. Haywood recounts her tales with much vivacity, on the whole one is inclined to question the sincerity of her didacticism. Her paper represents an application of the club framework to a purpose far removed from that for which it was invented.

That the method affected the periodicals even in the second half of the century is clear from its use by Arthur Murphy in *The Gray's-Inn Journal*, which he published

1. *The Female Spectator* (rep. 1748), I, 56.
2. *Ibid.*, I, 4.   3. *Ibid.*, I, 108; II, 2, 35.

under the pseudonym of Charles Ranger from 1752 to 1756. In outlining his project, in Number 3, Murphy writes:

> Besides this, I belong to a club of *originals*, who meet once in each month, at the *Devil-Tavern*, near *Temple-Bar*. Every member of it is remarkable for some peculiarity in his manners and way of thinking, not contracted by an affected imitation of others, but absolutely inherent and native to each respective person. I shall take a proper opportunity to make the town acquainted with this society. It is probable that I may occasionally be able to derive from them materials, which, I trust, will not be disagreeable to the reader.[1]

Nothing further is said of the club of originals till Number 10, in which Mr. Ranger recalls his promise and gives an account of the society with characters of the members. Each gentleman has a particular idiosyncrasy not common in the author's age. Charles Ranger himself is unique in that he is neither a cheat nor a rake. Abraham Gulliver is a fearless and adventuresome traveler, descended from Lemuel Gulliver. Harry Wildair is a frolicsome man of fashion; yet he has a keen insight into the foibles of his type. Counselor Plastic is a Shaftesburian philosopher. And Mr. Allcash, who represents the successful man of business, occupies a position not unlike that of Sir Andrew Freeport in *The Spectator*. At the close of the description of the group, Mr. Ranger asserts that applications for membership in the club will be considered.

Murphy uses his imaginary society exactly as he had announced in Number 3; that is, he occasionally derives from it materials which are not disagreeable to the reader. In Number 14 Mr. Candid presides at a club meeting at which there is criticism of Rich's pantomimes and of current productions of Shakespeare. An oriental tale is related in Number 32 as told by Mr. Gulliver "at the last meeting of our club." Mr. Plastic, as temporary chairman

1. *The Works of Arthur Murphy* (1786), v, 25.

of the society, furnishes a critical essay for Number 44. Between these numbers, however, the group is forgotten, nor is there any attempt to connect it with the publication of the *Journal*. Thus in Murphy's hands the device is a purely casual matter, to be employed entirely at the author's convenience.

By this time the club framework had run its course.[1] It had begun in *The Athenian Mercury* as a means of securing belief in the information which Dunton and his collaborators had to impart. Defoe saw its value as a vehicle for the criticism of manners, and turned it to advantage in his Scandalous Club papers. *The Weekly Comedy* and *The Female Tatler* made experiments in dramatizing ideas by describing the actual meetings of their fictitious societies. In *The Spectator* all these possibilities were turned to account, with the important addition of lively characterization of the members. Here, too, the club was linked indissolubly with the publication of the periodical and was sustained throughout. The machinery of *The Lay Monk* so captured the fancy of its authors that the activities of the club took on a narrative interest. As a variation of the club form, the imaginary family was introduced into *The Guardian, The Grumbler*, and *The Champion*. The device eventually became so well established that writers often introduced an imaginary group which was not particularly adapted to their ends, and subsequently abandoned it. By the time of *The Female Spectator*, the fictitious society had lost its narrative quality and its dramatic power, and had become a perfunctory bit of traditional artifice, inserted largely out of deference to Addison and Steele.

1. Walter Graham refers in *The English Literary Periodicals* to club-like devices in *The Dublin Spy* (1753–1754), *The Yorkshire Freeholder* (1780), and *The Templar and Literary Gazette* (1773). He also implies (pp. 151, 161) that both *The Gentleman's Magazine* and *The London Magazine* advertised societies of gentlemen on their title-pages. This is not true of any copies of the two magazines that I have seen. It is true, however, of *The Critical Review* and *The European Magazine*.

CHAPTER V

The Club and the Author

POLITICS AND THE LITERARY PROFESSION

THE literature of Swift's day would not have been concerned with club life as it was had not many writers been clubmen themselves. The dean's experiences as one of the Brothers have been already touched upon. Some of his literary friends have been mentioned as belonging to other societies. The membership of a number of heretofore unnoticed authors, in clubs literary and non-literary, played an important part in their lives. Through clubs they made or fostered acquaintanceships both among themselves and with less professional wits. Their intimacies led to a free interchange of ideas, often to collaboration. Finally, the presence of men of letters in certain clubs was productive of patronage, which in turn affected the writing of those who enjoyed it.

During the reign of Queen Anne, the writer without independent means almost necessarily allied himself with a political party. His bread was not buttered on the side of nonpartizanship. His livelihood came most often from positions in the gift of Whig or Tory leaders. Before he was considered worthy of patronage he had to make a reputation for himself by producing some work of genuine literary merit, for which he was generally paid little. When his mark was made, he had often to defend his party with his pen in order to insure the assistance which would allow him the leisure to compose further masterpieces. The least he could do was to keep on the best possible terms with influential gentlemen of his political opinions. In most cases little sacrifice of principle was involved. The company in which the writer moved was of the best, and the game itself was exciting.

The effect of political activity upon the lives and works of the writers who engaged in it is plain enough. A glance at the controversial literature of the period shows poets, essayists, dramatists, and critics lined up in the opposing ranks beside courtiers and members of Parliament, engaging in bitter party controversy. On December 27, 1712, Swift drew in his *Journal* a dark picture of the result.

I met Mr Addison and Pastoral Philips on the Mall to-day, and took a turn with them; but they both looked terrible dry and cold. A curse of party! And do you know I have taken more pains to recommend the Whig wits to the favour and mercy of the ministers than any other people. Steele I have kept in his place. Congreve I have got to be used kindly, and secured. Rowe I have recommended, and got a promise of a place. Philips I could certainly have provided for, if he had not run party mad, and made me withdraw my recommendation; and I set Addison so right at first, that he might have been employed, and have partly secured him the place he has; yet I am worse used by that faction than any man.[1]

A few writers, like Pope, were not much interested in politics and had enough financial independence to keep reasonably clear of party entanglements. Certain others, like Congreve, had so much of the amiable in their dispositions that their lives were little affected by party animosities. These two men, however, stand out as exceptions; for most of the great names in the literature of the first two decades are linked firmly with one party or the other.

Under these conditions it is not surprising to find men of letters connected with political clubs. In some cases the

1. Swift, *Prose Works*, II, 406.

connection was simply that of satirist with victim; but it also occurred that groups made up solely of writers were brought together by the allying forces of profession and party. Again, literary men were found by statesmen to be of such influence and congeniality as to be worthy of membership in societies recruited chiefly from the nobility. Such was the case with the Kit-Cat Club, which was one of the first to use its wealth and prestige in patronage.

THE KIT-CATS AGAIN

Just how far the Kit-Cats went in this direction is difficult to say. We know that they once paid for effigies to be used in a demonstration against the Tories. We know that several members, particularly Maynwaring and Steele, were active pamphleteers on the Whig side. It is not unreasonable to suppose that the Kit-Cat Club directed the journalistic campaign of the whole party and rewarded such writers as Oldmixon, Boyer, and Ridpath. Positive evidence of this kind of patronage is, however, completely lacking, and only the likelihood of it may be insisted upon.

In the realm of wit the activities of the club are much clearer.[1] Almost all the members were men of taste, not a few were wealthy, a respectable number were themselves poets or dramatists. The astute Tonson knew as well as any other man in London where patronage could be most validly and charitably bestowed. Thus it is not strange to find that the Kit-Cats, early in their career, were linked with the theatre on the occasion of the death of the leading contributor to the drama of the preceding generation. May 13, 1700, was the day set for Dryden's funeral. By a general agreement, the leading theatres had decided to honor the great dramatist by suspending their activities for the day. When, therefore, the mercenary lessee of Dorset

---

1. Portions of the following discussion of the Kit-Cat Club have already appeared in *The Review of English Studies*, VII (1931), 56–61.

Garden let out that theatre, on the day of the ceremony, to be used for bear-baiting, there was great indignation in theatrical circles. A broadside poem entitled "The Patentee" was the result. The shocked author was particularly horrified by the fact that

> Butchers and Bailiffs now the Boxes fill,
> Where Ladies Eyes were Instruments to kill,
> Where Kit-Cats sate, and Toasters would be seen,
> These swoln with Wit, and those with Letch'ry lean.

The emotions aroused by such a spectacle are the easier to understand in the light of a letter, dated May 14, 1700, from Edward Hinton to his cousin, the Reverend John Cooper. Hinton states "that Dryden was buried by the Bishop of Rochester at the Abbey on Monday; that the Kit Cat Club were at the charge of his funeral, which was not great, and that Mr. Montague had engaged to build him a fine monument." [1] The letter adds the better known information that "Dr. Garth made a Latin speech, and threw away some words and a great deal of false Latin in praise of the poet." So varied and inaccurate were the contemporary accounts of the funeral that such statements are naturally to be viewed with a touch of suspicion. The fact, however, that Montagu, Garth, and Tonson, all of whom were Kit-Cat members, are known definitely to have been prominent at the poet's obsequies lends countenance to Hinton's statement.

One more connection between Dryden and the Kit-Cats is suggested in an honorary garland of verses entitled *Luctus Britannici: or the Tears of the British Muses; for the Death of John Dryden, Esq;* which was published June 20, 1700. The concluding poem of the volume, "To Dr. Samuel Garth, occasion'd by the much Lamented Death of John Dryden, Esq;" presents the views of its editors,

---

1. *Fifth Report of the Royal Commission on Historical Manuscripts* (1876), pp. 359–360.

Henry Playford and Abel Roper. The verses appeal to
Garth to take Dryden's place as guardian of young poets.

> Permit us then, our Dutious Zeal to prove,
> And make a Tender of our Tears and Love,
> As we with Sighs unfeign'd the Task pursue,
> And Weep him *Dead*, who still must Live in You.
> And who shall make us known, and stamp Esteem,
> On what we Write, since He's the Writer's Theme,
> Though 'midst our Verse no Fav'rite *Congreve* shines,
> Nor *Urwin* sends Auxilliary Lines.
> Though Title Page no swelling *Kitcat* Grace,
> And *Playford*'s Name, takes *Jacob Tonson*'s place.[1]

The lines concerning Congreve and Urwin refer to Will's
Coffee-house, Dryden's favorite haunt. The couplet that
follows them can only be taken as associating the Kit-Cat
Club with the dead monarch of wit.

How much the members had to do with non-dramatic
poetry is uncertain. The verses which they wrote in honor
of their toasts were, of course, famous in their day; and a
satirist of 1705, in accusing them of cowardice, remarked
that a Kit-Cat man "had much rather judge of *Addison's
Poetical History* of the Battle of *Blenheim*, than be in it,
and is fitter to write the Second part of the *Campaign*, than
to make *One*." [2] The last couplet of the verses to Garth
quoted above hints at some connection between the club
and Tonson's publication of poetry. Furthermore, a collection of Italian songs, of 1703, the titles of which are
strangely derived from the names of famous toasts and
the names of old English country houses, has one song
called "The Kitcat." [3] But such vague and curious clues
as these lead nowhere in particular.

With the drama, the case is distinctly different. The
passage excerpted from *The Patentee* shows unmistakably
that the Kit-Cats were theatre-goers. The often-quoted

1. *Luctus Britannici* (1700), pp. 51–52.
2. *A Kit-Kat C—b Describ'd* (1705), p. 3.
3. *A Choice Collection of Italian Ayres* (1703), p. 1.

passage in the prologue to William Burnaby's *Reform'd Wife* (1700) implies as much by bidding for their favor in a vague description of their meetings.

> *Often for change the meanest things are good,*
> *Thus tho' the Town all delicates afford,*
> *A Kit-cat is a Supper for a Lord.*
> *But if your Nicer tast resolves to Day,*
> *To have no relish for our Author's Play.*
> *Place some diverting Scene before your Mind,*
> *And think of that, to which you will be kind.*
> *So thus when heavily the moments pass,*
> *Toaster's to Circulate the lazy Glass*
> *By nameing some bright Nymph their draughts refine,*
> *And tast at once the joys of Love and Wine.*

By 1702 the club had begun to attend the theatre *en masse*. Tom Brown, describing a playhouse in that year, remarked that "the L[ord] D[orset] is known by his Ribbon, and T[om] D['Urfey] or some other Impertinent Poet, talking Nonsense to him, the L[ord] H[alifax] by sitting on the *Kitcat* side, and *Jacob* T[onson] standing Door-Keeper for him." [1] The passage indicates that one of the side-boxes was regularly allotted to members of the club, as it had been on the benefit night of which Prior had written two years earlier. [2]

On April 9, 1705, the new Queen's Theatre was opened in the Haymarket. This important theatrical event was brought about by the competition which had been long in progress between the playhouses of Lincoln's Inn and Drury Lane. In describing the struggles of Betterton's company against their more advantageously situated rivals, Colley Cibber gives the following account of the outcome:

To recover them therefore, to their due Estimation, a new Project was form'd, of building them a stately Theatre, in the

---

1. *Amusements Serious and Comical* (1702), p. 50.
2. See above, p. 40.

Hay-Market, by Sir *John Vanbrugh*, for which he raised a Subscription of thirty Persons of Quality, at one hundred Pounds
each, in Consideration whereof every Subscriber, for his own
Life, was to be admitted, to whatever Entertainments should
be publickly perform'd there, without farther Payment for his
Entrance. Of this Theatre, I saw the first Stone laid, on which
was inscrib'd *The little Whig*, in Honour to a Lady of extraordinary Beauty, then the celebrated Toast, and Pride of that
Party.[1]

The inscription to the "little Whig" at once suggests the
gallants of the Kit-Cat Club, which at this time numbered
approximately thirty; for the Countess of Sunderland, who
was so toasted, was a daughter of the Duke of Marlborough, himself a Kit-Cat member, and was a favorite among
the distinguished Whigs who made up the society.[2]

Evidence concerning the identity of the "thirty persons
of quality" mentioned by Cibber goes farther than this
tribute to one of the club's toasts. A satiric advertisement
of the "New Hospital in the *Hay-Market* for the *Cure of
Folly*" stated that "*Subscriptions will be taken in till* Lady-
day *next, at the Sign of the two left* Legs, *near* Gray's-Inn
Back-Gate," indicating that Tonson had something to do
with receiving the contributions. Shortly after the opening
of the theatre, a slender pamphlet appeared under the
title, *A Kit-Kat C—b Describ'd*. In drawing a satiric portrait of a typical member, the author remarked:

He Subscribes largely to the Building of *New Playhouse*, to
shew his Aversion to *Prophaneness* and *Immorality*;

and a little farther on:

He imagines no ane [*sic*] will doubt his *Conversion* from a Gentleman of *Indifferent* Abilities into a *States-Man*, after he has been

1. *An Apology for the Life of Colley Cibber* (1740), pp. 257–258.
2. Two toasts to Lady Sunderland were among those proposed at the club
in 1703.

a Principal *Contributor* towards the *Transforming* a *Stable* into a *Theatre*.[1]

The connection between the club and the new playhouse is here plain enough.

Even more definite is Charles Leslie's *Rehearsal* of May 12, 1705. After an introductory thrust at the opposition of the Whig party toward the established church, the Tory journalist points to the activities of the club by way of illustration.

> The KIT-CAT *Clubb* is now grown *Famous* and *Notorious*, all over the *Kingdom*. And they have Built a *Temple* for their *Dagon*, the new *Play-House* in the *hay-Market*. The *Foundation* was laid with great *Solemnity*, by a *Noble* Babe of *Grace*. And over or under the *Foundation Stone* is a *Plate* of *Silver*, on which is Graven *Kit Cat* on the one side, and Little *Whigg* on the other. . . . And there was such *Zeal* shew'd, and all *Purses* open to carry on this *Work*, that it was almost as soon *Finish'd* as *Begun*.

In concluding his attack, Leslie quotes from the "Prologue Spoken at the First Opening of the Queen's New Theatre in the Hay-Market," which was "said to be Written by Dr. G[ar]th, Chaplain to *Kit-Kat*, an Open and Profess'd Enemy to all Religion." The prologue appeared in at least two broadsides during the year 1705. In the margin of one of them, opposite the second verse of the couplet,

> More sure Presages from these walls we find
> By Beauty founded, and by Witt design'd,

there is printed the note, "Lady H— G—n." The lady in question may be easily identified with the "Lady H. Godolphin"[2] in whose honor Arthur Maynwaring had in-

---

1. *A Kit-Kat C—b Describ'd* (1705), pp. 2–3.
2. Lady Henrietta, a daughter of the Duke of Marlborough, married Francis Godolphin in 1698.

scribed some verses upon a wine-glass at the Kit-Cat Club two years before.

The interest of the club in the theatre did not cease with the building of the Haymarket. When not long after its opening the new playhouse turned to the production of opera, for which it was better adapted than for plays, the Kit-Cat Club continued its patronage; and we find Thomas D'Urfey hopefully dedicating his musical entertainment, *Wonders in the Sun, or, the Kingdom of the Birds* (1706), "To the Right Noble, Honourable and Ingenious Patrons of *Poetry, Musick, &c.* The *Celebrated Society* of the *Kit-Cat-Club.*" What may have been a club transaction in the interest of the opera appears in the letters of Vanbrugh to the Earl of Manchester in the winter of 1707–1708. Since the earl, a fellow-member of the society, was traveling in Italy at the time, Vanbrugh commissioned him in behalf of the theatre to employ two or three Italian singers for the coming season, in order to make the most of the tremendous vogue that Valentini was having in London.

That the theatrical activities of the Kit-Cats continued at least to the year 1709 is suggested by the well-known instance of their patronage given subsequently by Pope to Spence. "The paper was all in Lord Hallifax's hand writing," says Spence, "of a subscription of four hundred guineas for the encouragement of good comedies, and was dated 1709." [1] The document itself seems to have been lost, and with it all means of discovering the destination of the four hundred guineas. It may, however, have been to this appropriation that Mary Astell referred in the same year when she prefaced her *Bart'lemy Fair* with the ironic dedication to the Kit-Cats. The passage is as follows:

They [of the club] who desire to be more taken notice of, contribute perhaps to the building or repair of a Church, and shew

1. Joseph Spence, *Anecdotes, Observations, and Characters*, ed. S. W. Singer (1858), p. 257.

their Value for Religion by the Proportion between their Offerings
to the Temple and their Bounty to the Theatre.[1]

Beyond this point it is difficult to trace the relations between the club and the drama. During "the four last years
of the queen" the party struggle was so bitter and the
unanimously Whiggish Kit-Cat Club so loyal to its cause
that the energies of the members were bent on politics,
probably to the exclusion of theatrical projects. All that
is certain is that the society was responsible for building
the Haymarket Theatre, that the members frequently
honored the playhouse with their presence, and that they
were the active patrons of certain dramatists. How much
the playwrights of the club governed their policies and
who were the recipients of their bounty for "good comedies" are questions which cannot be easily answered until
the reappearance of the lost paper described by Pope.

THE CLUB AT BUTTON'S

The literary importance of the group of wits which
gathered about Addison at Button's Coffee-house was of a
totally different sort. They were the recipients of patronage, not the givers. Whether they may be said to have
been professional writers or not, every man of them but
one was interested primarily in literary pursuits. Their
significance as a club lies in the fact that though bound together partly by politics — they were in varying degrees
Whiggish — they stood together on critical matters,
helped each other in various literary projects, and on occasion even fought each other's battles.

Like many other early societies of gentlemen, Button's
can hardly, in the twentieth-century sense, be called a
club at all. Its organization was fairly casual. Since the
death of Dryden, Will's had degenerated, slowly but

---

1. *Bart'lemy Fair* (1709), pp. 12–13.

surely, from the meeting-place of London's most select
literary circle to the haunt of the idle "pretty fellow."
By 1712 party controversy was having the effect upon
writers' friendships that Swift noted to Stella.[1] Whig and
Tory authors who were on these terms could find solace
only in separate companies. Addison was among the first
to realize that the Whig men of letters needed an established rendezvous at which party animosities could not
place a restraint upon their conversation and at which
their literary endeavors could receive the stimulus of a
free interchange of ideas.

It was Addison who from his commanding position in
both politics and letters undertook to establish such a
Whiggish society. Mr. Dobrée's keen insight has produced a plausible explanation of Addison's conduct in the
matter.[2] His happiness depended on living in a company
that admired him, to whom he could talk, confident that no
unfriendly ear was listening. The coterie of friends who
made up the club had begun to worship at Addison's
shrine as early as 1710. In that year, according to John
Nichols, the Gentlemen's Society at Spaulding was
founded "with the encouragement of Secretary Addison,
Captain Steele, and others of Button's club."[3] Nichols
would have been more accurate if he had said "others who
were later of Button's club."

The seat of the "little senate," as it came to be called
after the success of *Cato*, was a coffee-house in Russell
Street, opposite Will's. Of the history of its proprietor,
Daniel Button, little is known. Whether he had been,
before 1712, a servant of Addison or of the Countess of
Warwick is after all of no great consequence.[4] It is gen-

---

1. See above, p. 231.
2. Bonamy Dobrée, *Essays in Biography* (1925), "The First Victorian,"
passim.
3. *Literary Anecdotes*, VI (1812), 6.
4. Compare Spence, *Anecdotes*, p. 199; and Johnson, *Lives of the English
Poets*, ed. G. Birkbeck Hill (Oxford, 1905), II, 122.

DR. GARTH AND MR. POPE AT BUTTON'S COFFEE-HOUSE

From Samuel Ireland's Graphic Illustrations of Hogarth

erally agreed that Addison established him at Button's as the first step towards founding the society of wits. Although the membership was not fixed, the regular group included Addison, Steele, Budgell, Philips, Carey, Tickell, Hughes, Davenant, Young, and Colonel Brett. Garth sometimes dropped in, and in the early days of the group Pope was a daily visitor. The latter gave Spence an interesting description of Addison's habits at this period.

Addison usually studied all the morning: then met his party at Button's; dined there, and stayed five or six hours; and sometimes far into the night.[1]

It was at these protracted meetings that copies of verses were presented for correction and essays for the latest periodical venture were planned. In addition, the conversation partook of the critical flavor which had permeated Will's during the régime of its old monarch. The gentlemen at Button's may have been responsible for the long-delayed production of *Cato*. How they made a success of Philips's *Distressed Mother* has already been told.

The whole occasion gives a pleasing picture of how loyally the little senate worked for the glory of its individual members, and with what a gentle hand Addison ruled his friends. Finally, when some pedantic curmudgeon wrote to *The Spectator* protesting against the epilogue, the letter was printed to be suitably pulverized in a later number.[2]

The name of Button's has been perpetuated chiefly through those papers of *The Guardian* which deal with the lion's head set up there to receive the letters of different contributors. Steele's picture of Daniel Button assisting young wits to deposit their contributions properly, and Addison's of Daniel's four-year-old daughter performing the same service for lady correspondents are too well

1. Spence, *Anecdotes*, p. 216. Cf. *ibid.*, pp. 148–149.
2. Dobrée, *Essays in Biography*, pp. 271–272.

known to require description.[1] Curiosity about the fate of
the lion's head has been great enough to inspire a writer of
the early nineteenth century to relate its history.[2] Less
widely known, and much more illuminating, is the glimpse
of Button's in Steele's *Englishman*, No. 36, where the
coffee-house appears as a Whig rallying-place. The Englishman tells of meeting Nestor Ironside there, and reading
him an attack on Marlborough out of *The Examiner*, in
order to hear the worthy old gentleman's defense of the
high character and "consummate capacity" of the duke,
in open defiance of the Tory journalist. The anecdote continues:

> The Sage was going on in his Discourse, when Mr. *Button*
> entred the Room, and told us, Mr. *S[tee]le* was come on his
> Crutches, after a Fit of the Gout, to wait upon Mr. IRONSIDE.
> We all rose to that ingenious Gentleman, and began to make
> him our Compliments of Consolation upon all the Calumnies
> that had been published against him, during his Indisposition.

This fictitious incident furnishes one of the few pictures of
a meeting at Button's.

A different phase of the activities of the society is revealed in Whiston's account of how Addison and Steele
assisted him, upon his banishment from Cambridge, by
employing him "to have many Astronomical Lectures
at Mr. *Button*'s Coffee-house, near *Covent-Garden*, to the
agreeable Entertainment of a good Number of curious
Persons." [3] Whiston tells also of an encounter which he
had there with Steele, after the latter had been elected to
Parliament. When Whiston accused Steele of making a
speech "to please the Court, but against his own Conscience," Sir Richard replied, " 'Mr. *Whiston*, you can

1. *The Guardian*, Nos. 98, 114.
2. Charles Richardson, *Notices and Extracts Relating to the Lion's Head*
(1828).
3. *Memoirs of the Life and Writings of Mr. William Whiston* (1749), p. 302.

walk on Foot, and I cannot.' Than which," adds Whiston,
"a truer or an acuter Answer could not have been made
by any body." [1]

Although the informal nature of the club at Button's
tended to keep it from the public eye, it was none the less
subject to satiric attacks. Steele's connection with the
club was one of the points on which he was ridiculed in *The
Character of Richard S——le, Esq*. The pamphleteer tells
us that when Steele fell heir to the property of his mother-
in-law, "he was told by the *Minor Poets*, his Companions
at *Button's*, That a Man of his Sense must undoubtedly
advance himself by being in the Senate." [2] A little farther
on, Steele is attacked in an ironic jeremiad for his abusive
method of dealing with *The Examiner*:

O! Ye Literati of *Button*'s Coffee-House! Ye Ladies of St.
James's! Ye Milliners of the *Exchange*! Ye Upholsterers of the
City! Ye Stock-Jobbers of *Jonathan*'s! Ye Neighbors of Sir
Roger, and Ye Family of the *Lizards*! Behold the Patron of
Learning! the Encourager of Arts and Sciences! . . . dwindled
on a sudden into an Author below the Character of *Dunton*!
below the Politicks of Ridpath! [3]

Charges of a more serious nature seem also to have been
directed at Button's. It was from unorthodoxy that Colley
Cibber defended the group in *The Non-Juror* (1718), when
he made Colonel Woodvil reply to the accusations of Sir
John.

Sir *John*. O! Perverseness! but there is no better to be expected from your Course of Life: This is all the Effects of your
modern Loyalty, your Conversation at *Button's*. Will you
never leave that foul Nest of Heresy and Schism?
Col. Yes, Sir, when I see any Thing like it there; and should
think myself oblig'd to retire, where such Principles were started

1. *Ibid.*, pp. 303–304.
2. *The Character of Richard S—le, Esq.* (1713), p. 5.
3. *Ibid.*, p. 10. Compare John Lacy's mock defiance in *The Steeleids* (1714),
p. 16.

— I own I use the Place, because I generally meet there in-
structive or diverting Company.[1]

The passage gives an excellent idea of what many Tories
thought of the club. The colonel's apology for frequenting
it may speak for the dramatist himself. In later years, at
least, he was often seen at Button's. In 1722 *Mist's Journal* contained "An Exercise on the Art of Punning, proper
to be read by all young Gentlemen who resort to Button's
to hear Colley quibble." An anecdote [2] involving him and
Colonel Brett also has the senate-house as its scene.

One incident which is supposed to have taken place at
Button's is rarely quoted from the jest-book in which it
occurs.

Two Gentlemen disputing about Religion, in *Button's Coffee-
House*, said one of them, I wonder, Sir, you should talk of Religion, when I'll hold you five Guineas you can't say the *Lord's
Prayer*, done, said the other, and Sir *Richard Steele* shall hold
Stakes. The Money being deposited, the Gentleman began
with, *1 believe in God*, and so went cleverly thro' the *Creed*; well,
said the other, I own I have lost; *I did not think he could have
done it.*[3]

Much of what is known concerning the literary activities
at Button's has come to light, strangely enough, in connection with two famous quarrels of Alexander Pope, the first
of which was said to have ended his attendance on the little senate. This initial affray, in which Philips was the
other principal, was opened by Pope in *The Guardian*, No.
40. How the younger poet, piqued by the neglect of his
pastorals in the series of critical essays in *The Guardian*,
wrote an ironic sequel subtly ridiculing the widely ac-
claimed Philips and managed its publication in the same

1. *The Dramatick Works of Colley Cibber, Esq.* (1754), III, 11.
2. Recounted by Thomas Davies, *Dramatic Miscellanies* (1784), III, 444.
3. *Joe Miller's Jests* (1739), p. 24. For other anecdotes of Button's, see H.
Westerfrölke, *Englische Kaffeehäuser als Sammelpunkte der literarischen Welt
im Zeitalter von Dryden und Addison* (Jena, 1924).

periodical has been related fully and delightfully.[1] Mr. Dobrée gives Steele credit for penetrating Pope's irony. Yet he accepts the story that Steele asked Pope's permission to use the anonymously submitted essay, protesting that he did not wish to use any paper where one member of the club was complimented at the expense of another. Steele's treatment of Pope as the injured person, if sincere, was most astonishing. On the other hand, it is a matter of some doubt whether Richard's sense of humor was capable of triumphing over his loyalty to his clique, even if the joke appealed to him very much indeed. If he did see through the essay, he must have realized that it would cause trouble. Thus he stands convicted of either a little knavery or a good deal of obtuseness. Mr. Dobrée's explanation of his behavior is certainly the more generous one.

The fortieth *Guardian* left no doubt whatever in the mind of its victim, and Philips's wrath was bitter. Pope's association with the Tory wits of the Scriblerus Club about this time gave his enemy an unusually good opportunity to calumniate him. Philips seized it at once, with a result that appears in a letter from Pope to Caryll dated June 8, 1714.

Mr. Philips did express himself with much indignation against me one evening at Button's Coffee-house, as I was told, saying that I was entered into a cabal with Dean Swift and others to write against the whig interest, and in particular to undermine his own reputation and that of his friends Steele and Addison.[2]

Addison and Halifax endeavored to straighten the matter out, according to Pope's letter, but Philips continued to talk against him at the Hanover Club. As often happened subsequently, Pope's indulgence of his spleen was a source of inconvenience to himself; for at the time he was collect-

1. Dobrée, *Essays in Biography*, pp. 268–270.
2. Pope, *Works*, VI, 209.

ing subscriptions for the forthcoming translation of the
Iliad from members of the Hanover Club. Since Philips
was secretary, the business had to pass through his hands.
Pope's story has it that Philips withheld the money paid
to the translator, with the mean design of making him ask
for it. "As to the secret grounds of this malignity," Pope
wrote to Caryll, referring to his *Guardian*, "they will make
a very pleasant history when we meet." The situation
eventually became so intolerable that a year later Pope
was dealing with the Hanover men through his friend
Jervas, having forsworn all business relations with Philips.
The full extent of the latter's animosity comes to light in a
letter from Broome to Fenton, written nearly fifteen years
later, in which Broome expresses surprise that Pope had
never been whipped for his bitter personal attacks.

> I wonder he is not thrashed: but his littleness is his protection;
> no man shoots a wren. He should rather be whipped; and it
> was pleasant enough in Mr. Ambrose Philips to hang up a rod at
> Button's *in terrorem*, which scared away the little bard.[1]

The exact time at which Pope ceased to frequent Button's cannot be ascertained.[2] In May, 1714, when he wrote
to Gay from Binfield, his greetings to his friends were followed by the cryptic remark, "Let them know at Button's
that I am mindful of them." [3] In view of the fact that the
quarrel had begun some months before and that Gay was
of the Scriblerus Club, not Button's, this sentence has an
ominous sound. Nor can one wonder at Pope's preference
for the Tory wits, who accepted him as an equal, over the
Whig society, in which he had to play second fiddle to
Addison. By the time the first section of the *Iliad* was
published in 1715, the estrangement was complete, despite
the continuance of outward civilities on both sides.

1. Pope, *Works*, VIII, 147.
2. Dobrée believes that Philips's threat had little to do with it.
3. Pope, *Works*, VII, 415.

It was over the translation of the first *Iliad* that a second literary quarrel arose in which Button's played an active part. The story, in its outline, is an old one. In 1715 the first four books of Pope's *Iliad* and a translation of Book I by Thomas Tickell were published almost simultaneously. The open rivalry of Tickell neither alarmed Pope greatly nor shook his faith in the superiority of his own Homer. His Tory friends hastened to reassure him on this score, Gay, Arbuthnot, and Swift being among the first to congratulate him on his success. What did annoy him was the seemingly competitive nature of Tickell's undertaking and the attitude taken by the Whig wits at Button's, who regarded him as having deserted to the enemy. Rarely has there been a more patent instance of the warping of critical opinion by party politics than appeared at this point. Addison, the literary dictator of the Whigs, came forth with the pronouncement which Gay summarized in merciless detail in his letter to Pope of July 8, 1715.

I have just set down Sir Samuel Garth at the opera. He bid me tell you that everybody is pleased with your translation, but a few at Button's; and that Sir Richard Steele told him, that Mr. Addison said Tickell's translation was the best that ever was in any language. . . . I am informed that at Button's your character is made very free with as to morals, &c., and Mr. A[ddison] says, that your translation and Tickell's are both very well done, but that the latter has more of Homer.[1]

No one now doubts that Addison's judgment, if sincere, was biassed. Nichol Smith would add to the party prejudice "a desire to check the growing fame of the other poet."[2] Certainly this idea was in the minds of Pope and the others who fostered the rumor that Addison himself had had a hand in the translation published as Tickell's.

1. *Ibid.*, pp. 417–418.
2. *The Letters of Thomas Burnet to George Duckett*, ed. D. Nichol Smith (Oxford, 1914), pp. xxviii–xxix.

The opinion of Button's Coffee-house was not that of modern critics, nor even of the Town at large. Lintot, Pope's publisher, sent him a copy of the rival translation with the statement that "the malice and juggle at Button's is the conversation of those who have spare moments from politics." [1] Indeed, we may accept with few reservations the happily worded passage in which Pope himself told Craggs of the controversy.

I (like the Tories) have the town in general, that is, the mob, on my side; but it is usual with the smaller party to make up in industry what they want in number, and that is the case with the little senate of Cato. However, if our principles be well considered, I must appear a brave Whig, and Mr. T[ickell] a rank Tory: I translated Homer for the public in general, he to gratify the inordinate desires of one man only. [2]

Earlier in the same letter the poet showed a full realization of the rôle played in the affair by party differences. He even implied that politics was undermining the spirit of bonhommie which had been the basis of the club's success.

The quarrel had a twofold effect upon the life of Addison. It left a breach in his friendship with Pope which widened until it resulted in the famous satiric picture of Cato and his little senate in the "Epistle to Dr. Arbuthnot." [3] Then, too, the controversy arising from Addison's uncompromisingly mistaken critical position was harmful to his prestige. The open apostasy of a writer as distinguished as Pope had already become must have hastened in no slight measure the decay of the society which sponsored the leading Whig poets. Addison's marriage, in 1716, also contributed to its decline. Doubtless he was in the unhappy position of finding his visits to Button's con-

1. Pope, *Works*, IX, 540.   2. *Ibid.*, X, 172.
3. Professor Sherburn holds that the failure of *Three Hours after Marriage* to maintain its original popularity was due to the opposition of the wits at Button's. See *Modern Philology*, XXIV (1926), 99.

sidered too rare by his old associates, too frequent by Lady Warwick.

That the little senate survived until 1718 is indicated by a rare pamphlet from the hand of Gay, which appeared under the title, *A Letter to a Buttonian K* * * from Sir James Baker, Admiral-General of the Fair-Sex, and late Secretary to the Toasts of the Kit-Cat-Club. Containing Some Observations on 'Squire Budgell's Letter to the Lord * * *.* Aitken has given such a complete account[1] of the piece that a general description of it is unnecessary. Though directed to Steele (the "Buttonian K* * * "), the pamphlet aims its attack chiefly at Budgell. Pretending to be a member of "the Assembly of *Belle-Esprits* at B——'s," Gay aims his shafts at Budgell's plurality of positions under the Duke of Bolton, his manner of enumerating his own virtues in his *Letter to Lord * * *,* and his plagiarism of some of his happiest expressions from the works of Pope, Addison, and Gay. Although the idea of writing the pamphlet was probably suggested to Gay by these verbal parallels, it shows clearly enough how association with Button's could lay writers open to attack from opposing literary groups.

As soon as the original club disintegrated, the house began to lose caste. A satire of the day, after describing the glorious days when the lion's head was first set up, concludes a lofty tribute to Addison with the couplet:

> But Button's now, since Addison is gone,
> In scandal deals, disdains to be outdone.[2]

The coffee-house survived for some time on its early reputation. *Mist's Journal* for September 9, 1721, contains a facetious will made by "the immortal Cato of the London Journal," in which the author's wit is bequeathed "to Mr.

---

1. *The Athenaeum*, No. 3228 (September 7, 1889), pp. 321–322.
2. Quoted in *Notices and Extracts Relating to the Lion's Head* (1828), p. 33. Burnet had hinted, as early as 1715 (*The Grumbler*, No. 7), that Button's was a seat of scandal.

Daniel Button of *Russell-street*, *Covent-Garden*, Coffee-man, to be by him held in Trust for, and to the Use of all the Gentlemen who are his constant Customers." In the same paper, on December 9, 1721, there was an advertisement to this effect:

Lost by a sudden jolt of a Hackney Coach, turning the Corner of Grubstreet, half a simile, two curious Rhymes, and an Alexandrine; all of which were designed to conclude the 4th Act of a Trajedy, which the World is at present in Expectation of: This is to give Notice, that whoever shall bring the above-mentioned Fragments to Button's Coffee-house, shall be well rewarded for the Whole, or proportionably for any part. N.B. They are of no Use but to the Owner.

A letter from "Timoret" to *The Plain Dealer* in 1725 laments that the classics had been elbowed out by the constables and that magistrates "strut about the Room, and shoot out their *Mittimus's*, like *Porcupine's Quills*." [1] There is also a threat to bring the dead lion to life again as a defense against the invaders. A reference to Button's in 1733 pictures it as the haunt of "fops and fools," [2] and so concludes sadly enough the story of the resort of wit over which Addison had once brilliantly presided.

Tory Patronage

Two clubs made up of Tories, Swift's Brothers and the Scriblerus Club, occupy places in literary history which make them comparable to the Kit-Cats and the society at Button's. Among the Brothers, the preponderant number were gentlemen of political importance, though Arbuthnot and Prior, as well as Swift, represented the literary class. Like the Kit-Cats, they were concerned with patronage. The Scriblerus Club was made up of Tory men of letters as truly as the little senate was made up of Whigs. Aside

1. *The Plain Dealer*, No. 102.
2. *The Manners of the Age* (1733), p. 492.

from these superficial resemblances, however, the Tory clubs had little in common with their Whiggish counterparts.

As Henry St. John promised Lord Orrery in outlining his plans for his society, the Brothers were much taken up with contemporary letters. When Swift wished to try the reception of his own literary efforts, he often submitted them to the club for their approval. On February 14, 1712, he gave Stella the results of one such experiment.

To-day I published the Fable of Midas, a Poem, printed in a loose half sheet of Paper. I know not how it will sell; but it passd wonderfully at our Society to-night.[1]

It became the regular thing, when dinner was over, for their printer [2] to put in an appearance, bringing with him whatever new pieces were just off the press for the discussion of the Brothers. On one occasion at least, he made a mistake which proved somewhat embarrassing to Swift. When the satirist had finished his "Windsor Prophecy," he showed it to Mrs. Masham, who desired him not to let it be published "for fear of angering the Queen about the Duchess of Somerset." Although Swift notified the printer, the word arrived too late. In the midst of a meeting of the society, he arrived with "dozens a-piece." "But I ordered him to part with no more," wrote Swift, and added complacently, "'Tis an admirable good one, and people are mad for it."[3]

Although Swift's pen is known to have been very much at the service of the Tory cause at this time, it is not easy to decide exactly to what extent the society influenced his endeavors. How naturally this influence sometimes came about, he reveals in his story of the composition of "Toland's Invitation to Dismal."

1. *Prose Works*, II, 337.
2. Probably John Barber.
3. *Prose Works*, II, 305–306,

Lord Nottingham, a famous Tory and speech-maker, is gone
over to the Whig side: they toast him daily, and Lord Wharton
says, It is Dismal (so they call him from his looks) will save
England at last. Lord-Treasurer was hinting as if he wished a
ballad was made on him, and I will get up one against to-
morrow.[1]

The occasion of his haste was the next day's meeting of the
Brothers, at which he wished to submit his verses. He
spent the next morning on the piece, and upon his return
to his lodging that night after the meeting he gave Stella a
gleeful account of its reception. The printer had come in
before they broke up and brought the ballad, "which made
them laugh very heartily a dozen times."

The fact that such clear examples of club influence are
not numerous in the *Journal* cannot vitiate the inference
that Swift's political tracts of this period were definitely
stimulated by his connection with both the Brothers and
the Saturday Club. Such polemical masterpieces as *The
Character of Lord Wharton* and *The Conduct of the Allies*
would be inconceivable as the work of the Irish clergyman
were he not granted the background gained by his attendance at these two Tory clubs; and it is not unlikely that
the very suggestions for such tracts came from his court
associates at the meetings. Such a conjecture is most
tempting in the case of *The Examiner*. This very theory,
in fact, seems to have occurred to some of the opponents of
that political organ, if we may judge from the pains Swift
took to destroy such notions in order to preserve the
anonymity of the periodical. In Number 19 he wrote:

I am often violently tempted to let the world freely know
who the author of this paper is; to tell them my name and
titles at length; which would prevent abundance of inconsistent
criticisms I daily hear upon it. Those who are enemies to the
notions and opinions I would advance . . . are so generous

1. *Prose Works*, ii, 294.

and candid, to allow, it is written by a club, and that very great hands have fingers in it.

And again in Number 24:

I have too much detested that barbarous injustice among the writers of a late party, to be ever guilty of it myself; I mean the accusing societies for the crimes of a few.

There is no reason to take Swift's protestation about the unity of authorship any more seriously than that about his titles. The suspicions of his contemporaries were partially justified.

If *The Examiner* is to be connected with either club from these statements, it must be with the Saturday Club. The Brothers had not yet begun to meet when Numbers 19 and 24 appeared, and the paper was so entirely the mouthpiece of the ministry that such a conclusion would be the more logical in any case. One more bit of evidence may be summoned in support of the conjecture. On October 2, 1711, Swift wrote to Stella, to whom he had not revealed his authorship of the earlier papers, the following statement about a collected edition:

I am sorry I sent you the Examiner, for the printer is going to print them in a small volume: it seems the author is too proud to have them printed by subscription, though his friends offered, they say, to make it worth five hundred pounds to him.[1]

It is difficult to conceive who these friends were, if they were not the ministers of the Saturday Club.

When the Brothers were assembled they took over the task of guiding the destinies of *The Examiner*. With their approval Swift probably directed much of the Tory journalism which deluged the country for the next two years.[2]

---

1. *Ibid.*, p. 271.
2. See D. H. Stevens, *Party Politics and English Journalism* (Chicago, 1916), pp. 30–40.

He also saw to it, when he could, that the Brothers paid for the defense of their party. Early in 1713 Stella received the following information:

> Our Society met to-day at the Duke of Beaufort's: a prodigious fine dinner, which I hate; but we did some business. Our printer was to attend us, as usual; and the Chancellor of the Exchequer sent the author of the Examiner [Oldisworth] twenty guineas.[1]

By this time the Brothers had become the financial mainstay of their party's henchmen in Grub Street.

Although it is not always possible to trace the munificences of the society to their recipients, it is clear enough that the members not infrequently discussed the merits of those who wrote on their side and rewarded such writers as seemed worthy of encouragement. The *modus operandi* in such cases is apparent in a passage in the *Journal to Stella* in which Swift complains at the expense of the program.

> It cost me a guinea contribution to a poet, who had made a copy of verses upon monkies, applying the story to the Duke of Marlborough; the rest gave two guineas, except the two physicians [Freind and Arbuthnot], who followed my example. I don't like this custom: the next time I will give nothing.[2]

Swift's objections seem at times [3] to have been tinged with jealousy. His compunctions about contributing, however, arose out of his natural thriftiness. They vanished when the assessments came to be made according to the wealth of the various members. The club as a whole was inclined to be liberal. It was the recalcitrance of the Earl of Oxford, on whom they largely depended for state money, that caused the only discouragement to their efforts in behalf of authors. At one time Swift wrote indignantly:

1. *Prose Works*, II, 440.
2. *Ibid.*, p. 316.
3. *Ibid.*, p. 353.

Our Society does not meet now as usual, for which I am blamed: but till Lord-Treasurer will agree to give us money and employments to bestow, I am averse to it; and he gives us nothing but promises.[1]

At the next meeting he proposed a message to Lord Oxford, asking him to "give a hundred guineas to a certain person," to accompany a subscription from the club. This appeal was successful, and two weeks later Swift was able to report that the lord treasurer had promised them a hundred pounds "to reward some others."

The most definite and complete record of the club's transactions with any one writer is the dean's account in the *Journal* of his efforts in behalf of William Diaper. It begins with the entry of March 12, 1712.

Here is a young fellow has writ some Sea Eclogues, Poems of Mermen, resembling pastorals of shepherds, and they are very pretty, and the thought is new. . . . I think to recommend him to our Society to-morrow. His name is Diaper. P— on him, I must do something for him, and get him out of the way.[2]

Swift carried out this benevolent plan. A few days later his protégé sent copies of his poem to the society, for which he was rewarded with "guineas a-piece" and hopes of further patronage. Nor did Swift's good offices stop there. On December 23 of the same year he entered in his *Journal* the following statement:

This morning I presented one Diaper, a poet, to Lord Bolingbroke, with a new poem, which is a very good one;[3] and I

1. *Ibid.*, p. 418.
2. *Ibid.*, p. 353.
3. The poem to which Swift refers was published in folio (1713) under the title, *Dryades; or, The Nymphs Prophecy*. The parts which describe the daemon-haunted vale
"Where fairy Elves, and Mid-night *Dryads* meet,
    And to the smiling Moon the Sylvan-Song repeat,"
are not altogether unworthy of Swift's admiration. The poem drifts into political allegory, however, and ends in a direct bid for the patronage of Wyndham.

am to give him a sum of money from my lord; and I have contrived to make a parson of him, for he is half one already, being in deacon's orders.

A statement in the *Journal* some weeks later concludes, pathetically enough, the record of Diaper's connection with the society.

I was to see a poor poet, one Mr Diaper, in a nasty garret, very sick. I gave him twenty guineas from Lord Bolingbroke, and disposed the other sixty to two other authors.[1]

Another literary servant of the Brothers was Mrs. Manley. The unfortunate lady had lampooned the great Whig leaders while they were still in power and had been persecuted accordingly. She had relieved Swift of *The Examiner* for a few numbers in 1711, and at his direction had written more than one Tory pamphlet. "Upon these accounts," she wrote to Lord Oxford in June, 1714,[2] "and the promises Mr. Barber [the printer] was ordered to bring me from a number of great men who were called, the Society for rewarding of merit, I had hopes that my poor endeavours to do service might have given me some mark of your Lordship's favour." And could she please have the promised sum of a hundred pounds? A week later she wrote again to express her extreme joy at receiving fifty "with commands of secrecy, which I shall punctually obey."

To identify with any certainty the other recipients of the club's financial assistance seems a hopeless undertaking. One of the most plausible possibilities is William Harrison, a bright young Oxonian whose fortune Swift set out to make in 1710. He introduced Harrison to men of influence, including Bolingbroke, aided him in an unsuccessful revival

1. *Prose Works*, II, 428.
2. *Report on the Manuscripts of His Grace the Duke of Portland*, v (1899), 453. A full account of the transaction is given by P. B. Anderson in an unpublished dissertation on Mrs. Manley which is deposited in the library of Harvard College.

of *The Tatler*, and finally found him a place on the embassy to the Hague. When Harrison returned to England in financial straits, on account of the non-payment of his salary, Swift procured for him the belated assistance of Bolingbroke and Oxford. The dean was also active in promoting the fortunes of Thomas Parnell and George Berkeley, whom he likewise introduced to members of the society. Whether these efforts had any concrete results traceable to the Brothers, it is impossible to say.

A particularly interesting feature of Swift's tremendous activity during his connection with the Brothers was his project for establishing an English academy. Stimulated by the success of the *Académie Française* and by a strong conviction that his native tongue was in dire straits for want of stability, he began his campaign soon after his return to England in 1710 by writing a letter to *The Tatler*. He attacked the "continued corruption of our style" by the pamphleteers of Grub Street, illustrating the insidious spread of the evil by means of a cleverly fabricated letter supposed to have been written by a man of quality, in which the satirist incorporated some of the contemporary abuses which he found objectionable. What alarmed him most was his belief that the literature of his day would be unintelligible to the readers of a generation or so later when the fashions had changed.

The idea kept turning itself over in his mind until it took a more definite shape. The following summer he wrote to Stella:

I am proposing to my lord [Oxford] to erect a society or academy for correcting and settling our language, that we may not perpetually be changing as we do. He enters mightily into it, so does the Dean of Carlisle; and I design to write a letter to Lord-Treasurer with the proposals of it, and publish it; and so I told my lord, and he approves of it.[1]

1. *Prose Works*, ii, 195.

Party matters engaged the dean's pen to the exclusion of such peaceful undertakings for a number of months. In November he told Stella that he was about to finish his *Proposal*. Not until the following February, however, did the work approach completion. At that time he gave the following account of his progress:

I have been 6 hours to-day morning writing 19 Pages of a Lettr to-day to Ld-Treas^r, about forming a Society or Academy, to correct and fix the English Language. (Is English a Speech or a Language?) It will not be above five or 6 more. I will send it to him to-morrow, and will print it, if he desires me. I dined, you know, with our Society to-day; Thursday is our day.[1]

The juxtaposition of this last remark is significant. Six hours composed a considerably longer morning than he was in the habit of spending at his writing. Why this extraordinary application on Swift's part? Nothing could be more plausible than that he was preparing the essay to read to the Brothers that evening, in the hope of securing their coöperation in the project. Two other passages in the *Journal*, similar to the one just quoted, bolster up the hypothesis that the club was connected with the projected academy. On October 30, 1712, Swift wrote:

Our Society hath not yet renewed their meetings. I hope we shall continue to do some good this winter; and Lord-Treasurer promises the academy for reforming our language shall soon go forward.[2]

And again, on December 12 of the same year:

Our Society meets next Thursday, now the Queen is in town; and Lord-Treasurer assures me, that the Society for reforming the language shall soon be established.[3]

Although such evidence cannot be conclusive, it seems inconceivable that the recurrence of this relationship of Brothers and academy can be altogether accidental.

1. *Prose Works*, II, 340.   2. *Ibid.*, p. 392.   3. *Ibid.*, p. 398.

The publication of the *Proposal* was somewhat delayed by its submission to Oxford for corrections and by Prior's negligence in returning the manuscript when it was passed on to him. On May 10, 1712, Swift was at last able to tell Stella that the pamphlet was in the press and that contrary to a hitherto unbroken custom his name was to be signed to it. The essay was finally published under the imposing title, *A Proposal for Correcting, Improving, and Ascertaining the English Tongue; in a Letter To the Most Honourable Robert Earl of Oxford and Mortimer, Lord High Treasurer of Great Britain.* The tract is too well known to require any description; but it is pertinent to point out that Swift gave no hint about the nature of the society intended, beyond proposing the French Academy as its model.

Even before the *Proposal* was published, Swift and the Earl of Oxford, who seems to have been genuinely interested, had drawn up plans for putting the scheme into execution. "He and I," wrote Swift to Archbishop King, "have named above twenty persons of both parties to be members." [1] One would like to know who were deemed worthy of this distinction. According to a later letter to King, all the ministers promised their support, but by this time they were too busy to think of "anything beside what they have upon the anvil." Swift feared that his plans might all come to nothing. The Archbishop sensibly replied that it would be best to wait until the peace was settled before taking any further steps, and that it might be as well not to emphasize the imitation of the French institution until international prejudices had subsided. Swift's premonition proved to be justified. By the time the treaty of Utrecht was arranged, another storm had begun to gather on the political horizon. The project shared the fate of the clubs to which the dean belonged, and died with the ministry in 1714.

1. *The Correspondence of Jonathan Swift*, ed. F. E. Ball (1910–1914), I, 325.

The Scriblerus Club

While the Brothers were still functioning as patrons to the friends of the Tory ministry, a smaller group sprang up which eclipsed them both in fame and in literary fruitfulness. This was the little company known as the Scriblerus Club. The manner in which the two Tory societies have become confused [1] is easy to understand. Both were made up of men of the same party, and both claimed Swift and Arbuthnot as members. To add to the confusion, the Scriblerus Club occasionally invited certain of the Brothers to their meetings. Yet the two societies were one neither in purpose nor in membership.

Politics played somewhat the same part in the Scriblerus Club as at Button's Coffee-house. It was not an end in itself, but an inevitable force in bringing the friends together. Party pride is plainly visible in the numerous Scriblerian invitations to the Earl of Oxford, one of which began with the couplet:

> Let not the Whigs our Tory club rebuke,
> Give us our Earl, the devil take their Duke.[2]

Oxford's reply to one of these invitations shows even more party enthusiasm, as the first six lines will bear witness.

> I honour the men, sir,
> Who are ready to answer,
> When I ask them to stand by the Queen;
> In spite of oraters,
> And blood-thirsty praters,
> Whose hatred I highly esteem.[3]

It remained for Arbuthnot, in a letter to Parnell written in 1716, to sum up the feelings of the group in regard to party.

1. *E.g.*, by Colvile in *A Miscellany of the Wits* (1920), p. xxiii; and by Dobrée in *Essays in Biography* (1925), p. 292.
2. Swift, *Correspondence*, II, 416.
3. *Ibid.*, p. 417.

"Our love again and again," he wrote, "to the dear dean; *fuimus* tories; I can say no more." [1] At the time when the club was formed, however, the members were so near to satiety in matters political that they enjoyed Scriblerus as a relief from, rather than a further occupation with, party matters.

The name came from that of the fictitious virtuoso on whom the members were pleased to father their combined literary efforts. The designation seems to have arisen from the playful appellation of Martin which Lord Oxford coined as a synonym for Swift. When the name was later applied to the fictitious personage, a surname was added to indicate the mysterious gentleman's literary proclivities, and the whole latinized in deference to his scholarship. The character of Martinus Scriblerus soon became so definitely established that any member who wished to wield his pen in the interest of the club could assume it at will as a cloak of pseudonymity.

The end of all the writings of Scriblerus was to satirize false learning. Through him were reprimanded the pedantry of classical scholars, the absurdities of such antiquarians as Dr. Woodward, and the sophistry of the pseudo-scientists. Pope gave Spence, between 1728 and 1730, the following account of the origin of the scheme:

The design of the Memoirs of Scriblerus was to have ridiculed all the false tastes in learning, under the character of a man of capacity enough; that had dipped into every art and science, but injudiciously in each. It was begun by a club of some of the greatest wits of the age. Lord Oxford, the Bishop of Rochester, Mr. Pope, Congreve, Arbuthnot, Swift, and others. Gay often held the pen; and Addison liked it very well, and was not disinclined to come in to it. [2]

Although this account of the distinguished originators of the club may redound to its fame, the statement cannot be

---

1. Pope, *Works*, VII, 460.   2. Spence, *Anecdotes*, p. 8.

accepted as literally true. Party considerations are enough
to make the membership of Congreve and Addison look
very doubtful. There is no conclusive evidence elsewhere
to justify the inclusion of Oxford and Atterbury. The same
is true of Bolingbroke, who has also been credited with
membership.[1] The five who were really members were
Pope, Gay, Parnell, Swift, and Arbuthnot.[2] The letters of
these five to each other are full of references to their joint
lucubrations. Their correspondence with the others in no
way implies that anyone else had a hand in the enterprise.
The verse epistles to Lord Oxford which emanated from
the club make it clear that he was an invited guest, — an
interested and welcome onlooker rather than a participator. The most significant of the invitations, written from
Arbuthnot's room on March 20, 1714, survives in Swift's
own handwriting.

> The Doctor, and Dean, Pope, Parnell, and Gay,
> In manner submissive most humbly do pray
> That your lordship would once let your cares all alone
> And climb the dark stairs to your friends who have none,
> To your friends who at least have no cares but to please you,
> To a good honest junto that never will tease you.[3]

It is possible that some of the others mentioned by Pope
in connection with the club attended certain meetings as
guests and that their invitations were not preserved with
the care that was taken of Lord Oxford's papers. None of
them was as constant a visitor as the lord treasurer himself. Spence records that "he used to send trifling verses
from court to the Scriblerus-club almost every day, and
would come and talk idly with them almost every night:

1. Pope, *Works*, v, 233.
2. This is Aitken's view, expressed in *The Life and Works of John Arbuthnot*
(1892), p. 56.
3. Pope, *Works*, VIII, 225. The regular meeting-place, up to the time of the
queen's death, was Arbuthnot's apartment in St. James's Palace. Occasionally the club met at the lodgings of Swift's friend, Charles Ford.

even when his all was at stake." [1] Nor were his mediocre poetical efforts scorned by the club. Arbuthnot wrote to Swift, after the dean had departed for Letcombe in the summer of 1714:

The Dragon [Oxford] was with us on Saturday night last, after having sent us really a most excellent copy of verses. I really believe when he lays down, he will prove a very good poet. I remember the first part of his verses was complaining of ill usage, and at last he concludes:

> He that cares not to rule, will be sure to obey,
> When summon'd by Arbuthnot, Pope, Parnell, and Gay. [2]

Oxford was the only non-member who followed the activities of Scriblerus with any constancy. The other guests left no verses to commemorate the club's hospitality.

The precise time at which the original five drew together cannot be exactly determined. Ball asserts that the club must have been formed after the queen's arrival at St. James's in February, 1714. A letter from Pope to Gay, however, indicates that the collaboration had begun as early as October 23, 1713. The significant passage runs as follows:

Dr. Parnell will honour Tonson's Miscellany with some very beautiful copies, at my request. He enters heartily into our design. I only fear his stay in town may chance to be but short. Dr. Swift much approves what I proposed, even to the very title, which I design shall be, The Works of the Unlearned, published monthly, in which whatever book appears that deserves praise, shall be depreciated ironically, and in the same manner that modern critics take to undervalue works of value, and to commend the high productions of Grub-street. [3]

Here are four members of the club connected with a distinctly Scriblerian project. There is added evidence of an early formation in the statement of the booksellers to the

1. *Anecdotes*, p. 152.   2. Swift, *Correspondence*, II, 151.
3. Pope, *Works*, VII, 412.

reader, in the 1741 folio edition of Pope's prose works, to the effect that the *Memoirs of Martinus Scriblerus* were "the beginning of a considerable Work undertaken so long ago as 1713 by several great hands."

The brief period — hardly more than a year at most — during which Swift was able to meet with the club was the busiest of its existence. That this group of men of letters, some of whom had known each other for a comparatively short time, should come to accept each other on an equal footing and collaborate with the greatest zest and with no apparent rivalry is a matter for admiration. Yet so it came about. The wit of one inspired the other, and before Swift departed the memoirs of the fictitious virtuoso had gained sufficient impetus to keep him in Swift's mind through a number of years devoted to St. Patrick's Cathedral, Dublin society, and Irish politics. One odd phase of his position in the club appears in Goldsmith's *Life of Parnell*:

> The Scriblerus Club, when the members were in town, were seldom asunder; and they often made excursions together into the country, and generally on foot. Swift was usually the butt of the company; and if a trick was played he was always the sufferer.[1]

By way of illustration, Goldsmith tells how the club started out on foot to visit Lord Bathurst, who resided about twelve miles from town. Swift tried to avail himself of his superiority as a walker to arrive before the rest and secure the best bed for himself. When he was out of sight, Parnell took horse and going another way arrived before him. Upon the dean's arrival, he was informed by the servants that there was smallpox in the house. Fearing contagion he remained outside, while the rest feasted within.[2] It was not until after dinner that the others took compassion on

1. *The Works of Oliver Goldsmith*, ed. J. W. M. Gibbs, IV (1885), 170.
2. Goldsmith neglects to tell how the later arrivals gained an entrance without Swift's knowledge.

him and exposed their intrigue. The anecdote, if credible, is a surprising revelation of the intimacy of the five friends.

During Swift's sojourn at Letcombe in the summer of 1714, his friends in London kept him posted on the progress of Martinus. Gay wrote to him on June 8, "We had the honour of the Treasurer's company last Saturday, when we sat upon Scriblerus." [1] A few days later Arbuthnot gave him an account of the same meeting and added, "I am to meet our club at the Pall Mall coffee-house, about one to-day, where we cannot fail to remember you." [2] About the same time (June 18), Pope wrote to Swift in a manner which leaves no doubt that the work was continuing in the latter's absence. After expressing some curiosity concerning the dean's reasons for remaining at Letcombe, Pope remarked:

Dr. Arbuthnot is singular in his opinion, and imagines your only design is to attend at full leisure to the life and adventures of Scriblerus. This, indeed, must be granted of greater importance than all the rest, and I wish I could promise so well of you. The top of my own ambition is to contribute to that great work, and I shall translate Homer by the by.[3]

Swift, still troubled by politics, replied that he must be a little easy in his mind before he could think of Scriblerus.

Before the dean departed for Ireland, not to return for more than ten years, he was visited at Letcombe by Pope and Parnell, who styled themselves "the envoys to Dean Swift on the part of his late confederates." Knowing that they were followed by the thoughts of Arbuthnot, whose duties did not permit him to leave the queen, Pope gave him an amusing account of the visit in the form of a news-letter. The letter concludes with an epigram, which, as Pope says, "Dr. Parnell and I composed as we rode toward

1. Swift, *Correspondence*, II, 145.
2. *Ibid.*, p. 151.
3. *Ibid.*, p. 155.

the dean in the mist of the morning, and is after the Scriblerian manner."

> How foolish men on expeditions go!
> Unweeting wantons of their wetting woe!
> For drizzling damps descend adown the plain,
> And seem a thicker dew or thinner rain;
> Yet dew or rain may wet us to the shift,
> We'll not be slow to visit Dr. Swift.[1]

The jovial and productive meetings over the works of Martinus met their first obstacles in the fall of the Tory ministry and the departure of Swift for Ireland. With the dean in Dublin, Pope and Parnell at Binfield, and Gay and Arbuthnot in London trying to repair their damaged fortunes, meetings were of course out of the question. Their letters of this period take a reminiscent turn and show that for the time being they had lost their enthusiasm for the work. Even the cheerful physician was affected by the general gloom, and complained that Martin's "lucubrations lie neglected amongst old news-papers, cases, petitions, and abundance of unanswerable letters." The same letter to Pope, however, adds more hopefully that "Martin's office is now the second door on the left hand in Dover Street, where he will be glad to see Dr. Parnell, Mr. Pope, and his old friends, to whom he can still afford a half-pint of claret." [2]

There is little evidence that Scriblerus made any progress during the next few years. What may be an exception to this statement occurs in a letter from Pope to Caryll, written in 1716, where in recounting the various literary tasks that had been employing him the poet includes in his list, "*Item*, new designs with some of my friends for a satirical work, which I must have formerly mentioned to you." [3] But the reference may be to *Three Hours after Marriage*, which was produced early in the fol-

---

1. Pope, *Works*, VII, 470–471.
2. *Ibid.*, p. 473.   3. *Ibid.*, VI, 241.

lowing year. Correspondence between Swift and the others almost ceased between 1716 and 1722; and when Gay wrote to the dean for the first time in eight years, Swift querulously took him to task for recalling the pleasures of the gatherings over Scriblerus.

Much of this feeling was doubtless caused by the death of Parnell in 1718. Goldsmith wrote in his biography:

> It is probable the club began with him, and his death ended the connexion. Indeed, the festivity of his conversation, the benevolence of his heart, and the generosity of his temper, were qualities that might serve to cement any society, and that could hardly be replaced when he was taken away.[1]

It may have been out of their Scriblerian friendship that Pope undertook the task of editing Parnell's poetical remains and that Oxford readily permitted the edition to be dedicated to him.[2] Swift's visits to England in 1726 and 1727 brought about a happy reunion of the surviving members of the old club. But the ghost of Parnell still haunted them. While Pope, Swift, and Gay were at Twickenham, Pope received a letter from Lord Oxford's son which aroused painful memories.

> Now you three are together, I often think of the lines wrote in old times which begin,
>
> The Doctor and Dean, Pope, Parnell, and Gay.
>
> Only poor Parnell is gone; and I regret him the less because, by being the editor of his poems, you had an opportunity of making the finest copy of verses, and the greatest compliment, that ever was paid by a poet to any man.[3]

The society did not remain long intact, however, for when the business of the *Miscellanies* was done, Swift departed for Ireland never to return. He was not present to discuss

---

1. *Works*, IV, 171.
2. See Pope, *Works*, VIII, 186–187, where Pope acknowledges Oxford's kindness. 3. *Ibid.*, pp. 224–225.

with the rest the attacks on the club which the *Miscellanies* and *The Dunciad* caused.

It was inevitable that Pope's ill nature should reflect
upon the other members. In 1728 Nicholas Amhurst published, under the pseudonym of Caleb D'Anvers, a collection of satiric pieces entitled *The Twickenham Hotch-
Potch, For the Use of the Rev. Dr. Swift, Alexander Pope,
Esq; and Company*. The thrust at the club in general
occurs in the introduction. After lamenting the neglect
suffered by Butler, Lee, and Otway during their lives, Amhurst draws a savage contrast.

If I should now shift the Scene, and shew all that Penury,
and that Avarice changed all at once to Riot and Profuseness,
and more squandered away upon four Objects (an impertinent
Scotch-Quack, a Profligate *Irish*-Dean, the Lacquey of a Sup-
eranuated Dutchess, and a little virulent Papist) than would
have satisfied the greater Part of those extraordinary Men, the
Reader . . . would fancy them Prodigies of Art and nature.
. . . Instead of which this *Twickenham*-Club cannot be justly
intitled to any other Motto, than that of the honest *Roman*;

> *Odi Imitatores Servum Pecus.*

or, what an *English* Poet has said of *Longinus*, may be as justly
applied to them:

> *Their own* Example, *strengthens all their* Law,
> *They are*, Themselves, *the* Bathos *that they* draw.[1]

The four were linked again by Welsted in 1730 in *One
Epistle to Mr. A. Pope*. Welsted properly blamed Pope for
most of the personal abuse that appeared in the *Miscellanies* and *The Dunciad*, but the others did not escape untouched. He spoke of Swift as "a Fop in Rhime, and
Bungler in Affairs." Arbuthnot appears as

> That puzzling, plodding, prating, pedant *Scot*!
> The grating Scribler! whose untun'd Essays
> Mix the *Scotch* Thistle with the *English* Bays.

1. *The Twickenham Hotch-Potch* (1728), pp. vi–vii.

In professing pity for "ill-fated Gay," Welsted accused the club of fathering their worst pieces on Gay and appropriating his best to enhance their reputation. These attacks are manifestly unfair, but they show how firmly the bonds of friendship were forged anew when Swift revisited his old friends.

When Swift left England for the last time, his forebodings were gloomy enough. Arbuthnot attempted, early in 1729, to reassure his friend in Ireland. "As to the condition of your little club," he wrote, "it is not quite so desperate as you might imagine, for Mr. Pope is as high in favour, as I am afraid the rest are out of it. The King, upon the perusal of the last edition of his Dunciad, declared he was a very honest man."[1] We hear nothing further of the Scriblerus Club from the pens of its members. Gay died in 1732, Arbuthnot three years later. Only two of the original five lived to see the publication of their *magnum opus*, the *Memoirs of Martinus Scriblerus*.

Such is the outline of the club's history, many details of which can never be known. In spite of its vicissitudes, the association proved a fruitful one, and its literary remains command some consideration. They fall, roughly speaking, into three divisions: (1) the *Memoirs*; (2) the miscellaneous minor pieces to which the name of Scriblerus was signed; (3) independent works of the various members which carried out hints from the others. As the work for which the club was originally designed, the *Memoirs* deserves the first attention.

In the most nearly complete form which it ever assumed in print, the *Memoirs of the Extraordinary Life, Works, and Discoveries of Martinus Scriblerus* was first published in 1741.[2] To decide the exact time at which it was written is next to impossible. It is generally supposed to have taken

1. Swift, *Correspondence*, IV, 73.
2. See R. H. Griffith, *Alexander Pope: A Bibliography*, I, ii (1927), 426, 429, 434.

definite shape during the months when the club held regular meetings. Arbuthnot's letter to Pope, dated September
7, 1714, shows that the nature of Martin's personality
was generally understood, by its reference to the gravity
and moroseness of the savant; and the doctor's frequent
references to the lucubrations that were lying about his
study bear witness to the writing already done and to the
cessation of activity which followed the dispersal of the
members.

The difficulty comes in estimating just what had been
written when the club broke up. Courthope was of the
opinion that "all the evidence, internal and external, seems
to point to the fact that the Memoirs were composed during the sittings of the Club, and that when the first book
was completed it was put aside — perhaps because it was
not thought worth while to publish them till Pope included
them in the octavo edition of his Works." [1] There is more
than enough internal evidence to prove that this statement
is incorrect. The introduction to the *Memoirs* reprints a
letter from the great Scriblerus in which there is a reference
to the war with Spain. As Aitken has pointed out,[2] this
passage must have been written after 1739. The date
agrees with another statement in the introduction, that
several years had elapsed since the publication of Martin's
strictures on *The Dunciad* — that is, since 1729. It seems
likely that Pope wrote the introduction, or at least put it
in its final form, only a short time before it went into type.[3]

The reference to Philips's *Persian Tales* (1722) in Chapter IV also defies the theory that the *Memoirs* received
its final shape before the club ceased to meet. Furthermore, in describing the youthful accomplishments of

1. Pope, *Works*, x, 272.
2. *The Life and Works of John Arbuthnot*, p. 310 n.
3. Parnell wrote to Arbuthnot in September, 1714: "Yet art thou still, if
thou art alive O Scriblerus, as deserving of our lucubrations," showing that
the design of having Martinus disappear was already conceived; but the remark does not imply that the introduction was then in its final form.

Scriblerus in the domain of rhetoric (Chapter VI), his biographer refers to his treatise concerning bathos, "which he wrote at this time, but concealed from his father, knowing his extreme partiality for the ancients. It lay by him concealed," continues the account, "and perhaps forgot among the great multiplicity of other writings, till, about the year 1727, he sent it us to be printed, with many additional examples, drawn from the excellent live poets of this present age." [1] The chapter of which this quotation forms part of the opening paragraph is headed "Rhetoric, Logic, and Metaphysics." After this paragraph the biographer proceeds at once to a description of Martin's early excursions into logic and metaphysics. Thus it appears that a parallel account of his endeavors in the field of rhetoric originally began the chapter; that this section was greatly expanded into the treatise on bathos, called "The Art of Sinking in Poetry"; and that the introductory paragraph was inserted subsequently, probably by Pope, to fill the gap. Add to this the fact that Chapter XIII clearly presupposes the publication of *Gulliver's Travels*, and there can be no doubt that the *Memoirs* was completed long after the club had ceased its regular meetings.

The first appearance of Scriblerus in print occurred in 1723 in a rare little pamphlet of twenty-seven pages, the title-page of which reads as follows:

Memoirs of the Life of *Scriblerus. Scalpellum, Calami, Atramentum, Charta, Libelli.* By *D. S—t.* London: Printed from the Original Copy from *Dublin*; and Sold by *A. Moore* near *St. Paul's.* MDCCXIII.

Its unheralded appearance is the more puzzling because there seems to be no external evidence as to the sponsors of its publication, and because it bears so slight a resemblance to the *Memoirs* of 1741. The central figure of these earlier memoirs is Timothy Scriblerus, not Martinus. In its ma-

1. Pope, *Works*, x, 306.

terial, the book shows a kinship with the later version only in a single, astonishing detail. In the account of Timothy's birth, it is related that his mother, on the night before that momentous event, dreamed that she was delivered of an inkhorn, a circumstance which figures prominently in the story of the birth of Martinus. The 1723 prospectus — for it is little more — is almost wholly given over to a history of the Scriblerus family and their careers as literary hacks. Toward the end the author leaves the following caution with the reader:

I shall take my Leave of the Reader, intreating him, First, not to consider these Memorandums as a perfect History; that was not what I promised, but only look upon it as the Token of a Heart full of Gratitude towards a Man I acknowledge myself, to the last Degree, beholden to.[1]

In spite of the irony directed upon Grub Street and the virtuosi, the precise relation of this piece to the Scriblerus Club and to the final form of the *Memoirs* constitutes a baffling problem. Dr. L. M. Beattie, in an exhaustive dissertation on Arbuthnot,[2] holds that the club had nothing to do with Timothy Scriblerus or his *Memoirs*. Beattie cites a passage which seems to ridicule in turn Arbuthnot, Gay, Parnell, Swift, and Pope, the latter by name. It runs as follows:

So unbounded was the Genius of our young Student that he would one Day write a System of Physick; the next, a Comedy, or Copy of Verses; a third, would make a Sermon; the next, a Tale of a Tub, or Romance; but had this peculiar Turn in his Temper (whether it proceeded from natural Modesty, or Policy, I will not venture to determine) that he never would own his Productions, but always father'd them upon some body or other: I remember a Copy of his that appear'd under the Name of P——e, wherein he compliments a musical Lady, but the

1. *Memoirs of the Life of Scriblerus* (1723), pp. 26–27.
2. Deposited in the library of Harvard College.

World found him out here, and tho' they look'd upon it as one of his Juvenile Performances, every body said it was prettily done for one of his Bigness.[1]

If this sentence was not written by the Scriblerus Club, it was written by someone who knew the identity of the members and their intention to attack Grub Street. The writer must also have known that the memoirs of Martinus had been planned. Who could it have been? Again, if the Scriblerians looked upon the piece as satirizing them, why did no mention of it appear in their letters in 1723?

These difficulties would not arise if the club could be held responsible for the pamphlet. But in such a case another set of difficulties would appear. It is hard to see why the passage referring to the members was written if it was not intended as ridicule. And why was not the same family of Scriblerus used in both documents? Although a theory of either Scriblerian or non-Scriblerian authorship will admit some defense, neither is entirely satisfactory in the light of the known facts. The *Memoirs* of 1723 tends to obscure rather than illuminate the history of the club's master-piece.

There is some indication that the club meditated the publication of Martin's memoirs in 1727. In "Martinus Scriblerus, His Treatise of the Art of Sinking in Poetry," which appeared in the "Last Volume" of the *Miscellanies* in that year, there was an unobtrusive footnote which read:

Martinus Scriblerus, tho' of *German* Extraction, was born in *England*. *Vid.* his *Life* and *Memoirs*, which will speedily be Publish'd.[2]

The actual publication, however, hung fire for some years longer. A letter from Pope to Warburton shows that by October 27, 1740, the work was ready for the press;[3] and in

1. *Memoirs of the Life of Scriblerus* (1723), pp. 17–18.
2. *Miscellanies in Prose and Verse*, "Last Volume" (1727), p. 5.
3. Pope, *Works*, IX, 212.

1741 the *Memoirs* came out in three different publications.
A second and a third book of the *Memoirs*, relating to the
travels of Scriblerus, were advertised in one of Dodsley's
1742 editions of Pope,[1] but they were never published. So
ends the somewhat involved history of the history of
Scriblerus.

Concerning the authorship of the *Memoirs* it is possible
to do little more than outline the probabilities. That each
member of the club contributed something there can be
little doubt. Aside from the general heterogeneity of style,
there is what amounts to an admission of the plurality of
authorship in the introduction, which concludes archly:

> I dare promise the reader, that whenever he begins to think
> any one chapter dull, the style will be immediately changed in
> the next.[2]

The early testimony of Swift concerning the share of the
various members is more definite. In a letter to Arbuthnot
from Letcombe, before he returned to Ireland, the dean
summed up the situation thus:

> To talk of Martin in any hands but yours, is a folly. You every
> day give better hints than all of us together could do in a twelve-
> month; and to say the truth, Pope who first thought of the
> hint has no genius at all to it, in my mind. Gay is too young;
> Parnell has some ideas of it, but is idle; I could put together,
> and lard, and strike out well enough, but all that relates to
> the sciences must be from you.[3]

There is little reason to doubt any of these statements save
the compliment to Arbuthnot; and, as will appear later, the
tribute to his ingenuity was abundantly justified.

Gay's position seems to have been secretarial. Both

1. See R. H. Griffith, *Alexander Pope: A Bibliography*, I, ii (1927), 453.
2. *Ibid.*, x, 276. Compare the note to the episode of the Double Mistress
in *The Works of Mr. Alexander Pope, In Prose*, II (1741), 46.
3. Swift, *Correspondence*, II, 162–163.

Spence [1] and Goldsmith [2] assert that he "often held the pen." Pope remarked in a letter to Arbuthnot in 1714, after Gay had been deprived of his secretaryship to the Hanoverian embassy:

Our friend Gay will still continue secretary, to Martin at least, though I could be more glad he had a better master for his profit, — for his glory he can have no better.[3]

Although in view of the later history of the *Memoirs* Gay can hardly have put the book in its final form, many of the notes that gathered dust in the doctor's office after 1714 were doubtless in his hand.

The contributions of Parnell and Swift were mainly verbal and general; but such was not the case with Arbuthnot, who was by far the most ingenious and prolific of the collaborators. In one letter to Swift, he outlined enough satirical material on the medical profession to fill several chapters, none of which was ever printed. As he was supplied with a boundless fund of miscellaneous knowledge and was by all odds the best informed member of the club, his domain included other fields than medicine. One of his most promising ideas for a pseudo-scientific article was anticipated in a curious manner, which he described in a letter to Swift.

Whiston has at last published his project of the longitude; the most ridiculous thing that ever was thought on. But a pox on him! he has spoiled one of my papers of Scriblerus, which was a proposal for the longitude, not very unlike his, to this purpose: that since there was no pole for East and West, that all the Princes of Europe should join and build two prodigious poles, upon high mountains, with a vast light-house to serve for a pole-star. I was thinking of a calculation of the time, charges, and dimensions. Now you must understand, his proj-

1. *Anecdotes*, p. 8.
2. *Works*, IV, 169.
3. Pope, *Works*, VII, 472.

ect is by light-houses, and explosion of bombs at a certain hour.[1]

The doctor's wrong was avenged; for in the final chapter of the *Memoirs* is a thrust at Whiston which outlines the project as one of the "Works of the Great Scriblerus." Arbuthnot's readiness with suggestions eventually became a standing joke with the club. When *Gulliver's Travels* was published, Pope and Gay wrote to Swift that the doctor "says it is ten thousand pities he had not known it, he could have added such abundance of things upon every subject"; and more than a year later, when the success of *The Beggar's Opera* was assured, Swift inquired of Gay, "How is the Doctor? Does he not chide that you never called upon him for hints?" [2]

It seems safe, then, to assign to Arbuthnot those sections of the *Memoirs* which show a thorough knowledge of science, notably Chapters VIII and IX, and portions of Chapters I and II. He also wrote Chapter III, which satirizes the fate of Dr. Woodward's shield.[3] It is logical, in the light of his ability at projecting new works, to give him credit for the material in Chapter XVII, which treats briefly "Of the Discoveries and Works of the Great Scriblerus." How much more of the *Memoirs* he was responsible for is difficult to conjecture, though his share in the work is not likely to be overestimated.

The honor of conceiving Scriblerus belongs, Swift tells us, to Pope. When one considers the dean's comment on his fitness for the work and the nature of the material dealt with in the *Memoirs*, it is hard to believe that he was the creator of any great part of the whole. Between 1734 and 1736 Pope remarked to Spence: "I have so much of the materials for the Memoirs of Scriblerus ready, that I could

1. Swift, *Correspondence*, II, 186.
2. *Ibid.*, III, 359; IV, 12.
3. See L. M. Beattie, *John Arbuthnot*, III, 1028–1037.

complete the first part in three or four days." [1] His work, however, was chiefly editorial. He collected and revised the remains of Scriblerus and welded them into a printable form. He probably inserted the satire on the textual critics, notably Bentley, and he certainly added the allusions to lately printed books. The dispersal of the late additions shows that his revision was extensive. The finished product was amorphous enough; but such coherence as it had must have been due to his pen.

The *Memoirs of Scriblerus* by no means constituted the sole work that bore the name of the savant. Since some of his productions are of considerable interest, it may be well to enumerate them all in the chronological order of their publication. [2] In the second volume of the *Miscellanies* (1727) appeared the account of the lawsuit of "Stradling

1. Spence, *Anecdotes*, p. 133.
2. The following list of the works of Scriblerus was appended to the *Memoirs* in Dodsley's 1742 edition of Pope's *Works*:

PIECES *of* Scriblerus (*written in his Youth*)
already published.

An Essay on the *Origin* of *Sciences*, written from the Deserts of *Nubia*.

Περὶ ΒΑΘΟΤΣ: Martinus Scriblerus his *Rhetoric*, or, Of the *Art of Sinking* in Poetry.

VIRGILIUS RESTAURATUS: Seu Martini Scribleri, summi Critici, Castigationum in Æneidem Specimen.

Annus Mirabilis, or The wonderful Effects of the Conjunction of *Jupiter*, *Mars*, and *Saturn*.

The *Report* of a *Case* in an *Action at Law* concerning certain *Pyed*, or *Black* and *White* Horses.

Notes and Prolegomena to the *Dunciad*.

Bentley's Milton.

Others not yet published, *mentioned in the* Memoirs.

The Case of Queen *Esther*, with the whole Process of her *Purification*.

An Account of the wonderful Discovery of divers Diseases by *Setting-Dogs*, with a List of those Gentlemen

and Ladies at whom they sett.

A Proposal humbly offer'd to both Houses of Parliament, for a *General Flux*.

Scriblerus's REPORTS of certain extraordinary Cases in Law.

versus Stiles." The case therein described arose over a clause in the will of "Sir John Swale, of Swale-Hall in Swale-Dale, fast by the River Swale." The mooted provision bequeathed to Mr. Matthew Stradling, Gent., all the black and white horses belonging to the deceased. As Sir John was possessed of six black horses, six white horses, and six pied horses, the matter was highly involved, nor was it simplified by the discovery that the pied horses proved without exception to be mares. The satire on the courts of justice is of much the same nature as that in the trial scene of Chapter XV of the *Memoirs*. Dr. Johnson asserted that Pope wrote the piece "by the assistance, as is said, of Mr. Fortescue, afterwards Master of the Rolls." [1] In the same volume of the *Miscellanies* appeared the "Memoirs of P. P. Clerk of this Parish," a satire on Bishop Burnet's *History of His Own Time*, which Pope claimed as his own in *The Dunciad* (1729); [2] and in the "Last Volume" was "The Art of Sinking in Poetry," which was very largely the work of Pope. [3] Attention has been called to the fact that Chapter XV of the latter piece was extracted from the essay entitled "A Receipt to Make an Epic Poem," which forms Number 78 of *The Guardian*. There is something amusing in the fact that this bit of writing was used first in a periodical sponsored by the club at Button's and later in a work signed by Scriblerus, for whom Pope deserted Button's.

In the variorum edition of *The Dunciad* (1729), there appeared "Martinus Scriblerus His Prolegomena to the Dunciad." The quotations of critical opinion with which this introduction begins are selected with remarkable

1. *Lives of the English Poets*, ed. G. Birkbeck Hill (Oxford, 1905), III, 144.
2. II, 46 n.
3. The preface to Welsted's *One Epistle to Mr. A. Pope* (1730), which attacks Pope for indulging in satirical personalities, says that Swift *"never saw the Profund, till made publick, and Dr. Arbuthnot, who originally sketch'd the Design of it, desired that the Initial Letters of the Names of the Gentlemen abused might not be inserted."*

impartiality, some being highly laudatory and others pointedly abusive. Pope managed, however, to insert such ironic introductory passages before the quotations from unfriendly critics that their remarks were made to appear tasteless or absurd. This section of the "Prolegomena" is followed by Martinus's prospectus of the poem. He gives classical precedents for the genre, the method, and the style, defends the characterizations of contemporary poets, and shows the eminent fitness of the author for the work.

The pseudo-scholarly notes which accompany the text of the poem are, as has been frequently pointed out, satire on the textual critics of Pope's day, specifically Bentley and Theobald. Pope was responsible for most of these notes, though his friends had their opportunity to contribute and probably did. In June, 1728, Pope gave Swift the following account of his plans for the new *Dunciad*:

It will be attended with *Proeme, Prolegomena, Testimonia Scriptorum, Index Authorum*, and Notes *Variorum*. As to the latter, I desire you to read over the text, and make a few in any way you like best, whether dry raillery, upon the style and way of commenting of trivial critics; or humourous, upon the authors in the poem; or historical, of persons, places, times; or explanatory; or collecting the parallel passages of the ancients.[1]

Although Swift's answer contained no promise to comply with this request, Warburton insists that some of the notes are the dean's. And in the light of his long-standing quarrel with Bentley, it is entirely credible that he did not neglect his opportunity. Arbuthnot probably had an even larger hand in the annotations.[2] In this same volume was printed "*Virgilius Restauratus*,"[3] a piece made up of absurd notes on and emendations of the *Aeneid*, written

1. Pope, *Works*, VII, 134.
2. Beattie has treated this subject more fully in *John Arbuthnot*, III, 940–943.
3. Attributed by Beattie to Arbuthnot.

with the same satiric intent that characterized Martinus's notes on *The Dunciad*. It is only fair to remark that these notes, like some of the other minor pieces, cannot certainly be connected with the club except by the name signed to them in pursuit of the practise of fathering on Martinus all satire on pedantry.

The "third" volume of the *Miscellanies* (1732) contained two other works of Scriblerus. One was called "An Essay of the Learned Martinus Scriblerus, Concerning the Origine of Sciences. Written to the most Learned Dr. — F. R. S. from the Deserts of Nubia." According to the booksellers' preface to the reader in the 1741 folio edition of Pope's prose works, this tract was written by Pope, Arbuthnot, and Parnell. Spence has two entries regarding its authorship, one of which names only Pope and the doctor and the other all three.[1] The second work which appeared in this volume under Martin's name is entitled "*Annus Mirabilis*: or, The Wonderful Effects of the approaching Conjunction of the Planets *Jupiter*, *Mars*, and *Saturn*. *By* Mart. Scriblerus, *Philomath*. A Well-Wisher to the Mathematicks." This highly fantastic essay is based upon the prognostication that on the fatal day of the conjunction men and women would change sex. The opening sentence gives the date of the conjunction as December 29, 1722; and Professor Griffith shows that the essay appeared first in that year as a six-page folio pamphlet signed "Abraham Gunter, Philomath." He also refers to a contemporary ascription of the piece to "the famous Mr. P——" in *The London Journal* of January 5, 1723.[2]

This concludes the list of the minor works printed under the name of Scriblerus, which with the *Memoirs* make up the tale of the savant's literary monuments. If the fame of the Scriblerus Club had to rest upon these works alone, the group could hardly have attained its distinguished posi-

1. *Anecdotes*, pp. 126, 152.
2. *Alexander Pope: A Bibliography*, i, ii (1927), 566.

tion in literary history. The most productive feature of the meetings in Arbuthnot's study in St. James's was the habit formed among the five of offering and developing suggestions for new literary efforts. A single quotation from Swift's famous letter to Pope, dated August 30, 1716, is sufficient to show how fruitfully the practise continued when meetings were no longer possible.

There is a young ingenious quaker in this town who writes verses to his mistress, not very correct, but in a strain purely what a poetical quaker should do, commending her look and habit, &c. It gave me a hint that a set of quaker pastorals might succeed, if our friend Gay could fancy it, and I think it a fruitful subject; pray hear what he says. I believe further, the pastoral ridicule is not exhausted, and that a porter, footman, or chairman's pastoral might do well. Or what think you of a Newgate pastoral, among the whores and thieves there? [1]

Three of these hints actually materialized. As Warburton points out in regard to the first suggestion, "Gay did write a pastoral of this kind, which is published in his works."[2] It is the last of his eclogues, called "The Espousal," which presents the two young Quakers, Caleb and Tabitha. The dean himself used the idea of the servant's pastoral and wrote the verses on Dermot and Sheelah entitled "A Pastoral Dialogue." The last idea became articulate through the pen of Gay in *The Beggar's Opera*.

Less definite, though unmistakable, is the Scriblerian imprint[3] on the collaborative farce, *Three Hours after Marriage* (1717). Although Pope and Arbuthnot are definitely identified as Gay's anonymously mentioned assistants in the play, Gay himself has lately been given

1. Pope, *Works*, VII, 16–17.
2. *The Works of Alexander Pope, Esq.* (1751), IX, 15 n.
3. Curiously enough the name of Martinus Scriblerus's father was Dr. Cornelius Scriblerus, and the name of the virtuoso whom Plotwell impersonated in *Three Hours after Marriage* was Dr. Cornelius Lubomirski. This coincidence of given names may, of course, be entirely accidental.

most of the credit and blame for its composition. [1] Arbuthnot probably did little more than make suggestions for Fossile's more technical speeches. And Pope could not have done much of the actual writing, though the representation of Dennis as Sir Tremendous shows signs of his handiwork. As a matter of fact, the meetings of the club over the character of Scriblerus in 1713 and 1714 furnished Gay with enough ammunition against virtuosi and Grub-Streeters to enable him to write the play alone. Even the choice of Woodward (Fossile) as the false scholar *par excellence* had been made by the club at Arbuthnot's instigation three years before.

The conception of *Gulliver's Travels* may also be traced to the Scriblerus Club. According to one of Swift's more recent editors, "Swift probably intended 'Gulliver' to form part of the 'Memoirs,' in which, indeed, the travels of Scriblerus are identified with those of Gulliver. But when the original scheme fell through and the friends were separated, the project of writing a satire in the guise of a book of travels, though put aside for the time, was not forgotten by Swift. As his cynicism and misanthropy grew upon him, the idea appealed to him more and more. A passage at the end of the work suggests that it was begun about 1720." [2] Joseph Warton noted in editing the *Memoirs* that Swift changed "this work of humour, to a particular gratification of his spleen," and added, "but this is certain, that when he made so total an alteration in his design, he took care not to give one feature of Scriblerus to his Gulliver." [3] Something of the tone, however, and much of the purpose of the *Memoirs* survive in the attack upon pseudo-science in Gulliver's adventures at Laputa; and the fact that the surgeon's travels were afterwards appropriated by Martinus is enough to show the kinship between the two.

1. See Beattie, *John Arbuthnot*, I, 290–304.
2. Swift, *Prose Works*, VIII, xi.
3. *The Works of Alexander Pope, Esq.* (1797), VI, 183.

The significance of the club which so knit together the lives of five of the foremost wits of the time is not likely to be overrated. The *Memoirs* could not be deemed negligible, even if their sole claim to distinction were the fact that the opening chapter suggested to Sterne his account of the birth of Tristram Shandy. The minor pieces are written with spirit and humor enough to make them perpetually readable, slight as they are. But as Craik remarked in his life of Swift, the club's true claim to immortality rests upon its direction of the literary interests and creative efforts of the five ingenious writers who made up its number.

THE DECAY OF A TRADITION

As everyone knows, clubs did not cease to exist at the time of Swift's death. On the contrary, they became more and more numerous. Following the example of White's, many coffee-houses and chocolate-houses were converted into such exclusive clubs as Brookes's, Almack's, and Boodle's. In addition there were various informal societies without appropriated club-rooms, which did not differ materially from those of the reign of Queen Anne. Thus when Dr. Ralph Heathcote went to London in 1753, "in order to associate and converse with *literati*," he was shortly able to find his way "into a Society of Gentlemen, who met once a week, to drink coffee, and to talk *learnedly* for three or four hours." [1] This obscure group is of much closer relationship to the society at Button's than is Arthur's or the Cocoa Tree. The same is true of the club which William Cowper frequented to disperse the "gloomy thoughts led on by spleen" during his unhappy sojourn in the Inner Temple. The group, made up of Colman, Thornton, Lloyd, Hill, Cowper, and two others, used to dine together on Thursdays and adopted the name of the Nonsense Club. It is

1. John Nichols, *Literary Anecdotes*, III (1812), 537.

likely that Cowper's contribution to *The Connoisseur* had something to do with his membership in the club. His reference to it in a letter to Hill, written nearly thirty years after the society had dissolved, hints at what went on at the meetings.

The noble institution of the Nonsense Club will be forgotten, when we are gone who composed it; but I often think of your most heroic line, written at one of our meetings, and especially think of it when I am translating Homer, —

"To whom replied the Devil yard-long-tailed."

There never was any thing more truly Grecian than that triple epithet, and were it possible to introduce it into either *Iliad* or *Odyssey*, I should certainly steal it.[1]

Although the Nonsense Club attracted little attention, it must have been relished by its members much as the Scriblerus Club had been.

The more highly organized and more serious-minded English Club, described in *The Connoisseur*, No. 42, was formed to protect the language from corruption. Part of its energies were devoted to worshiping at the shrines of Spenser, Shakespeare, Milton, and other classic English poets. Furthermore, they "established a fund, from which handsome rewards are allotted to those who shall supply the place of any exotic terms, that have been smuggled into our language, by homespun British words, equally significant and expressive." The essay on linguistic purity which follows is vaguely reminiscent of Swift's *Tatler* (No. 230), and it is conceivable that the dean's attempt to found an academy was responsible for this description of the English Club.

Examples of literary societies accumulate rapidly. At some time prior to 1784, a "pleasing Society of very young men (for such they were)" was formed for the purpose of

---

1. *Letters of William Cowper*, ed. J. G. Frazer (1912), 11, 60.

reciting and criticizing the verses of the members. Their meetings proved so stimulating to creative effort that in 1784 they were able to publish a volume entitled *Poems by a Literary Society: comprehending Original Pieces in the several Walks of Poetry*. A number of different literary clubs claimed Dr. Farmer as a member, among others the Eumelian Club, to which Reynolds and Boswell belonged, and the Unincreasable Club, presided over by Isaac Reed. Dr. Johnson was a leading spirit in at least four societies at different periods of his life. Gibbon was the founder of a distinguished group called the Romans; the bluestockings met in various societies; and the last years of the century marked the rise of countless assemblies of more obscure reputation whose names are now almost forgotten. Even from this brief survey it will appear that the clubs themselves flourished enormously during the latter half of the century.

Their traces in literature are much less easy to follow than in the earlier stages of club history. The rakes, it is true, continued to call forth comment because of their sensational activities. There are also verses about clubs of less journalistic interest. Somewhat in the manner of Queen Anne's reign is one, described by Smollett in *Humphrey Clinker*, which gathered about the aged actor James Quin; and in Butler Swift's "Tyburn to the Marine Society" a club forms the object of satire as truly as the Calves-Head group had, almost fifty years earlier, in "Toland's Invitation to Dismal."

Such literary appearances as these, however, are much less frequent than in the early years of the century. Most of the later treatments of clubs can be accounted for as resulting from imitation of earlier modes. The attention given to them in *The Connoisseur* is certainly due to the fact that Colman and Thornton modeled their periodical after *The Spectator*. Goldsmith's essay on clubs in *The Busy Body* probably had the same inspiration. The satirical thrusts of Churchill and Butler Swift find numerous parallels in the works of their revered predecessors. The fictitious society of gentlemen, which had been so productive before the middle of the century, gradually came into disuse. Whereas the historian of clubs may find his material concerning the societies of Queen Anne's reign in contemporary essays, plays, poems, newspapers, and political pamphlets, after 1750 he must depend more and more upon memoirs and the records kept by the clubs themselves; this in spite of the fact that the club as an institution continued in a most flourishing condition.

The most obvious source of this singular change is to be found in the club itself. Early in the century a large number of the more important societies had been somehow connected with politics, which gave them a journalistic interest for the politically minded public. Men of letters had been drawn into clubs and had thus been provided with a complete knowledge both of their own societies and of the gossip connected with their opponents'. Under such conditions, the production of club literature was inevitable. William Cowper, looking back in 1781 to the days of his early Whiggish enthusiasm, described it to Newton as "apt to break forth into poetry. Prior's pieces," he continued, "were recommended to my particular notice; and as that part of the present century was a season when clubs of a political character, and consequently political songs, were much in fashion, the best in that style . . . were proposed to my admiration."

Cowper wrote as one recalling a different era. The decades which had elapsed since Prior's death had seen the gradual emancipation of the literary profession from party controversy. The political clubs themselves had passed one by one into oblivion, having served their usefulness. Thus were removed from the background of literature the societies which had been graced by the attendance of Swift and Arbuthnot, Congreve and Garth, Addison and Steele, together with many less distinguished groups, like the October Club, which had drawn the fire of the satirists.

Although the purely social clubs lived on, they too underwent a change. They became afflicted with by-laws, waiting-lists, blackballs, and other appurtenances of organization, until much of the spontaneity and intimacy which had characterized the earlier groups was lost. As the great clubs became more exclusive, the Town came to know less about them. Since the great world had become many small worlds, it was not so easy to know everybody as it had been in Swift's day. Men of letters became socially distinct from men of fashion, and the two classes no longer merged as freely as before. All these developments, coupled with the fact that the club was no longer arresting as a novel social institution, reduced its interest both to author and reader and had the effect of disengaging it from the literary fabric of the time.

Another force in the same direction was a deeper change which was taking place in literary fashions. There existed in the early years of the century "a literature not of this world, but of *the* world, of the *beau monde*, high life, fashion, society, the court and the town, the salons, clubs, coffee-houses, assemblies, ombre-parties." It was an age of satire upon manners and upon men, and clubs and clubmen came in for more than their share of attention. But when Churchill began his career as a satirist, his friend Lloyd had already written an imitation of Spenser; Thomas Warton's "Newmarket" contributed comparatively little to his fame; and one looks in vain for a preoccupation with clubs in the poetry of Akenside, Gray, and Collins. Thus the retreat of the society of gentlemen from the literary field was occasioned by two related impulses, — social evolution and a sweeping change in literary traditions.

INDEX

INDEX